BRIDGE TO LIGHT
Spiritual Wayfaring Towards Islam

"Invite all to the way of the Lord with wisdom and beautiful preaching, and argue with them in ways that are best and most gracious."

(Holy Qur'an 16:25)

BRIDGE TO LIGHT
Spiritual Wayfaring Towards Islam

Kathleen St.Onge

𝓛ight

New Jersey

Published by The Light, Inc.
26 Worlds Fair Dr. Unit C
Somerset, New Jersey, 08873, USA

www.thelightpublishing.com

Library of Congress Cataloging-in-Publication Data

St.Onge, Kathleen.
  Bridge to light : spiritual wayfaring towards Islam / Kathleen St.Onge.
     p. cm.
  Includes bibliographical references and index.
  ISBN 1-59784-074-2 (pbk.)
  1.   St.Onge, Kathleen. 2.   Muslim converts from Christianity--Canada--Biography. 3. Islam--Essence, genius, nature. I. Title.
  BP170.5.S7S76 2007
  297.5'74--dc22

                                                                        2006032241

ISBN-13: 978-1-59784-074-3

Printed by
Çağlayan A.Ş. Izmir, Turkey
April 2007

TABLE OF CONTENTS

Dedication..vii

Foreword..xi

Chapter I: The Journey to the Natural Call from Deep Within..............1

    The Homecoming 3

    The Time Spent..10

Chapter II: Healing the Dark Ages Inside the Modern Soul..................17

    The Dark Ages 19

    The Plague..25

    Justice – Part One – Pride 32

    Justice – Part Two – Prejudice..38

Chapter III: The Ego Trap 45

    Test of Ego – Part One – The View..47

    Test of Ego – Part Two – The Spider...53

    The Poisoned Heart...60

    The Battle Within 66

Chapter IV: Reflections on the Basic Tenets of Faith............................73

    The Fear Factor 75

    Helpers From Above 81

    The Instrument of Truth – Part One – The Revelation 87

    The Instrument of Truth – Part Two – The Confirmation 92

    Common Ground – Part One – The Opened Bible............................97

    Common Ground – Part Two – The Corner Stone 102

    On the Perfecting of a Prophet...107

    Jesus – The Barefoot Messenger...112

    These Last Few Days 120

    Resurrection 125

Chapter V: Nourishing Faith: Practice 131

    A Life of Prayer 133

    Vigilance 138

Hypocrites 141
On Sharing Truth...147
Abstaining from Alcohol 151
The Prohibition on Pork 155

Chapter VI: Clear Signs Around Us 161

Reason to Believe...163
The Smallest Mercies 168
Superstition 173
One Hell of a Gamble 178
A Throne Over Water...186
The Pulse of Creation 191
The Mosquito 197

Chapter VII: Evolution...203

Origins – Part One: It Becomes a Bird 205
Origins – Part Two: The Wing of Humility 215
Origins – Part Three - Those Who Compass It Round............225
The Blind Spot..235

Chapter VIII: Ethics and Values 241

The Journey 243
My Husband—My Brother 248
The Elders 253

Chapter IX: Diversity and Understanding 259

In Garments of Silk 261
Red, Black, and White 267

References..273

Notes...275

Index...282

DEDICATION

This book is dedicated to my husband, who was the first person to bring Islam into my life and the Holy Qur'an into my home; to my two sons, who have travelled the journey to this faith with me and have added their comments and insights to each text; and to my eldest, my daughter, whose different life path is a constant reminder of the importance of building and maintaining bridges of dialogue with which to hold our hearts together in the soft light of peace.

Some of the texts included here were originally written as individual articles, 17 of them appearing in an Islamic publication in the Greater Toronto area in 2002 – 2004 , Sunrise Newsletter, while another appeared in Pearls, an Islamic journal, in 2004, and a few were platforms for public presentations on Islam in Hamilton, Toronto, and Ottawa. Overall, writing for this book began in October 2002 and was completed in May 2005. The texts are provided here under various themes, not in the order in which they were written. As my knowledge and faith evolved, so did my writing style. The differences in texture and approach have been left deliberately, as a testament to personal growth.

I would like to thank various members of the Muslim community in Toronto who first provided me with books and answers to my many, many questions. In particular, I would like to mention Mr. Mehmet Gul, the respected former editor of Sunrise Newsletter, and Mr. Faruk Aslan, his esteemed predecessor, for their generous words of encouragement when I first began to write on this subject. I would also like to express my gratitude to many new friends from around the globe, who are gathered here in Toronto, perhaps the most multicultural city in the world, and who have offered me their company, their perspective, and their support. My dear friend and co-worker for a time, Suheir, in particular, nurtured my interest and ability in public speaking and always seemed to inspire my days with a verse from the Qur'an, sharing her superb fluency in both English and Arabic. My thanks also extend to the many individuals who have written and spoken to me over the years, both Muslim and non-Muslim, to indicate that the views presented here were helpful to them in better understanding Islam.

May God forgive me for any omissions or errors. I have tried to relate my comprehension of various points to the best of my ability, and I have endeavoured to check quotes carefully to eliminate faulty citations. Any discrepancies remaining are strictly mine and should not be taken as poor reflections on the blessed religion of Islam, the Holy Qur'an, or other Muslims.

May God also forgive me for often omitting or minimizing the usual blessings which should accompany any mention of the name of God or of the prophets. In traditional Islamic writings, for example, it is customary to see the phrase "Peace Be Upon Him," in Arabic, after every individual instance of a prophet's name, to demonstrate honour and profound respect. It is also a customary requirement to write "Subahana'Allah" (Glory be to God, to Whom all praise is due) after the word "Allah." In the interest of appealing to a largely western audience, however, this tradition has been applied less stringently than is normally the case, and written in English where used (as "pbuh") in order to reduce the burden on readers with no knowledge of Arabic or of this particular tradition. In addition, the word "God" has been used interchangeably with the word "Allah," as they clearly both refer to the same, and only, Creator.

Readers are strongly encouraged to consult the Holy Qur'an itself for clarification—and for pleasure. Among the vast tradition of Qur'anic commentary, the recently published interpretation, "The Qur'an with Annotated Interpretation in Modern English," by Ali Unal, is recommended, and I have personally found the translations by Abdullah Yusuf Ali and Marmaduke Pickthall to be highly accessible. There are also several excellent sites on the Internet which offer various translations next to each other to ensure that the reader is able to obtain the clearest and most consistent understanding of the Message. At islamawakened.org, for example, there are no less than 17 side-by-side translations of every line, along with a literal rendition of the original Arabic.

Other Internet sites which are particularly useful are mquran.org, for the English interpretation and exposition of the Qur'an, as well as a search by category and chapter; the excellent Qur'an chapter and word search hosted by the MSA at the University of Southern California (www.usc.edu/dept/MSA); muslimway.org, for a general understanding of Islam; pmuhammad.com, for details about the exemplary life of Prophet Muhammad; slife.org, for information about spirituality from an interfaith perspective; biblegateway.com, for Bible quotations; religioustolerance.org, for extensive information on various faith groups; and nationmaster.com, for world statistics on faith and values.

I am not a scholar of Islam by any stretch of the imagination. I am only an interested believer in God, and I have decided to study and learn what I can, in a way in which anyone might, primarily by reading, simply chronicling my studies up to now in these texts. In fact, all of us are urged to respect the value of reading and writing in coming closer to God:

> *Read! In the name of thy Lord and Cherisher, Who created-*
> *Created man, out of a mere clot of congealed blood.*
> *Proclaim! And thy Lord is Most Bountiful,*
> *He Who taught the use of the pen,*
> *Taught man that which he knew not…*
>   (Holy Qur'an 96:01-05)

God willing, I humbly submit this manuscript in the hope of supporting contemporary dialogue about the Creator of us all—One God and One God alone.

FOREWORD

This is a sincere believer's journey in heart and in spirit. The author reflects not only on her own experience of spiritual fulfillment and meeting with God in everyday life, but also on how deeply she is content with Islam on intellectual, theological, and practical levels. While exploring the logic behind the teachings of Islam as a western convert, she puts an emphasis on our finite capacities as humans, asserting the need to feel not only with our outward senses but also to discern and observe with the heart.

With her heart full of the Divine Light, she is able to use a fluent language in her careful interpretation of the Holy Book and the colorful pages of the Book of the Universe speaking of God in their own tongue. Pondering on the signs around us and thus being mindful of God is not an easy thing, particularly when it is with regards to ourselves, as stated in the Qur'an: *"Do they not reflect in their own minds? Not but for just ends and for a term appointed, did God create the heavens and the earth, and all between them; yet there are truly many among people who deny the meeting with their Lord (at the Resurrection)!"* (30:8) In another verse, God draws our attention to the significance of reflection, *"Those who remember God standing and sitting and lying on their sides and reflect on the creation of the heavens and the earth: Our Lord! You have not created this in vain! Glory be to You; save us then from the chastisement of the fire."* (3:191) With this in mind, the author, throughout the book, ponders on the purpose of the vast expanse of our existence in the world, the creation of the heavens and the earth, and the invitation to flee to God—a natural calling from deep within each one of us.

The author raises the awareness of intellectual inquiry into faith while surrendering to God's call, saying: "While acquiring belief through knowledge is an important duty, acquiring belief in what is beyond knowledge is a privilege." She focuses on the essentials of faith, the lawful and the prohibited in Islam, ethics, and spirituality in an eye-opening way, and she tackles head-on rather delicate issues, like evolution and the Trinity from the Islamic position, with a rigorous level of theological, spiritual, and rational investigation.

Thus, the author becomes a significant source of inspiration for journeying to the Light with her own spiritual wayfaring toward God. If the spirit of her articles were to be wrung out, what would result is her sincere longing and thankfulness to God. It is through these strong feelings that she has made hers a journey which may unseal the doors of other wayfarers' hearts and minds, as they undertake their quest. The perspectives in the articles are of exacting relevance to everyone, including people who are born into Islam in their reinvestigation of the religion, as well as new Muslims or interested seekers considering Islam and striving to discover the foundations of the religion.

Huseyin Bingul
Istanbul, September 2006

CHAPTER I

The Journey to the Natural Call from Deep Within

"Surely God loves those who turn much to Him, and He loves those who purify themselves." (2:222)

THE HOMECOMING

A friend of mine recalls being only marginally religious before embracing Islam—yet remembering to thank God for each glass of water. It wasn't something her family taught her to do— it was just something she thought she should do, as she felt the flickering light of Islam, submission to One God, inside her. For me, that overwhelming sense of thankfulness always came with the warmth of the sun. Yet I don't recall ever being grateful to God directly—it was more like a feeling of appreciation for a Greater Power. I was so occluded for so many years, it seems, about the role of God in my life. For decades, I lived like the lost people the Qur'an describes: *"In distraction, they will wander through the land."* (5:26) Why didn't I heed the signs better, or earlier? Why did it take me 40 years to realize, and honour, the fact that I owe absolutely everything to God?

As a child, I loved to retreat to my room early at night, just to think about God and pray. It was my little secret, and my cocoon of safety in a home filled with struggles which would take me decades to understand. I loved the Catholic sisters who taught me through elementary school. I was only a day student but I dreamt of being a boarder—hiding in closets after dismissal—just so I could live in a place filled with God, and go to the chapel in my pyjamas in the middle of the night. I treasured my first Bible, which they gave me: "Judge not lest ye be judged." Those were words to live by. When I was in Grade 4 or 5, the sisters decided to give up their habits for lay clothing, and I remember my father commenting on which ones looked sexy and which ones might as well have stayed covered up because there was "nothing good to see." My own feeling at the time was that some of what was special about them—and about my own life—was gone forever.

When I was three or four years old, my mother took me to visit a monastery, to chat with a family friend training to be a monk. I recall clearly the clacking of my little black shoes along the huge, stark expanse of glistening floors, and the feeling of peace, and safety, just like the feeling at mass. I always loved the smell of churches—the old, polished wood and the residue of frankincense—and as soon as I was old enough, I took myself to weekly services, usually alone. I used to daydream that I lived in the little back rooms behind the altar, and I never had to exit the doors into the real world.

I spent hours in reflection every day, usually too serious for my family, and I wrote poems about rocks and trees while I walked to school each day. It was enough to cause my poor mother to announce more than once, "You will never be happy in this life." One day, tired of one too many comments that I should be calling friends instead of just sitting there, I remember turning on her much too harshly, and speaking with a certainty I didn't know I had: "How do you know that I won't become one of the great thinkers, or one of the great philosophers of our time? Have you ever thought that not everyone wants to grow up to have this very ordinary kind of life, just doing what everyone else does? Have you ever considered that all of the people who change the world were children once? I like to *think*. That's what *I* like to do." I couldn't have been more than 10 or 11.

As I grew older, I shunned the *joie-de-vivre* lifestyle of my French-Canadian family more and more, and I began to withdraw. I started refusing to play guitar and sing for school plays, or for my father's business friends, telling him I wouldn't be a doll on display for men anymore. And at the age of 15, tired of dating already (begun at 12), I remember tearfully asking my mother when I could just get this business over with and get married. When my family consumed copious amounts of alcohol, I chose to drink less, sometimes abstaining for up to two years at a time, spawning waves of comments that I wasn't much fun. For years, I chose to be vegetarian rather than eat pork every day, and I relentlessly lectured my parents on the cruelty of immersing lobsters—their favourite—in hot water. I didn't care where the best sales were, or which salons gave the best haircuts, and I wore pale cotton clothes when the family wore flashy synthetics. At dinnertime, I relentlessly questioned virtually everything about politics and the emerging media.

At parties, I wanted to listen to Cat Stevens, my favourite, talk, and think quietly about the meaning of life, when my friends were into Jim

Morrison and augmenting their use of psychedelics and condoms. Increasingly, I found myself fractured from everyone and everything. My poetry became bleak and despairing, and even my parents began to detach themselves from me. My father predicted that I would "never find a husband dressed like that"— meaning like a hippie instead of a Barbie. And my mother threw vague curses that she hoped, one day, my daughter would give me as much grief as I was giving her.

From then, I continued to be, by all accounts, a sort of malcontent: an overachiever academically, and social enough to attract the bad boys— but not as popular as the girls who gave it all away. All in all, it seems I left a trail of dust behind me and I was not missed much when I left home at 17 to attend university. So when I fell into drugs, unstable relationships, and other self-destructive behaviours, I actually seemed to fit in better on visits back home. My tumble towards oblivion accelerated, and despite continuing academic excellence, which secured me three university accreditations, with highest honours, I became one of the most pessimistic individuals anywhere. I stopped going to church, and I began to openly challenge the concept of the Trinity, the ethics of consuming the "flesh and blood" of Jesus, and the gaudiness of Catholic churches. Falling ever faster, I relied on superstition, astrology and what seemed like psychic ability to guide me. Men scrambled for my attention in bars only until I opened my mouth and began questioning their purpose in life and their relative value in the universe. I tried to make friends among those whose beliefs seemed more meaningful than mine—embracing Native spiritualism and Judaism through friendships and social networks. Yet I refused to attach myself to anyone or anything permanently.

By the time I reached the age of 25, I had already been pulled away from death four times I knew of for certain—from drowning, acute depression, an attack at knifepoint, and a major accident. Through all these times, I had felt angels at my side, protecting me. So I somehow managed to change my lifestyle almost overnight by seeking refuge in the home of practising Buddhists who had become friends. I remained there long enough to regain my perspective and my health—about six months. Then, I journeyed alone for weeks, from Quaker to Navajo country, and from one ocean to another, until I settled far away from everything in my past, ripped hundreds of poems to shreds, and became a blank slate.

At that point, I chose a first husband deliberately on the basis of two key criteria: he had to abstain from drugs and alcohol completely, and he, too, had to be looking for the meaning of life. He and I never found God in our marriage, though, either separately or alone—as failed plans, bankruptcies, and interpersonal discord became our overwhelming distraction. Yet God was everywhere—and His compassion and mercy were woven through every day of poverty. Each time I was down to my last five-dollar bill, it seemed that the children won a food coupon in a draw at school, or someone dropped by with leftovers. Some of the items we found at yard sales and second-hand stores were so uncanny as to beckon me to reflect. Friends joked that if they needed something, they could just tell me, because everything I needed or wanted, I received. And, inevitably, when I was just at the point of despair, someone would drop by unannounced and invite me and my children for tea, or the sunset would be particularly beautiful that night. I felt like I was always being held aloft, like a feather in a soft breeze. I remembered the story of Jesus (Peace Be Upon Him) feeding the crowd with only a few loaves and fishes, and it gave me comfort and a sense of connection. Here I was I was living a parable, after all, but I somehow still could not get myself to the point of thanking God for it: *"God is full of bounty for mankind, but most are ungrateful."* (2:243) Instead, I looked to a vague sense of karma, trying to understand how it was that my needs always seem to materialize in the physical universe. I just never quite got it that it was simple indeed: God was watching, and listening, and showing me mercy: *"Put your trust in God, for enough is God as a disposer of affairs."* (33:3)

Ironically, it was during those years that I had to pawn my Cat Stevens records. I remember that day well, because the young man at the record store seemed educated and wanted to talk, despite my obvious poverty and babies in tow. We chatted about how consumerism eats away time by fuelling a false need to work and earn more than what is required, and how most people have no idea what life is really about. For just a moment, he looked at me as if he recognized something important, and I couldn't quite tell if he was happy because he thought he'd found a fellow spirit or reactionary. But as quickly as the look came, it went from his eyes. Another person seeing light as a flicker, I guess. The trail of my life was littered with them.

So I carried on as a mother, teacher, community member, and so on. Pagan friends celebrated their daughters' first menses—but I never joined them. I asked for the worship schedule at the local temple at least a half-dozen times, but I never attended. I browsed numerous books on Shamanism at the book store, but I never bought them. I did buy a deck of New-Age Tarot cards, but I felt ashamed to use them unless I had too much to drink. As I closed in on 40, I spoke to friends daily about the search for understanding, and how I could feel it so close, yet could not quite touch it. I even took my "inner child' to a psychiatrist for three weeks. When he suggested that pharmaceuticals might unlock the mysteries of my soul, I quit treatment then and there, believing the key to my soul was faith. After all, I could feel God around every corner—and the overwhelming sensation was one of magnanimous benevolence, like "Cat Stevens" once so aptly described:

> *I've sat upon the setting sun, But never, never, never, never,*
> *I never wanted water once. No, never, never, never.*[1]

And yet, I still I could not manage to understand God's message exactly. Faith, ever closer, kept eluding me—even when it came right up to my door. A practising Muslim joined the class I was teaching at the university, and this man eventually became my husband. Yet even after we were married, I watched with rather detached interest for over six months while he prayed and fasted, and I did not. Conversion was neither required nor expected. I remember being curious about the beautiful book he was reading so much, with its lovely letters and embossed pages—it was the closest I had ever been to the Holy Qur'an, in all those years of wandering. But it was in two languages I couldn't understand. Then, loitering in the university bookstore one day after teaching, I found an inexpensive paperback Qur'an in English in the aisle near the checkout, and thought it might be a good idea to discover what he seemed so interested in.

From the start, I found the Holy Qur'an remarkable, as "Cat Stevens" had, for everything I read about seemed to become a part of my daily life—and everything in my daily life suddenly seemed to be the subject of the verses I would randomly choose to read. Within days of opening the book for the first time, I started a process of remembering—

like a dam opening forth, one bit at a time—and all those moments of God's grace and guidance in my past seemed to start running together in my mind. Suddenly, I was five again, in my room alone, talking and listening to God, like the best secret of all. Only this time, I was holding on strongly to the feeling, and I was filled with certainty and awe:

> *"Whether you believe in it [The Holy Qur'an] or not, those who had knowledge beforehand, when it is recited to them, fall down on their faces in humble prostration, in tears, and recognize it as the fulfilment of a promise."* (17:107)

And so, I too became hooked on the Qur'an—the only book which can make me cry easily, even now. For I had spent much of my life wandering in futility, in a life which is really only as long as *"an hour of a day."* (10:45) I cried for my loss, my arrogance, and my blindness—and I cried for the generosity of my rescue, and for the beauty of this holy book: *"God has made the Qur'an a light to guide such of God's servants as God wills."* (42:52)

In truth, I feel as though my whole life prior to finding the Qur'an has been a near-death experience. I took the life I was given as a gift and I did everything to please myself in the short term—and virtually nothing to show my gratitude to God. Only accidentally was I ever deserving of mercy, for while I did have a strong conscience, I didn't choose my behaviours or my values based on God's instructions—only on a vague intuition, a kind of feeling of what was right. Tragically, I never once really tried to understand that God had planted these feelings in me, to be refined, developed, and applied towards worship in all its forms—devotion, righteousness, prayer, compassion, and charity—and in the knowledge of God itself. And then, though I had done so little to deserve mercy, God lifted the veil.

Ultimately, we have nothing except what God gives us, and through each act of mercy, God is really beckoning each and every one of us to the light. It isn't enough for any of us just to touch the light a little, and then lose it, as I did for so many years, and as so many of us do, in fact:

> *Did it take long to find me? I asked the faithful light.*
> *Did it take long to find me?*[2]

So like Yusuf Islam, I guess, I have a kind of time capsule, too—but mine is inside my heart. Everything God has touched—and God has touched everything—has left an imprint there which I have always been able to feel, even when I have not been able to hear it or see it. It's an odd parallel that "Cat Stevens" was in the shadows of my most troubled days, articulating the questions and pleas that filled my youth as I slid ever faster off the edge—and Yusuf Islam is on the strong, blessed shore of Islam now, as I am, too. Maybe, just maybe, when we are on a quiet path, we can hear the soft footsteps of someone just a little ahead of us on the same path. And just how it is that God connects us all and leads us gently towards our awakening is the great mystery underlying all of reality: *"God protects those who have faith, and leads them forth into light."* (2:257).

It has taken me decades to finally be able to live in a place filled with God—as I had wanted to do when I was very small—for that place is inside myself. And I regularly bring myself to prayer in the middle of the night, in my pyjamas, as I had always wanted. God's promise is so simple, and clear after all: *"Remember me, and I will remember you."*(2:152). For He has already *"written faith into the hearts of believers"* (58:22). All we need to do is let our hearts remember what our hearts have always known, for to God *"is the end of all journeys."* (2:285)

THE TIME SPENT

Whold we reach a certain age, we find ourselves looking back at our choices. One set of decisions brings us here, and another does not—or so it seems. When you accomplish something a bit distinctive, the questions are even more persistent—how did you first start to do this or that, or did you always know you wanted to do this or that, and so on. For example, people are always curious about conversion to Islam. How does someone seemingly give up a lot of freedom to become a Muslim? How do you start not caring about how beautiful you look to strangers, give up relaxing with a glass of wine after work, or stop going to parties and clubs—just for the quiet contentment of trying to live and pray well? And how does one go from being religiously uncommitted to trying to live each and every moment in God's light?

A famous convert, Yusuf Islam (formerly "Cat Stevens"), describes his journey from Orthodox Christianity to Islam, in 1977, after years as a worldwide, western-style music idol. He credits his transformation to a couple of near-death experiences (tuberculosis and drowning), as well as some key passages in the Holy Qur'an someone gave him. First, there was the startling stylistic beauty of the story of Prophet Joseph (Sura Yusuf): "These were not the words of a man," he says. Second, he felt an immediate connection to Chapter 26: *"And the poets, those straying in evil follow them. See you not that they wander distracted in every valley, and that they say what they practise not?"* (26: 224-226) "Cat Stevens" perhaps saw his reflection in these words, and the irony of his career as a pop poet, complete with "groupies" who pursued his life more than their own. Interestingly, one of his early songs had echoed this very sentiment:

Words, just words don't know. Words take you nowhere, nowhere to go, to go…[3]

And another song almost seems to have anticipated his momentous discovery of Islam:

…Don't you feel a change a coming, from another side of time
Breaking down the walls of silence, lifting shadows from your mind…
And the beauty of all things is uncovered again…[4]

In fact, countless songs from the early 70s echo his efforts to grasp an elusive "light" he could somehow sense:

…Mine is the sunlight, mine is the morning, Born of the one light, Eden saw play
Praise with elation, praise every morning, God's recreation of the new day…[5]

Now is the light of the world and the stars going out
Now does the blame for the disaster fall upon men…[6]

You've got too much deceit, deceit kills the light,
Light needs to shine. I said, "Shine light, shine light."….[7]

Take a look at the world, Think about how it will end…
Think about the light in your eyes, Think about what you should know…[8]

Sun is the reason all the happy trees are green
Then who can explain, The light in your dream[9]

Often, he even seems to be pleading for guidance towards that light:

Now, man may live, man may die searching for the question why.
But if he tries to rule the sky, he must fall….[10]

…Oh preacher, won't you paint my dream, won't you show me where you've been
Show me what I haven't seen to ease my mind.
Cause I will learn to understand, if I have a helping hand.
I wouldn't make another demand all my life…[11]

It seems evident that his inclination towards submission to God was just an extension of a feeling he'd had consistently all along:

…I listen to the wind, to the wind of my soul
Where I'll end up, well I think, only God really knows…[12]

And beyond this, "Cat Stevens" appears to have understood from early on that if he really wanted to find that light, he'd have to change a few things about himself:

Go climb up on a hill, stand perfectly still, And silently soak up the day
Don't rush and don't you roam, don't feel so alone, And in this way you will awake …
Don't let your weaknesses destroy you…[13]

I left my folk and friends with the aim to clear my mind out...
Then I found my head one day when I wasn't even trying...

Yes, the answer lies within, so why not take a look now?
Kick out the devil's sin, pick up, pick up a good book now.[14]

So the Holy Qur'an became the good book he'd been looking for all along, where his every thought found its source, and support: *"God will never change the grace which He has bestowed on a people until they change what is in their own souls."* (8:53) As he began reading the Qur'an, "Cat Stevens" began to see more and more that God was relating to him directly through this most unusual book, and he became instantly hooked on Islam—the faith practice set out in the Qur'an. Within a few months, he cast away a lifestyle driven by money and fame, sold his instruments for charity, and adopted a practising Muslim's life.

In effect, one could quote dozens of passages from "Cat Stevens" songs from about 1970 to 1974 and find evidence for the whisperings of Islam in his soul. It's a classic example of how Islam feels more like "remembering" than "changing"—why many people insist on the term "revert" instead of "convert," when it comes to Islam. And in the case of "Cat Stevens," there is really a unique opportunity to examine the path by which one person followed a glimmer of light coming from inside himself to find a place with God, where the light is always radiant:

> *The Parable of His Light is as if there were a Niche and within it a Lamp: the Lamp enclosed in Glass: the Glass as if it were a Brilliant Star, Lit from a Blessed Tree, an Olive, neither of the east nor of the west, whose Oil is well-nigh luminous, though fire scarce touched It: Light upon Light!* (Qur'an 24:35)

"Cat Stevens'" songs, in fact, are a fascinating sort of "time capsule"—historical evidence of God's guidance in the life of one man, and of a journey to become what Yusuf Islam is now—*"a lamp spreading light."* (33:46) Interestingly, "Cat Stevens" himself, far from being a religious scholar at the time (though he is now), or an ascetic seeking God's pleasure full-time (though he does now), was a man deeply immersed in western-style freedoms and material gifts, enough to be the envy of most people. True, he was a reluctant star—a relatively quiet and unassuming person who talked little during concerts and avoided visible excess. But he was, nonetheless, an idol for hundreds of thousands of young men and women who adored him—including me. Yet he completely overturned his life, just like that, in favour of a life of submission to God. In so doing, he realized a fundamental promise from God: *"If you turn away from them and the things they worship other than God...your Lord will shower his mercies on you and dispose of your affair towards comfort and ease."* (18:16)

Those who have never read the Qur'an tend to dismiss a story like this as simply one person's madness—or a sort of uninteresting coincidence. But those who have read it with an open heart get goose-bumps, or water wells up in their eyes. It's because they know the Qur'an has the power to do this to people—with just one chapter, one verse, or even one line. It seems, somehow, to rip away all of the layers of a person right to the core, and to deliver what each one needs to be able to turn the flicker of faith into a bright, blazing light: *"O mankind! Verily there has come to you a convincing Proof from your Lord, for We have sent unto you a Light that is manifest."* (4:174) Reading the Qur'an, in fact, one soon finds that each thought or concern one has about life on a given day is reflected precisely in the words one reads, as the Qur'an miraculously seems to anticipate each request and clarify each person's path exactly, for *"God is a witness of whatever portion of the Qur'an you may be reading."* (10:61) Of course, whether or not a person ever picks up a Qur'an at all, and whether or not the person reading it has a heart obscured by a veil of scepticism, or not, is entirely up to God.

The story of "Cat Stevens'" conversion is also particularly interesting because after this three- or four-year period where he was clearly sensing and grasping at the light within, his music for the next few years seems to chronicle his exploration of astrology, numerology, paganism, and other spiritual paths. It wasn't until 1977 that he finally "got it"—understood the message which God had been infusing him with before—and embraced Islam. So the natural question arises, if "Cat Stevens" was being so strongly guided, why didn't he find God sooner? Why is it that even when God is sending us signals loud and clear, we find it so hard to pay attention? What's stopping us?

In fact, it seems that most people are being effectively stopped. Consider a few statistics from a well-respected faith research group (religioustolerance.org). A shocking 31% of Canadians give the importance of God in their lives a rating of 5 or less out of 10, and 31% never pray—yet

81% of Canadians believe that God or some sort of "life force" exists. How is it, then, that they give the Creator they agree exists so little attention in their lives, and so little gratitude? Russia and East Germany are particularly interesting examples: only 12.4% and 9.2%, respectively, believe in God—but 18.7% and 11.1% believe in miracles. So who, exactly, do the non-believers think is delivering their miracles? And in country after country, populations believe in heaven more than God—in the USA, Northern Ireland, New Zealand, Norway, Great Britain, Russia, and East Germany. Is there any greater arrogance—or delusion—than to assume to deserve the great gift of eternal life, without ever serving God? As the Qur'an warns, *"We leave those who rest not their hope on their meeting with Us, in their trespasses, wandering in distraction to and fro."* (10:11)

So what are we doing, exactly, when we are too busy for the remembrance of God? Are we involved in massive humanitarian actions? Not usually. Are we contributing our time and efforts to the betterment of the world and its people? Hardly. The people who *are* doing these things— missionaries and philanthropists of all kinds—are, in fact, the sort of people who usually do remember God. In contrast, those of us who forget about God are busy working and taking care of our own lives—our needs, our families, our desires, and our goals. Or watching television. Or talking on the phone. We don't need statistics to tell us that the ordinary person these days is hardly ever involved in the pursuit of divine contemplation.

And yet all of us have God's blessing each and every day of our lives, whether we see it—or admit it—or not. And thus, we all have many invitations to remember God. There are the miracles all around us in ourselves, our families, every success we have, every beautiful sunset, every refreshing wind, and on and on. The list is infinite. Yet what do we call it when we are happy or we succeed? We say that we had a feeling we should do this or that, and we credit ourselves with intuition, or even psychic strength. But just who do we suppose has given us this gift of foresight, or the inclination towards our rightful fate? Or, we say that we are lucky, and that things just have a way of working out—but whom else but God could synchronize each and every event, in each and every life, to make even one moment work out exactly as it should? The logistics are mind-boggling. Or, we credit our own strengths for our successes—

it's because we are intelligent, or quick, or strong, or compassionate, or articulate, and so on. But where did these blessings come from, if not from God? Worse even is what we do when things don't go our way and we are unhappy. For then we blame stars, luck, our timing—and, especially, other people—never once thinking that perhaps God is intending for us a difficult test or a lesson, so that we can improve ourselves in the end.

Why is it that it actually takes most people a near-death experience, or a horrible crisis, or something quite out of the ordinary to shock them into seeing the truth, to remember the blessings of their life, to finally take time to talk with God, and to openly seek God's pleasure? It's because we just aren't looking for the "light" in our lives, normally. So if and when we see it, it is bound to seem sudden, fleeting, and unpredictable— even unnerving, or frightening. The Qur'an draws a parallel to a light-ning storm: *"The lightning all but snatches their sight. Every time light helps them, they walk therein. And when darkness grows, they stand still."* (2:20) And so, in between these flashes of light—flashes of insight into our hearts and our relationship with the one and only God—we live in utter dark-ness. We feel as though we are moving and making progress—in our homes, our communities, and our lives. But because we are not making enough effort to understand how it is God's light which guides each moment of our lives, we actually remain standing perfectly still, frozen on the path of faith, simply waiting for another flash of light.

CHAPTER II

Healing the Dark Ages Inside
the Modern Soul

"Verily in the remembrance of God do hearts find rest!" (13:28)

* * *

"True spiritual excellence is devotion to God as if you see Him; for even if you do not see Him, He certainly sees you." (Al-Bukhari, *Iman* 'Faith,' Hadith* 37)
[*Saying of the Prophet Muhammad (pbuh)]

THE DARK AGES

A dervish dancer whirls in a steady pulse, enveloped by his complete devotion. Through him flows the very cycle of life—one palm held upright towards God, and the other held down towards the earth. With every move, his dance becomes the continuum of existence, as gifts from up above pour down on humanity, and the circle of mercy continues from its origin to its end, its full extent unknown. Faith becomes rapture, and rapture, like a river with infinite ends, becomes the blood of the yearning heart. The dance becomes sacred, and effortless, each step engendering the next, each breath like another bead in an endless rosary. It is the most blessed surrender, the most rewarding trust, to let belief stir the soul into motion. And it is the ultimate prayer of this life to take each step in the name of God alone, to leave behind the music until the only sounds which resonate are the whisperings of divinity.

We don't need to look very far into western society these days to see that a lot of people are pretty unhappy—and a lot of the misery, it seems, is self-inflicted. There's always problems, divorces, drugs, broken homes, nervous breakdowns, unwanted babies, fights, etc. More and more, we become aware of rifts in the material, as it were, of our very material lives. And increasingly, we find it hard to explain the suicide of people who seemed to have it all; substance abuse even among the youngest and brightest; increasing numbers of people with no fixed address; and chronic depression among not just some, but the majority, of our population. The reality is that the average person in this culture is carrying an anti-depressant[1], and 15% of the population in developed countries in clinically depressed.[2] On any given day, about 13 million Americans are depressed[3] and Statistics Canada (1997) reports that almost half of Canadians (42%) were depressed for two months in a sample year, more than 20% were depressed half the year, and 13% were depressed for the entire year. Australian Government Statistics indicate that everyone will be affected by depression in their lifetime—their own or another's.[4] And the fastest-growing market for anti-depressants is pre-schoolers[5], while the rate of depression among children is a shocking 23%.[6] In fact, indications are that depression will become the number one killer worldwide after heart disease by 2020.[7] What is it about these times that bring about such pessimism, such a massive epidemic of self-hatred and self-detachment? For without a doubt, there is a growing sense that below the glittering surface of things around here, much is dark indeed. And by placing faith into the margins of our lives, secular culture has left many people grasping for light.

The evident proof is in the manifestations of despair all around us. There are men and women on this earth, for instance, who feel themselves walking with legs which have just been amputated, so deep is the habit, as there are countless elders who keep talking to a long-dead spouse, so deep is the bond. So, too, many people are committed to displaced rituals and feelings by their continuing yearning for the divine—though their faith has long been absent, perhaps since childhood. Faith, after all, is a need which society has told them is even more irrational than their behaviour. So they continue to be diagnosed with a variety of mental illnesses with names as complex as the high-profit pharmaceuticals designed to address them—though a closer look reveals a profound and disturbing reality: many of the sentiments and thoughts associated with clinical depression eerily echo the longing of a soul which is desperately seeking faith. But when a society is convinced that no one needs God, no one notices when someone does.

One of the first indications of someone who is suffering depression is withdrawal. Individuals begin to feel there is no point in talking to anyone, and they start to view their relationships and their daily existence as simply a façade. They separate themselves emotionally from friends and families as they grow in their conviction that no one can really understand or help them. They begin to experience life as though through a thick veil, as sounds and emotions become muted, and the world all around seems to grow more distant and increasingly meaningless. Food becomes tasteless, sexual interest is greatly reduced, and even pain seems muted, so that the depressed individual frequently seems to become injured, or even to injure himself, just to feel his own body, to try to connect with his own life. More and more, he finds himself moving surprisingly slowly through the motions of everyday life, almost in a robotic way, as though time itself had become a shadow above which he was suspended. The superficial attractions of this world seem trivial indeed, and it isn't uncommon to find the depressed soul has negligible regard for money, emptying his pockets when asked, even if there is nothing to eat later, and giving up what used to be his most valuable possessions. The individual in this condition seems worried about little—forgetting to pay bills, to show up on time for work, or to wear matching socks. Yet he is pleased with little, too, as he is enveloped in an overwhelming sadness about the state of the world, he loses his ability to laugh, and he becomes absorbed by the realization that life is not for amusement at all—but rather a very serious thing, indeed.

Yet isn't the soul in such a state strangely conscious of an essential fact, that our lives on this earth really are an illusion? Are we not all supposed to understand that the ornaments of this life are only a distraction, and that the rejection of the ego and material world are important steps on the path towards surrender? For the time we have here is nothing more nor less than a testing ground precisely orchestrated to achieve divine objectives. And at the end, we will be without our friends and families, alone at the mercy of our Creator, Who is always the only One Who can help us: *"Unless my Lord guide me, I shall surely be among those who go astray"* (6:77). Is not the depressed soul, then, in a surprising state of self-awareness, sensing that real life is beyond the bounds of the material sphere? And anyone who realizes this can easily become overwhelmed with grief at the state of this world—the breadth of ways in which we become lost, spending our existence grasping at futility, and the overwhelming deception on which lives of illusion are founded. Yet in seeing the veil without experiencing the Creator, the depressed soul is doomed to living on the edge of that boundary rather than passing through it into the light, remaining hopelessly and painfully disconnected.

Without any real security, fear becomes the greatest burden of the despairing soul. The heart feels oppressed—so the individual seems weak, tired, and without sufficient breath to cope with even the ordinary tasks demanded of him. He has trouble sleeping, struggling with deep anxieties, fearing for his personal safety. At times, he feels with the greatest conviction that the world harbours a tireless evil, waiting to envelop him completely. The individual, as a consequence, is unwilling to make future plans, feeling no certainty whatsoever about what the next minute, let alone tomorrow, might bring. He has increasing difficulty concentrating, and thus he begins to look for a thread of sense in the signs all around him, reading extraordinary meaning into simple events and nature—a bird reminds him that he cannot escape; a grey sky warns of bad news; a cold cup of coffee signals everyone's unconcern; and so on. And he begins to try to read signs in himself, too, feeling every pulse, imagining tumours and cavities forming, believing only that mysterious ends await him.

Yet it is not the realization of the devout that the heart is oppressed without faith, and that the future always brings only what God can know? Also, is it not each our task to seek meaning in the gift of our life, and in the attributes of Creation around us, so that we can, like true messengers of faith, become certain of God's benevolence and of God's presence in the world? And, most definitely, is not the devout soul willing to acknowledge that evil is a real force to be reckoned with: *"God is the Protector of those who have faith: from the depths of darkness He will lead them forth into light."* (2:257) The one in distress has indeed opened himself to the knowledge that the future is inherently uncertain, and that everything in us and around us has been sent to teach us something. Yet without faith, he is left tragically wondering about the content of the lesson, grasping at superstition, and internalizing his darkest fears—not for God, but for an all-encompassing nothingness. In such a condition, he falls further and further into a spiralling black hole from which the exit is ever-elusive.

And in that utter vacuum, the despairing one only finds the confirmation that life has no meaning. He reflects on his own existence and concludes he has done nothing of value, and nothing very well. In fact, he considers that he has committed a litany of failures, and wasted most, if not all, his time. Reviewing his history through his endless torment, he loses track of memories, confounding the past with what is recent, and merging the connections between what has happened with what has yet to come. Death becomes the overwhelming obsession, and the depressed soul may even become consumed with its planning, in intricate detail. Each day, each moment, seems certain to be the last.

Yet is not the individual in such distress feeling the ultimate reality that the end can come at any time, and the end will indeed be a time of judgment? Is it not a proper urge which we all should develop, to be among those who reflect on life every moment, and every day, always trying to improve in order to please our Creator? The believer knows that death is imminent, so he continually prepares for it by trying to be honourable and dutiful in his service, seeking forgiveness, and making the best preparations in his soul: *"Is there a doubt about God, the Creator of the heavens and the earth? It is He Who invites you, in order that He may forgive you your sins and give you respite for a term appointed!"* (14:10) As he prays for continued opportunities and blessings, he understands that time is beyond his mental grasp. For rather than being a line from his birth to his death, it is an infinite multi-dimensional fabric which allows the Creator to be present for everyone, everywhere, across time, and for what has happened anywhere to reverberate on what will happen next, while what happens next simultaneously echoes deep in the past. He is unburdened with existential angst because he believes that he exists because God wills it, and that is enough for him. Yet the despairing soul who torments about the purpose of life, while all the while sadly lacking the necessary faith and the reference to the Creator, remains, quite simply, only a man without answers.

Ultimately, by our very essence as humankind, we are bound to our Creator and to the reason for which we are alive. It is a natural calling from deep within us to seek the fundamental meaning of our existence as manifest proof of God's existence. Yet as our secular societies perpetuate the denial of this fact, we are collectively distracted into believing that this life is the primary objective of our being. The shameful result is that so many souls, while seeming to dance in the light of everyday life, actually harbour an inner darkness which precipitates them to the very edge of despair, and even death. There is only one remedy for what ails them—faith—yet it is virtually ignored as a clinical solution. In its place, society offers a range of anti-depressants, increasingly in the news for their devastating side-effects—including the very act of suicide which they are aiming to prevent.[8] Or, we try various forms of intervention such as Cognitive Behaviour Therapies, techniques which have been shown to have up to an 80% relapse rate in the long-term.[9] Meanwhile, prayer and devotional practice have been consistently found to promote good mental health in the long-term[10], and individuals and communities with defined spiritual beliefs and a sense of purpose about life demonstrate roundly better mental health.[11] Thus, it is evident that while the secular political winds favour the labelling of faith itself as a concern, it is, most assuredly, only the best of cures.

At the turn of the last millennium, a Muslim physician and scientist named Ibn Sina (Avicenna) wrote what is generally regarded, even among western historians, as being the first medical literature dealing with mental health. Rather than shunning sufferers, he prescribed their humane and compassionate treatment. It was a perspective born of his belief that mercy should be shown to all, and that the love and benevolence which breeds in a heart of faith can extend itself from one soul to another, to bring comfort, solace, and hope. Like the dance of the dervish, one hand takes what has been given to it by God, letting it become the fuel of his heart, then directs his other hand to be the humble servant of God, administering care, understanding, and grace. It is well-documented that the contributions of Muslims to European life helped to lift the Dark Ages, initiating the hope and vision of what we now call the modern world. And so may it be that the gift of faith, delivered so clearly in the holy message of Islam, may be the best hope for healing the dark ages inside the modern soul: *"Our Lord is the Lord of the heavens and of the earth: never shall we call upon any god other than Him"* (18:14). For in the end, a strong faith teaches the most important lesson of all: It is really of no matter that I am one, alone on my journey on this earth, but only that God is One.

THE PLAGUE

We're good at treating symptoms in Western culture, aren't we? We're concerned about how our children are having sex, so we dispense condoms in school bathrooms. We're concerned about drugs, so we offer free needles. We get infections all the time, so we take more and more antibiotics. In fact, our society has become the perfect example of crisis management, as most of us have been dulled into the kind of people who don't look very far into things, or very far ahead. Maybe that's why we find it amusing when children ask, "Why?" about everything—because that's a question adults seem to have little use for. Yet there is no shortage of things to ask "Why?" about—even on the nightly news. For example, why was anorexia almost unheard of a generation ago and now it's so common? Why was there no one with a peanut allergy in my whole school, and now the trend is "peanut-free" classrooms? And why is cancer so common these days? We've become so poor at asking "Why," that we think the "reason" we hear more about things is because we have better communications. But what if the real answer were quite different? What if it turned out that here in the west, where we pride ourselves on progress, we were actually very sick people? And what if it turned out that we were systematically being poisoned through our food supply—not by an act of bio-terrorism, but by a plague of mould caused by our own failure to ask "why?" soon enough, or often enough.

But plagues aren't a popular topic these days, are they? In fact, plagues went out of fashion about the same time that religion left the public schools and condoms came in. Now, mention the word, and people tend to joke or visualize hoards of locusts caused by a "freak of nature." It seems we've forgotten that plagues are real and we've been warned about them for millennia. Far from being biological accidents, *"plagues are sent from heaven"* (Qur'an 2:59, 7:162) as deliberate *"punishment from God"* (Deut 28:20-22)—and both the Bible and Qur'an recount the plagues on the people of Moses. The Bible advises believers on how to avoid mildew

(Psalms 91: 1-7), and Leviticus contains instructions for priests to destroy it. In the Qur'an, believers are told repeatedly about the importance of cleanliness (eg. 2:222), and the Prophet Muhammad warned that filth endangers peoples' lives and food leftovers can be dangerous.[12]

We've all had the chance to see mould growing on food—even in our refrigerators. The problem is that moulds release chemicals around us—and in us—that we don't see. Take a little time, some day soon, to check out mycotoxins on the Internet. This is the name given to poisonous substances produced by over 200 species of fungi. The references to the mycotoxins produced by the *Fusarium* fungi are particularly fascinating—and disturbing. *Fusarium* moulds attack various grains, such as wheat, rye, sorghum, maize, barley and oats, as well as soybeans, coffee beans, cocoa beans, oranges, grapes, melons, peanuts and other nuts, and some spices, to a lesser extent. Within just three days, when the crop is left wet in the fields or in storage (such as in the silos dotting the Canadian landscape), and the humidity level rises above just 15% - 20%, moulds grow to dangerous levels. The problem is actually most common in temperate climates, such as in Canada and the US, where most of the world's grain is produced and stored.[13] The problem is that you can't always see these moulds or their toxins at a glance—only at the microscopic or molecular level. Most times, the plants look normal and detection is impossible without expensive tests which growers and grain handlers are not eager to pay for—and even when grain is tested, sampling often fails to find *Fusarium*.[14] Yet conservative estimates are that *Fusarium* has now contaminated almost all feed corn and soft wheat supplies.[15]

The fungi dissolve cell walls in our bodies, absorb the cell content, and reproduce without limits, becoming the most severe threat of all time to human and animal health.[16] *Fusarium* infections can cause a reduction in the number of synapses per neuron and brain functioning, increased bacterial infections, overall suppression of the immune system, and "sick building syndrome." And in one way or another, *Fusarium* is definitively linked to tuberculosis, neurodegeneration of the cerebellum (bipolar disorder/schizophrenia), yeast infections of all kinds—on the hands, feet, genitals, etc.—lupus, asthma, multiple sclerosis, keratitis, endophthalmitis, arthritis, oesophageal cancer, breast cancer, prostate cancer, ulcers, stomach cancer, tonsillitis, sinusitis, otitis, bronchitis, asthma, pneumonia, kidney failure; liver cancer; lung cancer; testicular cancer; osteoarthritis; anorexia; diabetes; Parkinson's disease, mononucleosis, alcoholism, and AIDS.

The mycotoxins released by *Fusarium* mould—Zearalenone, Tricothenes, Ochratoxin A, Deoxynivalenol (DON), and Aflatoxins—have, in effect, turned our diets into our diseases. Zearalenone causes females to acquire pronounced female traits very rapidly—swelling of the vulva, mammary enlargement, increase in size and weight of the uterus, and behaviour suited to constant oestrus, resulting in precocious sexual development in girls[17] and premature puberty syndrome in general.[18] The oestrogen-like effect of the fungus also makes males more feminine, by lowering male libido, reducing the testosterone in blood, enlarging the nipples, and retarding testicular development.[19] Trichothecenes causes exactly the same reaction as radioactivity, with abdominal pains, chills, diarrhea, nausea, anemia, hemorrhage, and quick, painful death. Ochratoxin A is so potent that it can cause death just by inhalation.[20] It is extremely carcinogenic, nephrotoxic (causing kidney damage), immunotoxic (damaging the immune system), and teratogenic (causing non-inheritable birth defects).[21] Exposure to Ochratoxin A in the womb can alter DNA; the effect is dormant until puberty, when it begins to emerge and leads to cancer later in life.[22] DON ("vomitoxin") causes a loss of appetite and vomiting—anorexic and bulimic behaviours—leading to death. It is genotoxic (causing chromosomal abnormalities), it decreases resistance to other diseases[23], and it has been linked to the Gulf War Syndrome.[24] Finally, Aflatoxin is responsible for the deadly peanut allergy and also causes high fevers, liver damage, growth retardation, and decreased immunity; and it is related to anorexia, causing progressive emaciation, apathy, depression, prolapse of the rectum, and liver and kidney damage. Additionally, Aflatoxin is the most carcinogenic substance in existence.[25]

The idea that fungus causes cancer is actually not new, having earned Dr. Johannes Andreas Fibiger the 1926 Nobel Prize. He correlated cancer lesions to past injuries that hadn't healed, showing how pathogens multiply at the injury site, and some of those pathogens include mycotoxins. DNA can't replicate without DNA polymerase, and fungi are the best natural sources of polymerase.[26] In effect, the fungus is what allows cancers to grow. In a similar way, the fungus encourages the spread of AIDS by suppressing the immune system and allowing the HIV infection to establish itself.[27] Yet, tragically, most research dollars keep going to the pharmaceutical industry—companies which thrive on the economics of symptoms, not causes. Meanwhile, *Fusarium* is making cancer and AIDS "contagious" as the fungal environment which promotes these deadly diseases spreads through settlements sharing the same food supply. In essence, fungi have become "Trojan Horses"—allowing deadly diseases into our bodies and communities (Hurt, 2004). And as the two greatest killers of our time rage on, those with the largest stakes in agriculture seem content to talk about percentages of *Fusarium*-damaged kernels (%FDK) and "the cost of mycotoxin management"[28] — and Canada and the US continue to be the world's leading exporters of coarse grains. But how can we measure the cost of so many lives, so pointlessly lost?

Mould is a horrendously powerful foe—it can enter through food, skin, or breathing, and survive without food, in heat or cold, without air, indefinitely. It has no predators, and there is no 100% safe method of stopping it. Mycotoxins can even be transferred through the placenta and breast milk[29] and cause damage even in animals that were not exposed after weaning.[30] *Fusarium* is resistant to heat and cannot be destroyed by cooking or even by considerable levels of radiation. In fact, increased radiation seems to encourage fungal growth in some cases.[31] The implication is catastrophic, considering that the ozone layer is depleting, causing surface radiation to rise, and that many cancers are being treated with radiation. Further, the more exposure one has in a lifetime, the worse the symptoms get.[32] Obviously, any level of *Fusarium* is problematic.

In fact, we've been cautioned for hundreds of years about mould, as death coming from food: God *"splits the grain of the seed-grain and the date-stone. He brings forth the living from the dead, and is the bringer-forth of the dead from the living"* (6:95). Isn't it at least a bit interesting—even for those who don't feel terribly religious—that the Revelations warned humanity about this very problem long before the researchers ever did? Truly, only God can tell us what is clean and safe, and what is not: *"Have you not seen those who praise themselves for purity? Nay, God purifies whom He will, and they will not be wronged even the hair upon a date-stone."* (4:49) And truly, knowledge of God is the most important knowledge—the highest education. Thus, only the scriptures hold the real key to the remedy:

Abstention from Alcohol: All alcohol products contain *Fusarium*, and Fusaric Acid itself causes increased sensitivity to alcohol.[33] Heroine contains aflatoxins; the coca plant is often infected with *Fusarium*; and LSD/magic mushrooms are fungus. Without a doubt, *"intoxication is an abomination"* (5:90).

Eliminating Pork from the Diet: Swine are generally fed inexpensively using inferior grains—often, corn. And since most feed corn is contaminated, pork products are particularly dangerous. For example, in Quebec and Ontario, tests show excessive Ochratoxin A and sufficient zearalenone to cause the estrogenic response. Pigs accumulate *Fusarium* toxins in all their body tissues and pass these to consumers, whereas ruminants, like cows, degrade the moulds in digestion better than single-stomach animals like the pig.[34] As the Qur'an unequivocally states, *"the flesh of swine is an abomination"* (6:145).

Bee Products: Both propolis (hive sealant) and melittin (from bee venom) are the most powerful treatments against fungus in the body, even thought the mechanism is largely unknown, and these substances hold huge potential for the future treatment of cancers, arthritis, and other diseases.[35] Aptly, bees are highly esteemed in the Qur'an: *"There issues from within their bodies a drink of varying colour, wherein is a healing to men"* (16:69).

The scientific evidence is clear that following the instructions in the Qur'an would protect anyone against the worse illnesses of our day. And the greatest irony is that as researchers search for cures in multimillion dollar facilities around the world, the best solutions are all outside the laboratory—in our understanding of creation, and in our relationship with God. So, ultimately, if we just asked "why" a little more often, and looked for our answers in the scriptures a little bit more, we could save ourselves a lot of grief. The date palm is mentioned so often in both the Bible and the Qur'an, more than any other plant, so that it's like a constant, flashing light. By following that light, a little research reveals that date palms are suffering extensively from Bayoud Disease, a *Fusarium* mould infection—while the fruit, precious dates, are well-known as a cure for many fungal-related illnesses. It's the perfect metaphor for God's promise that we have been given "no disease without a cure"—and it's a clear signpost for all, informing us at once about the plague, the cure, and divine justice.

Sadly, our current lack of education is costing us a lot. Modern medicine, for example, relies heavily on antibiotics—but these are mycotoxins, and repeated use of antibiotics makes it more likely that we will be sicker in the future. The common pesticide, "Roundup," used extensively to "protect crops," actually increases the growth of *Fusarium* , spreading epidemics from field to field.[36] As part of its war on drugs, the US sprayed *Fusarium* on coca crops in Columbia which now threatens the Amazon rainforest, including countless as-yet-undiscovered medicinal plants.[37] Worse of all, we continue to overharvest, arguing for efficiency, so that grain production actually outstrips world population growth by about 16% —and mountains of unsold grain sitting on world markets become reserves of toxic waste.[38] In fact, it turns out that by ignoring the larger connection between fungus and death, we have allowed mycotoxins to take lives for years, disguised by the names of specific illnesses like "porcine-induced renal disease"—a fatal fungal infection of the kidneys caused by contaminated pig meat. It killed 20,000 in Croatia, Bosnia and Herzegovina, Yugoslavia, Bulgaria, and Romania in the last decade.[39] In the Balkans, where Ochratoxin A is highest in the diet, the rate of urinary tract tumours is also greatest. And Denmark, where pork consumption is the highest in the world, has the greatest rate of testicular cancer[40], while testicular cancer has been directly linked to the per capita consumption of pig meat generally.[41] In fact, all countries which rely heavily on pork products have the highest rates of cancer—notably Hungary, the Czech Republic, Denmark, Slovakia, Poland, Belgium, the UK, the US, and Canada. So why are we searching the globe for weapons of mass destruction when we are harbouring them on our own farms? It's the sickening truth that our enemies hardly need to conduct bio-terrorism against us—for we are killing ourselves.

It's time for a genuine self-examination—of our bodies, economies, and societies. We have succeeded in building the most efficient agricultural machines and processes in the world—and used these to exploit the good of the earth. We have built food and pharmaceutical empires with more political power than any Third World nation—and used these to drive our own prosperity. We have created the matrix for the distribution of goods worldwide—and inadvertently used it to spread hidden poisons. All the while, our ignorance and excess has caused us to waste precious food, and we have become the people of the scriptures: *"God sets forth a parable—a city enjoying security and quiet, abundantly supplied with sustenance from every place. Yet was it ungrateful for the favours of God: so God made it taste of hunger and terror in extremes closing in on it like a garment from every side, because of the evil which its people wrought."* (16:112) For food and terror have now become inextricably linked in our lives, as mould closes in on us from all sides, and our sustenance has become like that of hell, a food which *"will neither nourish nor satisfy hunger."* (88:07)

When life proves the scriptures, and the scriptures predict life, how can anyone deny the existence of God? Growing up as a Catholic, my favourite object in our house was a lovely wooden cross with Jesus on one side and a thin, sliding door on the other—like a secret and mysterious hiding place. Stowed away deep inside the space behind Jesus was a single, very old frond from a palm leaf, apparently brought from Jerusalem generations ago. It was, without a doubt, the most exotic thing in our home at the time, which was otherwise a composite of department store furnishings and middle class values. I loved to run the dry edges along my fingers whenever I chanced to take it down from the wall—completely unaware that the date palm was a sacred treasure for the whole world, not just for me. Fittingly, I suppose, that palm leaf was kept out of sight as my own family, like many people, ignored Biblical injunctions and never even considered reading the Holy Qur'an—thus, pork was our meat of choice, and alcohol was included at every table and occasion. What I understand now, but didn't understand then, is that life is really about much more than what we see, feel, or know on the surface—for everything can be a sign, a building block of faith. And our experiences with food—both good and bad—are just a way for us to learn what God is trying to teach us. Clearly, the lesson is that it's only through constant adherence that can we expect perfectly delicious, healthy sustenance which is not restricted by season or divine prohibition: *"A reward for the deeds of their past life... fruit in abundance, whose season is not limited, nor supply forbidden."* (56:24-33) And it's only when we stop trying to have heaven right here on earth, right now, that we can ever find it later.

JUSTICE – PART ONE – PRIDE

Years ago, I was strolling through the campus of the university where I taught when I was confronted with a petition to protest the stoning of Nigerian woman. She had been raped by her father and, being pregnant, was now guilty of sex outside of marriage, an offence apparently subject to the death penalty in this Muslim country. The treatment seemed terribly harsh and my heart ached at the thought. But I knew nothing about Islam or Nigeria. And there did seem to me to be hypocrisy on our part as westerners. After all, were we really in a position to lecture other countries about justice? Several women very close to me had been sexually abused by their fathers, though justice was never served on anyone. And I had already been stalked three times in my life—at one point, for months—and threatened with rape at knife point. How were our errors superior to anyone else's? The more I thought about it, the more I erased myself as a voice, as an opinion on anything.

First of all, it seems like a lot of crime goes unchecked around here. In San Francisco, only 28% of violent crimes are solved.[42] In fact, detectives are never assigned to robberies, assaults, non-fatal shootings, stabbings, or beatings—in other words, 70% of the crime. These incidents are reported, stamped "inactive" immediately, and packed into boxes. In Britain, only one of four cases where a parent murders a child reaches conviction because if the jury can't decide with certainty which parent did it, both get off.[43] In Canada, growing Marijuana commercially is deemed a "minor offence" with a typical $2000 dollar fine—what growers consider to be a sort of "license fee" on their $200,000 crops—a "cost of doing business".[44] In turn, only 19% of those who commit spousal assault are convicted in Canada[45], and 3.5 million American children continue to be abused or neglected in an average year.[46] Ultimately, only 45% of violent crimes and 18% of property crimes are actually cleared by arrests, as the probability of being caught for a crime has steadily declined since 1974.[47] In fact, it is now commonly accepted that crime "is not a particularly risky activity".[48] So why aren't we more concerned about our silent complicity in a system which allows so much crime to go unpunished? Why don't we collectively *"fear the trial that affects not only those who stray"*? (Qur'an, 8:25)

Second, the punishments levied on offenders are not really objective at all—a lot depends on age, for instance. If a pregnant woman is attacked and her baby dies, in most US states, no death has occurred because the foetus has no rights. In the last 10 years, the rate of juveniles in adult jails in the US has doubled, and almost 20% of those arrested are under 18.[49] In addition, the average American juvenile serves a longer sentence than an adult for the same crime, and the US is the only country in the world where someone as young as 17 can be given the death penalty.[50] In the 1990s, the US actually executed more juveniles than the other five top contenders put together—Pakistan, Saudi Arabia, Iran, Nigeria, and Yemen. Incredibly, in California, activists are attempting to lower the bar for the death penalty to 14—and in Texas, to age 11[51] — causing Amnesty International to name the US among its worst offenders.[52] Meanwhile, in Canada, though we have no death penalty, we are nonetheless relentless—locking up more juveniles for longer than any western country but the US. Objectively, can societies claim they understand justice when they shift blame away from adults and their institutions, and onto children?

Punishment also seems to depend on a person's colour. Sixty percent of prisoners in American jails are from minorities, and 82% of those executed on death row killed someone who was white.[53] Black people, who form only 12% of Americans, represent 42% of the prison population. Over 60 foreign nationals are awaiting the death sentence in the US, many denied legal counsel, and there has been a 75% increase in detainees by the Immigration and Naturalization Service since the 1990s.[54] In Philadelphia, for example, the chance of receiving the death sentence is four times higher if the defendant is black.[55] Contrary to the common idiom, then, it seems that justice isn't blind after all—for it does see a difference between black and white. So can we honestly say that our societies do *"not distort or decline justice"*? (4:135) In fact, Amnesty International has asked aloud how countries with poor records at home can dictate standards to foreign countries. In this regard, rather than travel the world to try to spread our ideologies and values, Canadians and Americans might want to do a little soul-searching right here at home. If we really cannot say that our criminal justice system is working, how can we dare to suggest that we know how to fix the problems of criminal justice systems elsewhere? The Qur'an cautions against this kind of arrogance: *"Do not hold yourself as being purified, for God knows best who it is who guards against evil."* (53:32)

There's no question that real justice is a big challenge. Certainly, the geography of North America compounds the problem—for the land is huge and wide, and the costs of effective policing are staggering. Demographics complicate matters further, for throughout this great land are scattered a larger mix of cultures and races than can be found anywhere in the world, sometimes creating conflicts and misunderstandings. We should hardly be surprised, then, when the American "melting pot" boils over, or the Canadian "mosaic" cracks a little. Well-intentioned people with stacks of certificates and qualifications are throwing themselves into the field of prison reform, from the volunteer pastors who minister to the inmates, to the freelance advocates who try to secure victims' rights, to the legislators and scholars who continuously examine and revise policies and laws. And still, with all of this expertise and good will, researchers are admitting that the current system is failing. What the western criminal system really needs is prompt deterrence, but this might compromise the highly valued procedural safeguards which are essential to establishing guilt. Meanwhile, Americans and Canadians are frustrated by the lack of restraints on criminal activities, and they tend to respond simply by increasing the severity of the penalties—longer prison times, and bigger fines. But the irony is that the bigger the sentence, the more likely it is to be appealed or plea bargained away.

Increasingly, those seeking real justice are telling themselves that the west needs a more effective alternative to recidivism than imprisonment.[56] Western experts maintain, in fact, that the permanent solution to crime is to remedy the three fundamental problems causing the high rate of crime.[57] First, people feel detached from the traditional bonds of community which used to check their behaviours. Second, the status of children has been expanded, largely through the media, so that they have become adventure-seeking consumers. Third, the economic system has

created a self-destructive underclass among minorities which feels powerless and frustrated. These are particularly fascinating statements for
Muslims to consider, for Islamic society is designed specifically to address
these issues.

First, Islam promotes a deep attachment to the family and community, and this is indeed a powerful check on behaviour. In Mecca, the centre of pilgrimage, for example, it is commonplace for shopkeepers to
leave their stores unlocked while they attend prayers. Compare this with
the heartless looting that takes place after a hurricane strikes a commercial centre in the US. Second, the status of children in Islam is clearly
limited, in that children have duties to their faith and their parents, and
conspicuous consumption is prohibited. This doesn't mean that every
Muslim is pious and reasonable in his or her spending—but every Muslim
should be. Third, the economic system in Islam, properly applied, erases class barriers as the richer one is, the more one is obliged to donate,
and people are not to be judged on their physical or financial attributes.
In fact, the variety of races, colours, and cultures are considered a blessing in Islam: *"God made you into nations and tribes, so you may know each other and not despise each other—the most honoured of you is the most righteous of
you"* (49:13); therefore, all people are to be guaranteed their dignity and
treated with equity. Again, the point here is not that all Islamic countries
are perfect states, which they sadly are not, but that if Islam were practised exactly as it should be, they would be. For Islam is a different kind
of criterion, adhering closely to the revelations and requiring a lot of
effort and self-restraint on the part of the individual in order to integrate
with his or her community and nation.

What is the net result of the self-restraint fostered by Islamic values?
A comparison of crime rates makes an important point. The rates of
assault per one thousand people in Saudi Arabia, Malaysia, and Turkey, for
example, are .19, .18, and .78, respectively. In contrast, for Canada, the
US, and Britain, values are 7.25, 7.7, and 7.5, respectively—ten to thirty
times higher. The rate of robberies per one thousand people in Saudi
Arabia, Malaysia, and Turkey is .02, .63, and .02, respectively, while for
Canada, the US, and Britain, it is .83, 1.41, and 1.58, respectively—up to
80 times higher. The rate of rape per one thousand people in Saudi Arabia,
Malaysia and Turkey is .00, .05, and .01, respectively, while in Canada,

the US, and Britain, it is .8, .4, and .9, respectively, 20 to 100 times higher. For fraud, the rate per one thousand people in Saudi Arabia, Malaysia,
and Turkey is 0, .08, and .15, respectively, while for Canada, the US and
Britain, it is 2.65, 1.28, and 5.31, respectively—up to 500 times higher. The
total crime rate per one thousand people provides an interesting summary—7.23 in Malaysia, 1.24 in Yemen, 7.14 in Qatar, 4.2 in Turkey, and 4.2 in
Indonesia, while the rates are 23.8 in Canada, 62.7 in France, 76.0 in
Germany, 81.5 in the US, and 86.0 in Britain. In every single case, the
crime rates in non-Muslim countries is 10 – 80 times greater than in
Muslim countries. And of the 10 most "murderous nations" in the world,
not a single Muslim country is among them.[58]

It is particularly noteworthy that these Muslim countries actually
have very different approaches to crime and punishment based on how
closely they follow the Islamic Code of Law (*Shari'a*) in the Holy Qur'an,
clarified through the teachings of the Prophet Muhammad. In Saudi
Arabia, *Shari'a* is followed more rigidly, for instance, than in Malaysia,
where Islamic courts are available along with civil courts, depending on
jurisdictions and offences—a dual system which is common to many
Muslim countries; and Turkey does not enforce Islamic Law at all. The
common point between these countries, however, is the prevalence of
Islamic morals among the majority—morals based on self-control, respect
for chastity and sobriety, and the importance of personal honour.

Ask ordinary Canadians and Americans about this, and they will
easily admit that self-restraint, chastity, and sobriety are not their most
commonly-held values. For this reason, Islam looks harsh and confining
to them, and they feel oppressed at the thought of so many personal restrictions. What's interesting, though, is that despite the bad press and the
fact that "*Shari'a*" has now become one of the most negative terms in the
English language, Islamic values are willingly upheld by millions of people around the world who feel more comfortable living in societies with
limits on personal and interpersonal behaviours. Why? Because Islam is
very effective in reducing rampant criminality, allowing respectful and
law-abiding individuals to feel safe. In fact, many important lessons can
be learned from the Islamic Code of Law (*Shari'a*), and these should be
on the table when Canadians and Americans are trying to brainstorm
solutions to the current problems with their justice systems.

These days, I can't help but be reminded of an old phrase from the 70s and 80s—that the key to happiness is to "go back to basics." All over Canada and the US, back then, people were trying to re-learn the meaning of life, by growing vegetable gardens, job-sharing, and going for walks instead of watching TV—some even moved into secluded communities with rules and practices completely different from the rest of society. It seems people had begun to realize that something was missing, or that something they knew long ago had been forgotten—and that their values were not very satisfying. As a result, that time bred a whole stream of "seekers"—people who quit high-paying jobs to live on farms, or sold everything they had to go climb a mountain in Tibet—each in their own way, looking for the paradigm which would give meaning to their lives again. That paradigm is faith. Back then, some people found it, and some people didn't. Now it's time to wonder if we all should try to go back to basics ourselves. For despite—some would say, because of— the rampant promotion of anti-religious sentiments in western culture, growing numbers of people feel depressed, scared, confused, dissatisfied, and angry. Are we ready to consider, then, that in the rules of life set forward in the revelations, there might be a remedy to the endemic pain of secular societies?

JUSTICE – PART TWO – PREJUDICE

The first seven years of my schooling, I attended a private Catholic school. There were a lot of rules—about everything from the length of our skirts, the polish on our shoes, how to curtsy, how to address the sisters and Mother Superior, how to write, and so on. There were always a few girls who complained their skirts were unfairly long, and they rolled them up at the waist, only to get caught by Sister Genevieve in the hallway with a measuring stick. They'd be given hundreds of lines to write, then a phone call would be made and they'd be sent home, suspended for days until they formally apologized. It was a lot of fuss and embarrassment, so those girls who argued a lot remained the minority. Most of us were happy there, getting high scores and enjoying all kinds of little incentives and rewards from the sisters, like field trips and special performances. And justice was fair. Even though I was respected, I was whipped 10 times on the hand with a metal ruler in Grade 2 because a boy behind me had spoken to me. For in all the rules was an inherent promise— compliance equals success. Then, one day at the end of elementary school, the sisters announced the school would be closing at the end of the year. So I was transferred to the local public high school, where kids were smoking drugs at recess and experimenting with LSD at parties in Grade 7 and 8. Two brothers brought knives to school in their boots, and no one dared to stop them. It doesn't take much to figure out who rules in an environment like this. The girls who wanted their skirts shorter got to wear whatever they wanted, and they soon became among the first to lose their virginity, at ages 12 and 13, some at the back of the school playground. A few teachers got away with dating the grade 11 and 12 students and bought drugs from kids who then became "untouchable"—passing classes they never attended. If you studied, people called you names and put you in lockers, or assaulted you in the hallways or after school. Anarchy ruled and success became elusive, as kids overdosed, got pregnant, dropped out of school, and ended up in juvenile detention or detox. But the lesson of those years was a priceless one I would not soon forget. For when people who are trying to live well are more at risk than those who are causing chaos, hasn't something gone terribly wrong? This is the question Canadians and Americans are increasingly asking themselves about their own justice systems.

The reality is that our prisons are bursting at the seams. The US incarcerates more people than any other western country and was holding more than 1.7 million people in its jails in 1996, triple the number from 15 years prior. The current rate of incarceration is 699 per 100,000 people, higher than any other western nation. Far from being above criticism, Canada is a shameful second, at 118 per 100,000 people. In California, the smallest prison holds over 3500 people, and prisons are routinely operating at 200% capacity, as the US population continues to soar. It's not unusual for prison guards to be watching over 300 prisoners, and for 25% of the population to just sit idly all day as programs are full to capacity. Of course, these conditions have led to rising violence and widening abuse. Amnesty International has harshly condemned prison conditions in the US for numerous violations, including abuses by US police and prison officials; incarceration of refugees as criminals; sexual abuse of women prisoners; excessive force used in maximum security units; shackling of prisoners for hours or days, including pregnant women; unfair treatment of minorities by the judicial system; and the retaliation individuals face when they try to denounce the problems.[59]

The truth is, both Canadian and American statistics reveal a bleak, persistent cry for profound, long-lasting solutions. Suicide is the eighth leading cause of death among American men, and 72% of those who commit suicide are white—presumably those with the most social advantages. In men aged 15 – 24, suicide is the third leading cause of death. In fact, in the US, suicide kills 1.5 more men every year than homicide.[60] That's one suicide every 17 minutes—and the Canadian rate is comparable, according to Statistics Canada. So why are people who claim they have so much going for them ready to throw it all away? Even more tragically, unhappy as they are, ordinary Canadians and Americans commit unspeakable horrors against their own families. Nearly one-third of American women, and one-third of Canadian women report being physically or sexually abused by their husbands or male partners[61], and one-third of American female murder victims were slain by husbands or male partners in 1996.[62] In the US, 1.3 children are sexually abused by a family member every minute.[63] One in five children murdered is killed by someone in the family[64], and the US ranks first in the world for child maltreatment deaths—Canada is in a shameful 9th place. In addition, the US and Canada embarrassingly rank 4th and 9th, respectively, for child injury deaths. Yet there is not a single Muslim country among the top 20 offenders in either category.[65] So why do people who have all the options in the world make the worst possible choices? Could it be that open social boundaries don't actually yield masses of happy individuals?

As a culture, we may have to ask ourselves difficult questions about what, exactly, we're trying to protect. Muslim society is designed to protect family, honour, and religion as fundamental human rights, and it views promiscuity and alcohol as the biggest threats. To achieve protection of these rights, it's true that personal liberties are restricted for the benefit of the majority, and statistics show that there will be times when a limited number of individuals will be severely punished to protect the fundamental rights which Islamic society has decreed to be the most important. In contrast, secular society aims to protect individual freedom and personal endeavour above all, and promiscuity and alcohol are tolerated—even supported by media and advertising. To achieve protection of these rights, the safety of the majority is put at risk, however, as statistics clearly show that substance abuse encourages crime, that overt sexualization fosters sexual violence—and, worst of all, that the personal freedoms which end up being defended the least are often those of the least empowered.

Interestingly, the very industries at the root of the problem have such a powerful voice in the west that no one dares to suggest a "crime tax" be imposed on alcohol manufacturers, or on the media, music, and fashion industries, who keep alive the fantasy that alcohol is normal and sexual freedom is always a good thing. Increasingly, for example, Canadians have been insisting that tobacco industries subsidize the national health care system since so many medical costs are incurred by smokers. Meanwhile, more than 45% of rapists are under the influence of drugs or alcohol[66], alcohol is directly involved in 2/3 of sexual assault cases, and alcohol is the leading cause of death and injury in teens and young adults.

In fact, Americans estimate that alcohol use costs society more than $86 billion dollars a year, when the entire "Desert Storm" operation in Kuwait and Iraq only costs the US $60 billion.[67] Is it really so radical a thought to have the industries that support crime directly subsidize the criminal justice system? For *"blame is against those who oppress men with wrongdoing, and insolently transgress beyond bounds in the land."* (42:42) As the boundaries of what is considered wrongdoing keep widening, and the media and advertising keep encouraging younger audiences to transgress, will we hold ourselves accountable?

The truth is that we will never be able to learn anything from other people's values if we aren't first ready to admit that something may be wrong with our own. Are we willing to consider, even for a moment, for example, that even though we think it's a problem that women in Islamic countries are required to have an escort in public, it's also a pretty big problem that every single minute, a woman unescorted in public in this culture is being raped?[68] Even though we don't like how Muslim parents try to control their children so much, are we willing to admit that we don't like how our own kids are so out of control, with 64 teen pregnancies per 1000 births in the US—the highest rate of any country in the world[69]—and one in five teens carrying a gun?[70] Even though we think it's ludicrous that people value chastity so much that they are ready to kill for it, are we ready to consider that it is ludicrous that one of every three girls and one of every five boys will be sexually assaulted in our culture before they turn 18—half before they turn seven?[71] Even though we think it's a shame how Muslim adults seem so serious and don't seem to know to just relax at the end of the day with a couple of beers or a glass of wine, can we agree that it's a shame that almost 50% of our teens use marijuana or other drugs[72], and 87% of our teens use alcohol?[73] Even though we wonder about the quality of education Muslim kids are receiving in Islamic schools, are we willing to wonder why, despite their education, 240,000 to 360,000 of our own kids in college today will die of alcohol-related causes?[74] And even though we think it's horrific that someone might lose their life for committing a murder, are we horrified at all that someone who has been proven, beyond a shadow of a doubt, to have mutilated innocent children might be living in a family neighbourhood again someday? Maybe these hard questions have something to do with how many Canadians and Americans are becoming Muslims—converting at the rate of almost 30,000 a year in the US alone.[75] Is it possible, actually, that ordinary citizens are beginning to ask themselves tough questions about what is right, and what is best?

There's an idiom that seems to capture our predicament exactly: "Thunder only happens when it's raining." It's from an old song from that seeker period of our cultural history, actually. It seems that we have an ongoing situation here, a background of discontent and hopelessness which is generating constant, thunderous bursts of violence in communities across Canada and the US. And the thunder won't stop until the rain stops. It just might be that secular culture, which promises so much, actually fails to deliver the most essential human need—hope. And without the hope that something better waits beyond this life, people are unable to deal with—or avoid—substance abuse, victimization, marital breakdown, uncontrolled pregnancies, abortions, addictions, drunk drivers, stock market crashes, and all the countless other perils of societies built on serving the freedoms of those who are best and fastest as getting what they want. Thus, we shouldn't be surprised when Islam is the fastest growing religion behind bars.[76] Is it possible that those who fall through the cracks of our society are the most ready to believe that their society is failing, too? Is it possible, then, that those who have experienced the broken promises of a secular world are the ones best able to understand that the real promise of recovery and self-improvement, for genuine hope and redemption, is only with God?

First and foremost, therefore, Islam recognizes that punishment alone cannot ensure compliance—a righteous system involves a partnership between the individual and the larger community, with both intending to the best of their abilities to comply with the scriptures. Thus, a just society must make it possible for all individuals to be spared from unemployment, poverty, homelessness, hunger, discrimination, and violence. And Islam upholds that a system which allows for rampant lawlessness will have failed in its duties and thus will have to shoulder the blame for the crime itself, for *"whoever helps in an evil cause shares in its burden"* (4:85). Thus, it may be necessary to punish one person to prevent many from being at risk from further offences or from the enduring negative influences which breed fear and disrespect within individual communities. In turn, the individual in such a society must develop and uphold a genuine attitude of contempt towards crime. It is for this reason that Muslim morals are unambiguous: society is about individual duties more than individual rights, and raw pleasure and immediate gratification are not factors in the equation: *"You may dislike a thing that is good for you, and you may love a thing that is bad for you"* (2:216).

If our western system could demonstrate diminishing criminality, cost-effectiveness, or a feeling of safety among our populations, we might have an argument to make abroad. But as it is, high-profile suspects run free, our prisons often fail to heal or reform those in their charge, lawyers have become profit seekers in the trade for testimonies, and the majority of Canadians and Americans are sceptical, frustrated, and even discouraged about their own criminal justice systems. So when our soldiers, legislators, and diplomats try to do good by promoting western influences and morals on missions abroad, Muslims can only reply, *"How strange it is for me to be calling you to salvation when you are calling me to the fire."* (40:41) Isn't it time for those of us living in western societies to admit that maybe, just maybe, we all have something to learn about justice? May God be our Teacher.

CHAPTER III

The Ego Trap

"And walk not in the earth exultant, for you cannot rend the earth, nor can you reach the mountains in height." (17:37)

* * *

"The strong one is not the one who overcomes people, the strong one is he who overcomes his ego." (Al-Haythami, from his hadith collection of *Majma' al-Zawa'id*)

TEST OF EGO – PART ONE – THE VIEW

One of my clearer memories of childhood is from a day in second or third grade, when we read a short story about two destitute brothers who torment themselves over what to buy their mother for Christmas. One boy overspends somehow to buy his mother a necklace, while the other spends a modest amount and buys her a new pail and mop. We were all supposed to agree that the boy who bought the necklace showed his love for his mother better than the other. I was the only one in the class who disagreed. I said that the mother, given her circumstances, probably didn't have much use for fancy jewellery and might wish the money had been spent on food. On the other hand, because she would use the new pail and mop every day, these were good gifts because they didn't waste money and would make her everyday life more beautiful. I was silenced quickly with cold stares from the teacher, and from classmates—better luxury than reality, it seemed, and better to feed vanity than necessity. And so it was that I discovered one of the key values of my culture: ego is everything.

The idea of ego, after all, is central to western ideology. Defined, ego is a collection of thoughts, feelings, ideas, beliefs, and habits which are neither stable nor permanent, yet which we consider to be our very essence. Ego isn't real—yet it's what we use to interpret and deal with all of our reality. It's something we're encouraged to do right from the beginning in western culture, as we read Greek and Roman myths full of huge ego-battles, and children's stories with the central theme that if you believe in yourself above anything, nothing can stop you. As we mature, we develop a complete concept of just who we are—we are our egos, in other words—and we work hard to protect our egos at all costs. To do this, we develop selfish desires and limited beliefs through which all of our actions—and reactions—become guided. And when our ego's desires remain unfulfilled, or our ego is threatened, we react aggressively to defend it, generating unhappiness among the members of the larger egos of which we are a part (our families and communities) —those with whom we share some common ego properties, like a mutual valuing of a particular sport, culture, political position, and so on. Through our egos, we try to have control over the things around us—in other words, the ego gives us a kind of illusion of strength which reduces the unpredictability of the world. In this way, it becomes what some researchers call the "god within" –but it also becomes our own worse enemy at the same time. That's because the ego's constant search for gratification keeps us preoccupied the life of this world and addicted to specific outcomes. We become obsessed with everyday events, feelings, and activities so that we can maintain or improve our egos. Putting the ego first like this fosters a sense of "independence" inside each one of us by which our "self" seems and feels really separate from our body, and even from the world all around us. As a result, most of us who are raised in the western mindset pursue a life path guided by our needs and wants, not by a higher set of morals, as we each become our own personal judges, deciding what is right and wrong.

In theory, being able to decide independently on the relative merits of every action might seem like a good thing, and it would be easy to assume that ego delivers contentment. But consider the sad statistics. Facing an increasingly secular globe, the World Health Organization predicts that within 20 years, half of all disability around the world will stem from mental illness.[1] Ironically, in Nigeria, one of the poorest places on earth, and a religious Muslim nation, 45% of people report being "very happy," compared to 32% of Canadians.[2] In Bangladesh, the heart of the third world, also conservatively Muslim, 67% of people are "quite happy," which only 55% of Canadians and 53% of Americans are.[3] And in El Salvador, though destitute by western standards, the life satisfaction rate is roughly equal (7.2) to that in Canada (7.6) and the USA (7.4).[4] Curiously, then, it seems that following and satisfying one's ego—the main preoccupation of most westerners—does not necessarily generate unlimited happiness.

In fact, ego seems to lead to a lot of unhappiness, even according to those who think life should be centred on our egos. The psychological literature—as well as popular novels and movies—is filled with catastrophes, like relationship problems, traumas, death, illness, public embarrassment, failure at work or school, and so on, which apparently rob us of ego strength, deflating or fading our egos. There is also the ever-present problem of defending clear "ego boundaries"—not just with others, but within ourselves. When these are disturbed, we may fall victim to various psychoses, or internal conflicts. An individual who suffers from such difficulties will usually be recommended for "ego-state therapy," where practitioners try to resolve the conflicts in order to reintegrate the personality. Therapy frequently involves hypnosis or journaling to the "child within," as well as the new trend of "self-help"—the ego assisting the ego, so to speak. All in all, it seems that in western society, when we are mentally unwell—a seemingly common occurrence—the diagnosis usually revolves around some sort of problem with the ego. In fact, we have dictionaries full of ego disorders: denial, displacement, intellectualization, projection, rationalization, reaction formation, regression, repression, sublimation, suppression, and so on. So psychotherapy—available in over 200 varieties—is designed to strengthen weak egos which lack enough "ego-support" or "ego-maintenance" in their everyday lives. And western life is seen as an interplay between egos—some have even called it a "game"—where we learn to get our needs met while we manage and manipulate other egos.

It's an interesting view, really, because the fundamental assumption is that we should all want to have strong egos. But there are prominent faiths where ego is actually not valued, the most obvious being Islam and Buddhism. Not surprisingly, the west lumps these value systems together under the title of "honour-and-shame-based traditions," concludes that they build fragile egos, and implies they are inferior. In other words, the sovereignty of the ego is seen as a kind of cultural evolution. And in the context of un-repressing the ego to act out its full potential, western secular society eliminates the idea of shame, rather than shameful behaviour itself, because of its conviction that strong egos yield success. In this way, we ensure that ego continues to be the main paradigm by which we hold ourselves together—inwardly and outwardly—and the cycle continues.

So, determined that ego should be the proper cornerstone of all human development and relationships, we design institutions whose main reason for existence, in fact, is to protect this very perspective. Consider the current educational system in the west, for example. Modern teacher training places a huge amount of importance on Erickson's theory of human development, and according to this framework, ego integrity is a critical step in maturity. As a result of this theoretical grounding, schools in Canada, the US, and other western countries consider it their responsibility to ensure proper ego development. The diagnostic tests used to assess and place children in school programs are designed by the educational system itself. So whenever they are used, researchers (not surprisingly) find a correlation between ego resiliency and early school success. The results confirm what teachers notice all the time in their classrooms: the child who has been raised in a more insular, traditional setting, in the company of close family more than preschool buddies, does have a harder time "fitting in." The supposition we're always making is that the child who knows how to assert and maintain his own ego among his classmates has somehow been better prepared for life. It just isn't even a point for discussion in educational circles that our assumption is itself a value judgement on what kind of childhood—and adulthood—best serves humanity's purpose.

Consistent with our decision that ego development is the supreme personal achievement, we foster interventions which help egos reach their full potential, ostensibly to ensure health, happiness and social competence. When we stumble upon individuals who seem to have weak egos, who are unsure of their abilities, or have trouble working inside our model, we recommend them for counselling, where specialists work to restore their egos, or even help them to "discover who they are"—i.e., find their egos. Therapists investigate their relationships and recommend friendships and life choices which will ensure ego maintenance—loved ones according to whether they will boost or destroy ego ("ego-validation") and groups according to the relative strength of the other member egos ("ego-stratification"). Yet the implications for increasingly multicultural schools and communities are devastating. For by definition, psychotherapy and western-style educational counselling can only help those who believe in, and want, ego strength. These practices can do little to heal—and much to hurt—anyone who believes that the ultimate purpose of the ego is to nullify itself.

So how did this obsession with the ego in the west get started anyhow? We don't need to look any further than the man Time Magazine (1999) dubbed "The Century's Greatest Mind"—Sigmund Freud. It doesn't seem to matter that Freud's original research is now highly suspect and he has been accused of experimental fraud, or that some studies have demonstrated that Freudian "therapy" can be worse than no therapy at all. The influence of the man on western thinking is permanent and pervasive. Through Freud, the average person in western society learned to consider ego identity as the triumph of maturity, and to think of life in terms of two drives—sex (the "life force") and aggression (the "death force"). Freud's view of the world led to new definitions of human nature in terms of ego growth, ego boundaries and ego defences. An individual apparently was made up of ego states, each with a unique history depending on various life experiences and influences. Accordingly, a problem would easily result when ego states came into conflict or did not communicate with each other, usually due to some childhood trauma. Freud's ideas ultimately led to what's been called the "genitalization of psychopathology"[5] because his unique and most recognized contribution seems to have been the notion that everything that happens in someone's mind is ultimately sexual, and that we are all a little crazy. Cynically, some people have accused Freud of providing better absolution than any priest ever could, because thanks to him, every dark sexual fantasy could be considered a natural result of a parenting error. Suddenly, sexuality became the most important human dimension, and mental illness became coffee-table talk. Critically, the Freudian worldview had no use for religion—which he considered a "neurosis," a "universal obsessional ritual," a "mass delusion," and an "infantile illusion." And so, Freudian psychology easily led whole generations towards atheism, as it promoted its three powerful anti-faith mantras: we are the centre of the universe, we are the goal of the universe, and we are the masters of ourselves. Thus, a new kind of polytheism was born—with each ego idolizing itself—a world where the only remaining sin was repression, and the most dangerous, disease-causing factor was guilt. And it is precisely this toxic mix of self-adulation and blamelessness which came to form the underpinning of western life.

So now that we are obsessed with ourselves and our sexuality, it's pretty obvious that we are a long way off from the life models the prophets gave us—Abraham, Moses, Jesus, Muhammad, Noah, and the rest—peace be upon them all. In fact, our lifestyles are starting to be a better reminder of the people who are not at all the heroes of the Holy Books—like the

Pharaoh, and the citizens of Sodom and Gomorrah. It's something the average person doesn't like to think about really, but we can't hide the fact that the ego-fest which is consuming us in western society is the picture of everything we have been told not to do, and we have become exactly what we have been warned not to become. Even someone who hasn't picked up a Holy Book in years would have to admit this. But try and warn anyone that our society, our culture, is headed down the wrong path and you will get some odd looks. It's because somehow, in being so focussed on ourselves, we've collectively decided that the message of the Holy Books— if we even read it or somewhat believe it—is for another set of people, not for us. We don't seem to be willing to consider at all, even just for a minute, that the message is *"a reminder to all the worlds"* (38:87), for *"God has revealed from time to time the most beautiful Message in the form of a Book, consistent with itself, yet repeating its teaching in various aspects,"* (39:23) and *"for every message is a limit of time, and soon shall ye know it."* (6:67) We are even invited to travel the earth—not to lavish in hedonism in luxury resorts and work on our tans, but so we can figure out what this life is all about: *"Travel the earth and see what was the end of those who rejected truth,"* (3:137), though *"superior in strength and population, (30:9)—* see *"how many towns We destroyed which exulted in their life of ease and plenty,"* (28:58). Without doubt, it is the collective destiny of humanity to achieve a deep faith in One God. Yet we have effectively moved religion to the archives of our lives. And, ultimately, if we just keep looking in the mirror, our view will never improve.

TEST OF EGO – PART TWO – THE SPIDER

Have you ever noticed how most people hate having their photograph taken? Try to record someone on video, and they become even more self-conscious. Quickly, they want to have a look at what you've just shot or taped, and their reaction is predictable. "Oh—I look so fat," Or, "Oh—I look so old," Or, "Do I seriously sound like that?" And so on. The really amazing thing is that this new mediated reality becomes their truth. They may be attractive, but if the clip shows otherwise, they now believe they aren't. They may have thought they had a pleasant voice or manner, but if the recording suggests they don't, they believe they don't. It's hard to know why this is so, but we give the media a lot of credibility. We let it interpret and re-interpret our world—even though we know it's an impure witness which layers a veil on everything. In other words, despite knowing "the camera adds ten pounds," or that recording technology can make the worst singer sound good, we still give the media preference over reality as the ultimate arbitrator of our egos.

The western media, in fact, has worked hard to fuel this dependence and our myopic view of reality. First, big egos are everywhere—in video games, music videos, talk shows, sitcoms, cartoons—and most especially, advertisements. Products and images are designed specifically to boost or prop up our faltering egos, and to keep us focused on trying to be as gorgeous, powerful, individualistic, and popular as possible—selling us everything from tighter abdomens to peace of mind. The commercial slogans capture the easy philosophy of the times: don't take life too seriously, the best therapy is laughing, play hard, have fun, relax, take time for yourself, go for it, you only live once, look better, feel good, do it now, focus on yourself, get your needs met, enjoy yourself while you can, take it one day at a time, take it easy, why wait for tomorrow, stop apologizing, take ownership, just do it, you're worth it, etc. Repeated enough times, these messages have become core popular beliefs, effectively bumping any pearls of scriptural wisdom right out of our collective consciousness.

What the commercials are doing, really, is selling us our own culture—telling us what we should look like, think, feel, and do in order to be who we are, right here, right now. And the threat is issued repeatedly in print, on air, and on the web that taking life too seriously will actually lead to death—from cancer, diabetes, high blood pressure, stroke, heart attack, immune disorders—you name it. As a result, the media almost seem justified in turning life into comedy—from Jerry Springer to the ever-popular "reality shows." Now, every mistake a human might make, and every absence of heart or conscience, simply increases a program's popularity. It's because humour has become a powerful tool in our efforts to become Supermen and Wonderwomen—invincible egos powered by the pleasure principle. The result is that even the most shameful behaviours—drunkenness, infidelity, promiscuity, dishonesty, and so on—have become just a way of getting what we need out of life. Through the power of suggestion, we are being collectively deluded into thinking that our egos can secure our futures—and we even have insurance companies selling us guarantees that we can somehow keep what we have indefinitely. The western worldview asserts, then, that a solid ego can essentially make its own fate. In this way, the ego has become man's ultimate solution to salvation anxiety, and the western media's message is dangerously clear: we are responsible for our own happiness, and happiness is the ultimate goal. And yet, there could be nothing further from the truth.

Interestingly, we've actually been warned about the media for a long time. The Bible has stern advice: *"Thou shalt not make unto thee any graven image, or any likeness of any thing that is in heaven above, or that is in the earth beneath, or that is in the water under the earth"* (Exo 20:4, Deut 5:8, Lev 26:1-2, etc.). And the Qur'an relates the following: *"And indeed We bestowed before on Abraham his portion of guidance... When he said to his father and his people, 'What are these images, to which you are devoted?' They said, 'We found our fathers worshipping them.' He said, 'Indeed you and your fathers have been in manifest error.'"* (21:51-54) On one level, these are direct admonitions against polytheism in all forms—idolizing everything from imaginary protectors, to popular leaders, and even ourselves. But even beyond this, these are clear instructions against making or watching images, becoming devoted to them, and continuing to do so just because that's what most people do. And if a decree is issued so clearly in the Holy Books, it shouldn't be taken lightly by anyone. Yet most ignore it completely. True, most Muslims generally follow the prohibition a little more closely than most Christians and Jews—Muslim households usually don't display pictures on the wall, for instance. But almost every home still has a television—and most families own a camera. What's the risk of ignoring the ban on images? Only God knows for certain. But one thing is sure: the excessive image-consciousness of western society, and the obsession with the ego, is actively nurtured by virtually every single magazine, newspaper, website, television program, advertisement, music video, and movie. The media, in other words, fortifies the ego trap which threatens to invalidate our lives.

Critically, the traditional *spiritual* perspective on the self is really the opposite of the popular western one. It's a view "eastern" religionists believe—including the world's billion-plus Muslims—one where the ego is something which has to be surrendered, not strengthened. According to this perspective, the ego is nothing more than a way for us to deceive ourselves, a false basis for security, and a powerful barrier to the Divine. Individuals with strong egos are pitied, not admired, because they're slaves to their bodies, habits and activities, and they want things which aren't useful for eternal life. In other words, a life of faith has little to do with the everyday sorts of problems which bring people to psychotherapists, and hardship and guilt are important opportunities to correct our failings. So values are promoted over ego, through honouring time, understanding and acting on the teachings, and defending what is good in ourselves and others. Thus, while western society is busy growing egos, a life of submission actually requires the ego to get much smaller—even to the point of erasing itself. And spiritually, what's undesirable is anything which threatens our souls—not our egos. It's a radically different position which argues that real happiness comes from devotion, not desire, and real security comes from our Creator, not ourselves.

The traditional *scriptural* view of the self is also completely opposed to the popular western position. For the Qur'an and Bible present detailed directions and parables which explain that ego-centredness prevents us from seeing that our purpose is more than our existence in this world. It's only when we let go of our egos that we can understand how real contentment doesn't depend on the gratification of our wants. Rather, it's an inner attribute which completely rests on our relationship with God. The ego model, in fact, challenges the idea of fate which is so central to Christianity, Judaism, and Islam, that, *"In his heart, a man plans his course, but the Lord determines his steps"* (Prov 16:9), and that man's happiness depends on God's mercy, not on his own ability to supply his desires: *"How many are the creatures that carry not their own sustenance? It is God who feeds them and you: for He hears and knows all things"* (29:60). Tragically, the average person in the west thinks about himself more than God, and chases after worldly goals rather than trying to understand God's goals for him. He sets his worth by how close he is to those goals, rather than on how close he might be to God. And he *forgets* that our purpose on earth is to glorify God, not ourselves.

Unfortunately, among the various empty lusts and lapses that cause humanity immeasurable suffering, forgetfulness is surely one of the worst. Following the creation of Adam and Satan's refusal to prostrate before Adam while they were all still in the Garden, Satan tempted Adam to the forbidden tree: *"Assuredly We have made a covenant with Adam (and forbidden him to approach a tree in the Garden), but he acted forgetfully."* (20:115) In fact, this happened even though God had compassionately forewarned Adam and Eve against Satan's power of temptation: *"O Adam, surely this is an enemy to you and your wife; so let him not drive the two of you out of the Garden, lest you become distressed."* (20:117) But mercifully, again, God forgave Adam, and his story becomes an excellent example of the importance of seeking immediate repentance when we fall into error chasing after the random caprices of our own egos, as we turn to our Creator, *"The One Who accepts repentance and returns it with liberal forgiveness and additional reward."* (2:35)

There's a particularly lovely remembrance of the Queen of Sheba's conversion from polytheism to monotheism in the Qur'an—and a version also appears in the Bible (1 Kings 10:1-13, 2 Chron 9:1-12). The Queen, having received Solomon's message, decides to visit him. Her throne is mysteriously brought to Solomon's court before her visit, yet somehow disguised almost beyond her ability to recognize it: *"Disguise her throne, and let us see whether she is able to find guidance or is among those who are not guided. When she (the Queen) arrived, she was asked: "Is your throne like this?" She said: "(It looks) as if it is it."* (27:41-42) This beautiful story speaks to the elemental truth of the existence of the Creator and the common origins of faith across nations and time, though we often have difficulty recognizing the signs of our own souls in one another's symbols and in the natural evidence all around us, as we are so poorly served by the facades and postures generated by our own egos. Suitably, then, while the Biblical account focuses on how dazzled the Queen was about Solomon's riches, the Qur'an explains in the most mystical way how she walked towards what she thought was a lake until Solomon pointed out that it was actually a palace made of smooth glass, and not a lake at all. Startled, she seemingly realized then and there the veil of illusion she'd been operating under, and submitted her whole self to God, exclaiming, *"O my Lord! I have indeed wronged my soul."* (27:44) And so it was that a person with all possible worldly attainments—beauty, fame, money, power, etc.—came to understand the thin veneer of her "reality" and surrendered her ego. In fact, the Qur'an is full of all kinds of information about how we each can deal with our egos. And the Islamic viewpoint is particularly useful for anyone trying to move beyond the mirror because it harmonizes both the spiritual and scriptural views:

Understand that the ego is limiting: *"Shall we tell thee of those who lose most in respect of their deeds? Those whose efforts have been wasted in this life, while they thought that they were acquiring good by their works,"* (18:103-104) and *"those who love the life of this world better than the hereafter."* (16:107) *(See also 9:38 13:26, 14:3, 28:60, 29:25, 29:52, 29:66, 40:39, 45:35, 52:12, 79:38, etc.)*

Avoid vanities and luxuries which inflate our egos: *"It is those who believe in vanities and reject God who will perish in the end,"* (29:52), for *"Of what profit to you were your hoards and your arrogant ways?"* (7:48) *(See also 2:188, 6:141, 7:31, 9:24, 28:76, 34:37, 43:32, 53:48, 56:45, 57:20, 64:15, 74:45, 102:1, 104:2, etc.)*

Demonstrate personal humility to reduce our egos: *"And swell not thy cheek for pride at men, nor walk in insolence through the earth; for God loves not any arrogant boaster."* (31:18), *"nor defame nor be sarcastic to each other, nor call each other by offensive nicknames."* (49:11) *(See also 2:96, 3:75, 9:108, 16:23, 17:37, 23:76, 25:63, 31:18, 35:10, 38:2, 40:60, 57:23, etc.)*

Let guidance from God—not our egos—decide right from wrong: *"Who is more astray than one who follows his own lusts, devoid of guidance from God?"* (28:50), or *"one who takes for his god his own passion or impulse."* (25:43) *(See also 2:54, 2:112, 3:20, 4:125, 12:87, 17:14, 18:23, 31:22, 38:26, 64:16, etc.)*

Accept that everything we have is from God—not ourselves: *"Nor strain your eyes in longing for the things We have given for enjoyment to parties of them, the splendour of the life of this world, through which We test them"* (20:131), for *"such days of varying fortunes We give to men by turns."* (3:140) *(See also 2:155, 4:32, 5:48, 6:165, 8:25, 8:28, 8:42, 18:7, 20:131, 21:35, 24:38, 25:20, 29:2, 34:21, 38:34, 47:31, 67:2, 75:36, 76:2, etc.)*

Numerous passages in the Qur'an, in fact, state explicitly that our purpose on earth is to glorify God, not ourselves, and this fundamental certainty was a great trust of the prophets themselves: *"It is not (possible) for any human being unto whom God had given the Scripture and wisdom and the prophethood that he should afterwards have said unto mankind: "Be servants of me instead of God." But (what he said was): "Be you faithful servants of the Lord by virtue of your constant teaching of the Scripture and of your constant study thereof."* (3:79) Typically, then, though Prophet Muhammad was undoubtedly and *"verily of noble nature"* (68:4), he always, and only, wanted to be a servant of God—nothing more or less. A famous recollection of his life describes the visit of a foreign envoy to Medina. Anxious to relay his diplomatic correspondence, the visitor asked of a small gathering, "Who is the master of these people?" The reply came from the mouth of the man whose very hands were serving food to his Companions, Prophet Muhammad, who simply explained, "The master of a people is the one who serves people." Thus, here is a pure and enduring message for us that in order to fulfill our mission in life, we have to rise above the limitations of our egos. We also have to understand that the really important gifts we have at our disposal, with which we can help others and ourselves towards a better life, have nothing whatsoever to do with our external selves. In addition, we need to realize that support from God goes a long, long way—on into eternity—a lot further than the supports we invent for ourselves. Finally, we must remember that the real goals we should strive for in this life exist completely outside the realm of the ego.

Ultimately, then, the personality God prescribes for us is a far cry from the one Freud describes. So how will we reform western man into the image which faith—not psychology or the media—requires? And how will get away from thinking that we really just need to believe in ourselves, when the truth is that we really need to believe in what is beyond ourselves, to *"believe in the unseen"* (2:3). For in using our egos for security, we have become like the spider, *"who builds to itself a house—but truly the flimsiest of houses is the spider's house, if they but knew"* (29:41). Maybe it's time we admitted that serving our egos hasn't served us well at all— and that it is the Freudian schema which is the infantile illusion, not religion. Maybe it's time we understood that paradise was never meant to be right now, but later. And maybe it's time we realized that, in the end, it isn't our vanities which will be counted but our virtues—for the purpose of this life is not to dominate the testing ground, but to overcome it.

THE POISONED HEART

Everyone knows the deadliest toxins are the ones you don't notice until it's too late—those that come into your body in little doses, over time, like mercury, lead, and radiation. Some toxins are so crafty, in fact, that they make you want more—like nicotine. It's an astounding thing that people crave the very poison that is killing them—at the rate of over 400,000 yearly in the US alone.[6] Certainly, smoking is the most quoted culprit these days—but not by any means the only one. Alcohol is obviously another, as are countless narcotics and prescription medications. Again and again, the pattern of the most effective poison is there: the more it's ingested, the more it's desired. Yet there are many, some might say lesser, poisons in our lives, as well—common substances we crave which can harm us in certain doses, like salt, fat, and even caffeine. The American Medical Association (2005) predicts that diet will overtake smoking as the number one killer in the US. Yet anyone who's had to restrict a food for health reasons will testify to how hard it is. Even people who will die if they keep eating fats find themselves sneaking a quick burger. It seems that we can easily avoid drinking industrial cleaners, and our chance of dying in something big and obvious like a motor vehicle accident is only about 1 in 6000. But the "lesser" poisons in our lives—these have the most dangerous hold on us. For evil really is seldom a huge and flagrant thing, easy to identify and avoid. Instead, evil is a subversive, whispered sort of thing which nudges us slowly away from what is right. And what is hard to notice is hard to defend against. I can easily remember not to kill my neighbour, for instance, because the evil of it is so evident. But I have a much harder time resisting the urge to be jealous of her youth. The evil seems so commonplace, almost benign. And yet it is these small ills that I commit each and every day—the ones I barely notice and seldom ask forgiveness for—which will be my undoing. The devil, as they say, is in the details.

Evil is hardly a popular topic of mainstream conversation these days. Yet western society is certainly no different from any other in having a lot of ideas about what the devil might actually look like. And like most cultures, we've drawn our images from popular literature. In fact, western ideology formed much of its concept of hell not from the Holy Bible, but from Dante's "Inferno." More than just a "great literary masterpiece," however, the text is a bit of a devil itself—for it remains one of the boldest examples of hate literature. The two main characters Dante contrived to be writhing in hell, in indescribable pain and grotesque horror, were named Muhammad and Ali, as Dante directed his poem against Islam and the threat it apparently posed to 13th-century Catholicism. It's impossible to know the degree to which these negative images of Islam may have rooted themselves in the western psyche. But certainly, Hollywood's contemporary takes on hell and the devil are no more realistic and no less self-serving than Dante's. For Satan has become the hottest-selling ticket of all, as horror movies consistently reap immeasurable profits, each season representing evil in more varieties, with progressively better special effects. Ask children to draw Satan these days, and they will easily sketch a red creature with horns or a hideous monster. It's a convenient model for the masses. For sure, if you saw such a being coming towards you, you'd run away. And if it tried to tell you something, you'd try hard to get far enough away not to listen. So we are well convinced now that if we don't see such a thing coming towards us, we must be on the path of good, or pretty safe at least. Much like Dante, Hollywood has dulled our senses, shrouding real evil in ridicule and exaggeration, and thus it has made us complacent and unguarded. Yet the real Satan is nothing like his caricature. And in expecting Satan to be huge and dramatic, we have left ourselves completely open to real evil as it moves in quietly through the cracks in our lives—discrete, insistent, and devastating.

In the scriptures, Satan is generally described as a spirit whose purpose has been determined by God, and the Bible and Qur'an give very little physical description of him. Since he is cunning (Eph 6:11) and masquerades (2 Cor 11:14), we cannot rely on a physical shape anyhow—certainly not on the stereotypical image. And his real job is hardly that which the media has assigned to him either—that of overturning homes and vehicles, casting fire on everything, or causing people violent injuries.

Satan's advance is actually something far subtler, as he is a deceiver who watches us from a place we cannot see (7:27). And rather than doing horrible things to us directly, he tries to command us to destroy our own lives steadily and slowly by getting us to say and do what is wrong (2:169)— as he assaults us incessantly (6:112, 7:200, 7:201, 17:62, 41:36), and "whispers into the hearts of mankind."(114:5). His gain is pathetically obvious: we will forget what it means to be righteous, we will hurt ourselves or others, and we will waste or lose the gifts and opportunities which God gave us, including time. After awhile, our lives will become limited by ill health, poor choices, a depressed mind, absent spirituality, and negative relationships. And thus we will effectively lose our ability to be happy, healthy, complete people, with thriving and satisfied souls, seeking God.

The Qur'an actually gives a detailed account of how Satan was given instructions to test man with limited authority granted to him by God (14:22, 17:62-64, 34:21, 38:82)—and the Bible concurs that God created good and evil (Deut 30:15, Isaiah 45:7). Thus, in Judaism, Satan is viewed as an "angel with a dirty job" who serves as our evil inclination, trying our devotion. In Christianity, he is a liar and deceiver who fights the Word of God (1 Thess 2:18, 1 Peter 5:8, John 8:44, Rev 20) and attempts to lead men astray. And in Islam, Satan is described a "jinn" (spirit), rather than an angel—a persistent enemy (2:168, 17:53, 35:6, 43:62) who is continually trying to reduce our desire and capacity to live as believers. It is a key point in Islam that God created both mankind and jinn to worship Him (51:56), and that both men and jinn are limited (6:130, 55:33)— sometimes inspired by evil and delusion (6:112, 7:179, 11:119), and sometimes honourable and submitting (37:158, 72:1-14). Satan's aim is not so much to destroy the pleasures of this life for us—in fact, he often encourages us to give in to sensuality and worry-free bliss. Rather, his objective is to destroy the pleasures of the next life for us. And in the end, he will admit, *"I had no authority over you except to call you, but you listened to me— then reproach me not, but reproach your own souls"* (14:22).

Exactly what Satan commands some people to do is obvious from the evening news—horrific crimes are perpetrated daily by individuals drawn into evil. Some will even state that they heard voices beckoning them to commit atrocities. As a society, we capture these events neatly as psychological illness so that we don't have to relate these individuals to ourselves—and we don't have to consider the explanation which faith holds for the battle against evil going on inside every one of us. Thankfully, the numbers of people who succumb to extreme evils are few in the world. Most people are tempted by wrongs which are seemingly more "civilized." Listen to gossip for a minute, for example, and it is inviting to join in. Gossip a bit to keep the audience, and it is easy to embellish for dramatic effect. Do that consistently, and you will find yourself lying inadvertently. And just like the smoker who doesn't notice the toxic smell of cigarettes, everyone's resistance lessens when the heart is already poisoned. The logical extension is that after awhile, Satan's job gets easier. The chronic liar hardly needs to be tempted anymore, in other words, for the addiction to wrong has become self-managing. And this is the fundamental pathology of evil. For it is not a vicious assault on human consciousness, but rather a gradual erosion of a person's will, which leaves *"a stain on their hearts from the ill that they do."* (83:14). And such is how so many of us come to be among those *"in whose hearts is a disease"* (2:10, 5:52, 8:49, 9:125, 22:53, 24:50, 33:12, 33:60, 47:20, 47:29, 74:31).

Be hard-working, for example, and you will one day find yourself jealously guarding your workload and comparing it to everyone else's. Stay frustrated for a little while longer, and you will eventually find yourself justified in giving less than your best effort, as you begin to slide into laziness, perhaps even dishonesty. Be a considerate individual who calls others to check on them and you'll find yourself wondering, one hard day, why no one is calling you. Upset, you may re-examine good relationships and people, looking for faults, and you may form a new friendship with someone who isn't particularly kind, just because he or she shares your negativity, as you slide into backbiting, and perhaps even cruelty. Be the sort of person who normally goes to the mosque, church, or synagogue and helps the community, and you may one day find yourself noticing all your friends and neighbours enjoying a day off. After a bit, you may begin feeling particularly tired and exasperated with everyone, thinking no one does as much as you. You may start reducing your own involvement as you begin to slide into apathy, perhaps even alienation. In each and every case, you had the option of remaining a decent, hard-working person, or a caring, compassionate individual, or a devoted and committed one. But instead, the whispers of evil slowly eroded what was the most righteous part of you, as Satan chalked another victory—not quite as vivid as killing you right out, perhaps, but just as effective. For in the end, only God knows how you will be judged. But in abandoning what is the best in yourself, you will have abandoned your best chance at eternal life, as God makes *"the suggestions thrown in by Satan but a trial for those in whose hearts is a disease"* (22:53).

And so goes the average life, as the devil creeps into the small things, causing us to become infinitely lost—not so much through violations of major sins, like taking others as God, murder, stealing, and so on, but through the minor compromises we make in our daily lives, the things we let slip by and we let ourselves slip into, one whisper at a time. We may have a relatively healthy body, yet start to become aware that we are short, overweight, pale, and so on, for example, and become increasingly self-conscious. Our home may be warm and comfortable, but if all of our acquaintances have a bigger one, we may start to feel jealousy. Our spouse may be a loving, supportive individual, but if he or she becomes suddenly burdened with problems, we may begin to seek the intimacy of others, perhaps even leading to indiscretions. We may endure many sacrifices because of our families, only to begin to incline towards self-pity or self-indulgences. We may have experienced a difficult childhood ourselves, and thus begin to feel entitled to anger against our own children. We may do much to help a constantly needy friend, only to begin to feel justified in distancing ourselves "for his own good." We may feel we have done so much for others without recognition, only to be tempted towards a bit of boasting or self-promotion. We may take every effort in the world to avoid wasting food and recycle, only to notice that neighbours throw a lot out, and become a little more careless ourselves. We may try to get involved in our cities, to improve conditions, only to watch the news and begin to feel powerless, then hopeless. We may feel that we have already given enough to charity, and so choose to withhold what we could easily keep giving. Each time we behave in this way, we lose the precious opportunity to be grateful to God for what we have been given; we fail to maintain our characters at the highest possible level; and we trade a temporal reward of ease for the greater reward which God promises: *"If they had kept their Faith and guarded themselves from evil, far better had been the reward from their Lord, if they but knew!"* (2:103) Most critically, each time we act this way, we engage in behaviours which encourage more of the same: vanity, self-pity, self-indulgence, self-promotion, and all of the other means by which we end up nurturing our egos rather than our souls. And such is the victory of Satan over each one of us—one drop of poison at a time, adding *"doubt to our doubt,"* (9:125), as it were, until we risk dying *"in a state of unbelief."* (9:125)

So how can we defend ourselves against evil—against an enemy who is so persistent and knows us well, and who stands in ambush so very close to us that we don't even notice his approach? The answer is faith. Without a doubt, faith encourages a constant effort towards what is best and provides enduring comfort and protection for *"those who believe and put their trust in their Lord"* (16:99), since *"if any believes in God, God guides his heart."* (64:11). For those who choose instead not to believe in God and don't try to exert self-restraint, the downward spiral is almost inevitable, since *"If anyone withdraws himself from the remembrance of the Most Gracious, We appoint for him an evil one, to be an intimate companion to him"* (43:36). Ultimately, then, it simply comes down to each one of us and the relationship we want to have with our Creator. If we seek to live out our purpose on earth with a sense of honour, dignity, gratitude and duty, then we need to remain vigilant against even the smallest hint of evil inside us, and around us, and learn to avoid it or overcome it. It will be a life-long, continuous battle, and we won't actually find out if we've won until the end. Perhaps that's how come so many people feel that a life of faith is hard work—too hard—and they succumb to the path of least resistance, rather than striving for *"the path that is steep"* (90:11-12). But the message from God is clear: *"O man! Verily you are ever toiling on towards your Lord, painfully toiling, but you shall meet Him"* (84:6). Surely, the effort is great. But the reward is surely greater.

THE BATTLE WITHIN

We are obsessed with our limitations in this life, aren't we? From the time we can talk, we push our parents to stay up later, go out longer, and venture further. We see money providing the freedom to do anything—and we worry about getting old or sick because that would reduce our freedoms: less mobility, less strength, and fewer choices. It's because we define ourselves from childhood in terms of "can-do" statements—I can walk, I can eat all by myself, I can drive a car, I can succeed at this job, I can buy this house, etc. What we don't seem to realize, though, is that we are actually a lot like balls inside an old pinball machine. Sure, we can hit new and successive targets—but in the end, we are still just bouncing off the edges of the confined space of our existence on earth. The Holy Qur'an explains one aspect of the pilgrimage ritual which confuses westerners—when Muslims run back and forth between Safa and Marwa, two mountains in Mecca. Yet the Qur'an tells us, *"Safa and Marwa are among the Symbols of God"* (2:158). For there could be no better metaphor of the trap of this life than having believers running to and fro between boundaries, inside the *"sacred precinct of Mecca"* (2:196, 5:1-2, 5:95-96)—itself a bounded space—as we each spend our lives running about within the boundaries God imposed on us in the world He created for us.

In fact, trying to discover and test our boundaries has been a longstanding human pursuit. History records our attempts to discover the curvature of the earth, the source of the Nile, the exact placement of the Indian continent, a northern passage around the globe, and to protect the boundaries we already have through various battles and wars. Our obsession with figuring out what's beyond our limits is legendary, too, as we continue to explore ideas about angels, alien life, parallel universes, String Theory, and even the hallucinogenics which distort the edges of consciousness. The fact that our life is defined by numerous sets of opposites actually invites us to think about boundaries—night and day, male and female, heaven and hell, good and evil, sea and sky—for these seem metaphorically like opposing pillars, the Safa and Marwa in our lives, between which our entire reality plays itself out. Among the world's holy books, the Qur'an is particularly specific in detailing the boundaries confining us: the barrier between salt and fresh water (25:53, etc.); our growth in the womb within three layers or *"veils"* (39:6); the deliberate construction of night as a veil over the day (7:54); the *"entrance"* of heaven (78:19); our hearts as wrappings around our faith (2:88); the division of man into nations (49:13); the boundary between the spirit world and mankind (55:31); the partition between life and death (23:100); and the wall between believers and hypocrites (57:13). In addition, we can only see God indirectly, from *"behind a veil"* (42:51), and creation itself is described as the very beginning of boundaries: *"Do not the unbelievers see that the heavens and the earth were joined together as one unit of creation before We clove them asunder?"* (21:30)

Even a quick study of the prophets and their missions (peace be upon them all) reveals the critical importance of the boundary as a symbol: Moses crosses the sea to escape from the Pharaoh; Noah loses all boundaries in a massive flood; Abraham abandons his wife and son at the utmost edge of the territory; Jesus is raised to God when his mission has ended; Adam experiences somewhat the reverse, being displaced from the company of God to earth; and Satan crosses over, too, as he descends on mankind. In addition, Muslims believe Prophet Muhammad ascended to heaven briefly at a difficult point in his calling, reaching *"the Lote-tree of the utmost boundary"* (53:14), arriving at the *"farthest mosque,"* (17:01), as heaven itself is set by boundaries.

Boundaries do not only describe our physical context, but our internal qualities as well. For it is the essence of belief in One God that there should be limits on our behaviours. These are the basis for the commandments and the instructions directing us towards what is best— for example, with regards to what can and can't be eaten. The Holy Books, then, are basically codes of law— restraints on humanity. And the books include examples, analogies, and historical support simply to make clear the details and importance of these restrictions. In keeping with the symbolism of these walls around us, those who rebel against God's rules are considered "transgressors" because they effectively cross boundaries (2:190, 2:194, 2:229, etc.). The whole idea of faith, then, is to understand and respect the limits set forth by God, to learn to live comfortably within them, and to see even them as a blessing. And ultimately, it's the extent to which we individually agree to live within these restrictions that defines us as religiously orthodox, conservative, moderate, liberal, non-adhering, and so on.

Anyone who values faith, then, ends up being a "boundary guard" of sorts—upholding divine law in his or her own life, and protecting belief in a wider context, by speaking to others about God, trying to model and encourage positive living, becoming involved in political activism in support of righteous causes, spreading inspiration, and so on. In this way, believers become God's vicegerents on earth, for which purpose God created the first man: *"Behold, thy Lord said to the angels: "I will create a vicegerent on earth... And He taught Adam the names of all things."* (2:30-31). In other words, protecting divine boundaries is a key responsibility of anyone wishing to engage in a meaningful relationship with God: *"O you who believe! Be you helpers of God"* (61:14; see also 47:7, 49:15, 61:11). And this, in fact, is the core meaning of the Islamic concept of "jihad," one of the most contentious political and media topics this decade.

In common usage, the word "jihad" denotes a "religious war" unique to Islamic practice. However, the world's historical record is clear: fighting for religion is hardly an Islamic invention. And tellingly, the word "jihad" *never* actually occurs in the Holy Qur'an. In fact, the dictionary meaning of jihad is "to strive," and in daily practice, this means praying, eating right, giving to charity, avoiding envy, and so on. It also means working hard to build places of prayer and engaging in public efforts to remind people of their duty to God—such as through weekly discussions and interfaith dialogues. But if we are forced by corrupt laws or persistent oppression to commit murder, worship idols, or break another of God's commandments, or if we are forcibly removed from our homes and lands, where we can freely practise our religion, then we may be permitted self-defence. However, even under such conditions, the rules of engagement are very limited, for we *cannot* claim a general difficulty with or within a society, simply fighting those we don't approve of: *"When angels take the souls of those who die in sin against their souls, they say: 'In what plight were you?' They reply, 'Weak and oppressed were we in the earth.' They say, 'Was not the earth of God spacious enough for you to move yourselves away from evil?' Such men will find their abode in Hell—what an evil refuge! Except those who are really weak and oppressed—men, women, and children—who have no means in their power, nor a guide-post to their way"* (4:97-98). So it is our duty to avoid fighting without proper justification: *"Fight in the cause of God those who fight you, but do not transgress limits"* (2:190).

If a fight is absolutely necessary because of devastating oppression and the absence of other solutions, then one is permitted a very disciplined, very limited engagement lasting only long enough to restore equity: *"And fight them on until there is no more tumult or oppression, and there prevail justice and faith in God; but if they cease, let there be no hostility except to those who practise oppression"* (2:193; see also 8:39, 22:39, 26:227, 49:9). In addition, the believer must always be very sensitive to the plight of his adversary, for if his adversary indicates a desire for peace, he must be obliged immediately: *"But if the enemy inclines towards peace, then incline towards peace, and trust in God: for He is One Who hears and knows all things."* (8:61; see also 49:9). And the believer engaged in combat must also avoid vengeance and senseless violence, such as through the wanton destruction of the environment and livestock, or through the killing of innocent people, as we are all encouraged, under all circumstances in this life, to retaliate only with equal or *lesser* force than that which we have suffered ourselves: *"The recompense for an injury is an injury equal thereto in degree: but if a person forgives and makes reconciliation, his reward is due from God: for God loves not those who do wrong,"* (42:40). Therefore, even as we defend the boundary of faith, we have to keep our own behaviour within the boundaries of good conduct, as God's rules for all of mankind and for our world are consistent with one another: *"God has revealed from time to time the most beautiful Message in the form of a Book, consistent with itself, yet repeating its teaching in various aspects."* (39:23) Most critically, we are reminded to hope for peace as a blessed choice: *"It may be that God will grant love and friendship between you and those whom you now hold as enemies."* (60:7)

Tragically, however, the concept of "jihad" has been incredibly distorted—both by those who practise it and by those who condemn it. The rampant terrorism plastered in the news today does not represent Islam, just as the infamous and violent crusades—the religious wars of the Middle

Ages—do not represent the kind hearts of devoted Christians around the world, including banners of humanity such as Mother Theresa, Martin Luther King, and Nelson Mandela. Real "jihad" is about striving, as *peacefully* as humanly possible, to uphold a safe perimeter around the practice of monotheism. Real "jihad" is primarily about the daily struggles within ourselves and within our own societies to avoid succumbing to our weaknesses, rather than the battles which fill the pages of history. And real "jihad," therefore, is not primarily about securing geographical dominance, but about securing the dominance of the soul over the ego. So while the word may be cited so frequently in Arabic, the concept is owned by no language. For the defence of faith is part of the fabric of all humanity—a controlled and measured response when one is prevented by mankind (including our own selves) from submitting to God. And, critically, it is this very protection of one's belief in this life which becomes the key to safe passage across the greatest boundary of all, into the next life.

So the question really becomes, how can we properly defend faith, in ourselves, in our societies, and on this earth? That's the question we urgently need to ask ourselves. In our lives, we abandon our duties to God so easily. That, in fact, has become one of the hallmarks of western culture—the wall we ourselves have built between what is secular and what is spiritual—the so-called separation of church and state which we credit as the foundation of modernism, but which in fact has amounted to locking the door of the house while leaving the children outside on the street. A quick look at the world around us reveals absenteeism from devotional services, the breakdown of families, usury and financial oppression, millions of needless deaths everyday through starvation and disease, random violence, and so on. These things only happen when we fail to understand that the protective envelope around our faith must include all of our actions, thoughts, words, and intentions—not exclude them—and when we are unable to comprehend that we are supposed to defend faith, not to defend ourselves from faith.

In a state of confusion, like guards unsure of what we are supposed to be defending, most of us have in effect, abdicated our responsibility to protect our trusts in this life, as instructed by the divine commandments: join no partners with God; be good to your parents, children, spouses, and neighbours; do not be indecent, either openly or secretly; do not kill except by way of justice; conduct your business fairly; speak justly; and respect and fulfill the covenant of God for you on this earth by being steadfast in worship, spending of your sustenance out of love of God, and being patient in pain, suffering, and adversity (2:177, 6:151, 70:23-38). Thus, though these commandments are actually almost universally held, people of all faiths around the world sometimes easily take up arms against each other, committing acts of atrocity which effectively capture our inhumanity rather than our humanity. Confucius, that paradigm of timeless wisdom once said, virtue lies in attacking the evil in oneself rather than the evil in others. And while there will be catastrophes in the history of the world where overt battles in the defense of faith will be our responsibility for a time, the internal battles for the defense of faith in our own hearts will be our duty always.

CHAPTER IV

Reflections on the Basic Tenets of Faith

"The Messenger believes in what has been sent down to him from his Lord, and so do the believers; each one believes in God, and His angels, and His Books, and His Messengers: 'We make no distinction between any of His Messengers (in believing in them).' And they say: 'We have heard (the call to faith in God) and obeyed. Our Lord, grant us Your forgiveness, and to You is the homecoming.'" (2:285)

* * *

"He is not a believer who does not love for his brother what he loves for himself." (An-Nawawi, from his famous "Collection of Forty Hadith")

THE FEAR FACTOR

Personally, I have to admit that I'm a bit claustrophobic. I really don't enjoy elevators too much, though I still ride in them. Unlike a lot of other people, though, I'm really not very afraid of snakes or insects because I think they're marvels of creation. I guess we're all afraid of different things, and fears can come and go, depending on our experiences. Anyone who's been bitten by a pit bull is probably afraid of them now, and anyone who's watched a dangerous predator, like a wolf, care for its young might soften their heart a little. Fear is such a potent thing, though, isn't it? You can tell someone a thousand times that a particular type of spider is virtually harmless, but if they're afraid, they won't calm down until it's chased away. In fact, fear almost seems to be the one emotion that can really detach us from our common sense and self-controls—people will go through all kinds of screaming, random movements and convulsions, hyperventilation, and even loss of bladder control when they are frightened. Without a doubt, fear is a powerful thing. My eldest, a practising Christian, tells me that Islam is a lot about fear, actually. She says that's because a lot of people are afraid of Muslims. And even more so, a lot of people think that Muslims don't love God—they're just afraid of Him. Watching the news night after night, I have to admit she might be onto something.

The idea that the general public is afraid of Muslims is becoming fairly self-evident. New words have sprung up in the language of even the average person on the street—words like "jihad," "National Security" and "Racial Profiling." As a Canadian and a mother, I'm *extremely* interested in national security. Diversity and tolerance have always been the anchors of our national character—the essence of the "mosaic" we use to describe ourselves, and the best thing about Canada. My family is related to the first European settler to this nation—Samuel de Champlain—whose full name was apparently Samuel de Champlain de la Touche de Saintonge. My forefathers built the national railway and defended this great country through wars, and I have lived here all of my life. As for the USA, more than half my family is there, and for about 20 years of my life, I crossed the American border from Quebec more often than I ever crossed a provincial boundary, heading down to New England to ski, New York and Boston for concerts, and so on. But things are a bit different now. Now I wear a head scarf, and people with head scarves get searched and held up at the border, no matter what direction they're coming from. It's not a new story, actually. Canada once excluded Chinese, Jewish, and Japanese individuals, for example, through rather similar periods of panic. Now it seems that Muslims are front and centre, experiencing all of the classic difficulties which go with this kind of paranoia: problems getting jobs, apartments, mortgages, immigration status, and so on; distrust among the general public, especially (but not necessarily) among the less informed, less educated, less urban and/or less travelled; and redefined public policies which segment society and justify, somehow, the selective application of commonly held rights. Definitely, I had to agree with my daughter: Canadians, for the most part, are afraid of Muslims.

Yet it was actually her second point which really gave me something to think about—the idea that Muslims fear God, and that Islam is a religion of fear. I had also heard, over a year ago, the expression that "Christians love God, but Muslims fear God." So she wasn't alone in thinking this. But where were these sentiments coming from? And was there any truth to them? The first assumption seemed true enough, for there really wasn't any question in my mind that Christians love God. Raised as a Christian, and surrounded by Christians in my extended family, workplace, and neighbourhood, I could comfortably say that Christians do love God. Love, in fact, features as the primary emotion directed towards God, and that which God directs towards believers. In truth, the relationship is often likened, by Christians themselves, to that between a loving Father and his children. Evangelical preachers even raise the level of love to that of rapture in their sermons, as followers are embraced in love for each other and the love of the Creator. But what about the second assumption? Did Muslims love God, too, or was our relationship with God really more about fear? Strictly from personal experience, I had to admit that as a Muslim now, I did fear God in a way I hadn't before, and I fear Him increasingly as my faith deepens. But my daughter was raising a pretty big issue here, and it would take a bigger answer than that—something outside my own reference—to resolve it.

Of course, the word "love" occurs in the Holy Qur'an—but not that much, in a way—only about 70 times. It's used primarily in reference to warnings about our attachment to the things of this life: *"You may love a thing that is bad for you, and dislike a thing that is good for you."* (2:216), and *"By no means will you attain righteousness until you give freely of that which you love."* (3:92; see also 3:14, 14:3). It's also used to describe the emotion which we need to share within our families: *"He created you and made his mate of like nature, in order that he might dwell with her in love"* (7:189) and *"love those near of kin"* (42:23; see also 30:21). Finally, it's used to describe some of the wider relationships we have with others: *"You will not be able to guide everyone you love."* (28:56) And how much talk of love was there in the Bible? Hundreds! There were 267 in Young's Literal Translation; 280 in the King James Version; 511 in the New International Version; 588 in the New Living Translation; and 653 in the New International Reader's Version.[1]

And what about the word "fear"? It occurred a lot more than "love" in the Qur'an—about 284 times (www.msc.edu) Yet it also occurred more than the word "love" in the Bible, actually: 385 times in the King James Version and 333 times in Young's Literal Translation, for example. Oddly enough, though, it only occurred 120 times in the New International Reader's Version—the same version which had the highest incidence of "love"—almost double the average.[2] Maybe my daughter was right, after all. Maybe Christianity was more about love than Islam. But I couldn't help wondering, too, why it was that some Bible versions had wildly different counts of such critical words—one version, for instance, clearly had more than twice the number of occurrences of the word "love" than some other versions. Could it be that "love" had been introduced a bit here and there, when the actual word or meaning intended might have been something a bit different, at least in some of the cases? Was it possible, in fact, that the overwhelming urge to deliver "good news" was overcoming the "real news" from God?

At any rate, it seemed worthwhile to reflect a little more deeply on the meaning of "fear" itself. Without a doubt, fear is the most urgent response we have—visceral, complete, and severe. And the purpose of fear as a response is always the same, in every species of living thing: survival. Fear is the alarm inside each living thing which demands an immediate response in order to escape danger, real or perceived. So fear, although highly uncomfortable, is also incredibly useful. Without fear, we would perform all kinds of actions, and put ourselves in all kinds of circumstances each day which would actually present a threat to our health and well-being. How else can we explain how "fearless" individuals expose themselves to untold risks through dangerous stunts and so-called extreme sports, and how very young children touch hot stoves, play with matches, and run out into traffic? Without fear, we are in constant danger. Considered in this way, fear is a great mercy.

So what does Islam specifically instruct believers regarding fear? Quite simply, it tells mankind to fear God, and it explains why that is critical to our survival:

- *"Fear God and know that you will be gathered unto Him." (2:223, 2:281, 5:96), 6:72, 58:9, etc.)*
- *"Fear God and know that He is well acquainted with all things." (or "He sees well all that you do," etc.) (2:231, 2:233, 5:7, 5:8, 33:55, 49:1, etc.)*
- *"Whoever follows My guidance, on them shall be no fear nor shall they grieve." (2:112, 2:262, 2:274, 2:277, 3:170, 5:69, 6:48, 7:35, 7:49, 10:62, 41:30, 43:68, 46:13, etc.)*
- *"Fear Me and Me alone." (also, "You feared men but you should have feared God," and "Fear not the beings they associate with God.") (2:40, 2:41, 2:150, 2:189, 2:197, 4:77, 4:131, 5:3, 5:44, 6:81, 7:65, 9:13, 16:051, 22:1, 23:23, 23:32, 23:52, 26:106, 26:142, 26:177, 33:37, 33:39, 39:16, 65:1, etc.)*
- *"Fear the penalty of a Mighty Day." (Or "Grievous Day," etc.) (6:15, 7:59, 10:15, 11:3, 11:26, 11:84, 14:14, 24:37, 26:135, 29:36, 39:13, 39:24, 40:32, 46:21, 76:7, 76:10, etc.)*
- *"Fear God and obey [the prophets]." (3:50, 26:108, 26:110, 26:124, 26:126, 26:131, 26:142, 26:144, 26:150, 26:163, 26:179, 43:63, 57:28, 71:3, etc.)*

- *"Fear God that you may prosper." ("Receive mercy", etc.) (3:200, 5:100, 7:63, 8:69, 36:45, 39:10, 39:20, 49:10, 49:12, 64:16, 65:2, 65:4, 67:12, etc.*

- Fear and Gratitude: *"Fear God that you may show your gratitude."/ "Fear Him who has bestowed on you freely all that you know." / "Fear Him who created you and generations before you." (3:123, 26:132, 26:184)*

- Fear and Trust: *"Fear God, and on God, let believers put all their trust." / "Fear God if you have faith." "Call on Him with fear and longing in your hearts." / "Fear God, in whom you believe." / "Fear God, and listen to His counsel."/"Fear God that he may grant you a criterion to judge right from wrong." (5:11, 5:108, 8:29, 60:11)*

- Fear and Honesty: *"Fear God and be of those who are true in word and deed."/ "Fear God and always say a word directed to the right." (9:119, 33:70)*

The overwhelming point to be extracted from all of these references is that just like the fear which keeps us from swimming in an electric storm, or walking in the middle of the highway, or running into a burning building—only deeper and infinitely more potent—the fear of God is intended as a blessing to keep us alive, or more precisely, to keep our souls alive. In other words, God is watching us at all times, and we will be returned to Him for judgement. While we live on this earth, we have to trust in God and live as believers, true to the Message, in gratitude for all we've been given. At the point of return, we'll have much to fear if we've failed in the purpose for which we were put on this earth—to worship God. On the other hand, if we've followed God's guidance, then we'll have nothing to fear in the end. It's a simple cause-and-effect thing, really. Fear God now, and be safe. Fail to fear God now, and you'll have much to fear later.

As a warning, it does resemble the type of counsel which dutiful parents or teachers give children at critical junctures—to exercise care in the present to avoid tragedy in the future. Inherent in this idea of fearing God, then, are the recognition of the awesome power of God in the universe He created, as well as the acknowledgement of the consequences we've been promised for submission (i.e. heaven) or transgression (i.e. hell). If we walk around thinking we're automatically perfect, or we presume to be already saved—like the spoiled child who thinks he deserves everything, so becomes complacent, self-indulgent and disrespectful—then we risk committing errors which will ultimately cost us our eternal lives. And it's critically important to remember that this idea of faith and effort going hand-in-hand is not uniquely Muslim, for the Bible articulates it clearly: *"Faith by itself, if it is not accompanied by action, is dead."* (James 2:17). It's because submitting to God's authority—through observance and belief in Judgement Day—are basic expectations of all of those who practise monotheism—pillars of belief for the People of the Book, in fact. And just as the Qur'an delivers God's instruction to fear Him that we might be saved, so does the Bible: *"What does the Lord your God ask of you but to fear the Lord your God, to walk in all His ways, to love Him, and to serve the Lord your God with all your heart and with all your soul."* (Deut 10:12) So if Islam is a religion of fear, then so are Judaism and Christianity, for we are all supposed to be in awe—and yes, in fear—of God. As Prophet Moses, whom we all share, said: *"Do not be afraid. God has come to test you, so that the fear of God will be with you to keep you from sinning."* (Exodus 20:20). So this fear of God is not only the greatest mercy, but the only real hope we have for everlasting salvation.

Ultimately, we are all instructed by scripture to reflect so that *we "will understand the fear of the Lord and find the knowledge of God."* (Prov 2:5) If we worry so much about softening God's Message for popular consumption that we forget to be afraid, we'll be no better than those, historically, who have deliberately manipulated the Holy Books to selectively emphasize, or de-emphasize ideas: *"There is among them a section who distort the Book with their tongues. You would think it is a part of the Book, but it is no part of the Book. And they say, "That is from God," but it is not from God"* (3:78). Genuine adherence must be to the whole message (3:19), then, and not just to some part of it—and fear is a big part of that message.

So that, in a nutshell, was the answer I presented my daughter with, one lovely spring day. Are Muslims afraid of God? You bet. And we're extremely happy and thankful about that, actually.

HELPERS FROM ABOVE

So here we are, trying to defend the walls around our souls, and it isn't easy. There's garbage being hurled at us each day—temptations and distractions which cause damage of varying proportions, and to which we must attend. And so we try to seek forgiveness for our indiscretions, and we try to self-correct and self-improve. Well, we try anyhow—or sometimes, anyway. And while we're trying to plug the holes with our fingers, new cracks are forming—character weaknesses like laziness, jealousy, rage, impatience, aggression, and so on, by which we end up chipping away at the wall from the inside. As the idiom goes, "With friends like that, who needs enemies?" We are so worried about the individual threats which various faith groups represent for us—Christians worrying over Jewish and Muslim influences, Muslims worrying over Jewish and Christian influences, Jews worrying over Muslims and Christians, monotheists worrying about the effect of polytheism in their communities, and so on. Yet in effect, we ourselves are our own worst enemy. For within our individual faith groups, within our communities and homes, and within our own lives, we are actually destroying ourselves through inattention, lack of effort, negligence, carelessness and a general disregard for the importance of maintaining a healthy soul and a strong faith even—and especially—in this day and age.

Certainly, protecting belief is a formidable task, and historically, man has inclined towards a life of ease and short-term gains. Protecting what's best in ourselves requires constant vigilance and effort, but we're weak from daily stresses and the business of this world. As a result, we let our boundaries erode, just as the edge of even the highest cliff wears away over time. Thus it has become remarkably easy for us, both individually and communally, to be what the Dead Sea Scrolls refer to as "seekers of smooth things"—people looking for a simpler way to live, a world free of religious limitations and obligations. Hundreds of years before the advent of Jesus, the Scrolls predicted Christianity would find

itself overwhelmed by those seeking to nullify the codes of law and
invite to a simpler way, with few duties or boundaries. But Christianity
is certainly not the only religion succumbing to such pressures. This is,
in fact, a phenomenon plaguing every faith group in the world, as young
people distance themselves from their parents' faith, adults find themselves drawn away from prayer by other commitments, and mass values
overwhelm us all. Yet a simple analogy—and warning—comes from inside
and around us, in the cells which comprise every living thing. Cells are
surrounded by walls of varying permeability, according to their kind.
Any cell whose membrane is compromised by infection, pollution, etc.,
will either begin to let in substances to which it was previously impervi-
ous, or to let slip out substances which the cell actually requires. Over
time, the result is disease and death, for the integrity of the membrane as
a barrier is the key to all cell life, and hence, all life: *"Verily in the heavens
and the earth are signs for those who believe, and in the creation of yourselves..."*
(45:3-4) Yet we frequently—sometimes permanently—compromise the
integrity of our own personal boundaries, as we abandon our posts as
guardians of faith, walk away from our beliefs, and cease to improve our
characters. In doing so, we open ourselves to the slow death of our souls
and the shameful realization that as God's vicegerents on earth, we are
not very effective at all.

Fortunately, God knows us better than we know ourselves, and He
ensures that His purpose for creation is executed perfectly, despite our
human ineptitudes, and despite the resistance of so many who reject faith,
and who reject God: *"God will not allow but that His light should be perfected, even though the unbelievers may detest it."* (9:32). Anticipating our shortcomings, God created helpers to assist us and to aid in the cause of faith.
Around the world, these beings—far more vigilant guardians of the boundaries of life and faith than we can ever be—are known simply as angels:
*"It was We Who created man, and We know what dark suggestions his soul makes
to him: for We are nearer to him than his jugular vein. Behold, two guardian angels
appointed to learn his doings learn and note them..."* (50:16-18; see also 82:10-
12). Angels, therefore, have been appointed to carry the burdens of faith
which we so often fail to carry ourselves, to redirect us and protect us
along the path to God, and to help spread God's mercy and benevolence
to all mankind.

It's interesting that around the world, irrespective of people's particular faith orientation, angels are viewed as positive forces capable of intervening in our lives when there is fear, danger, or despair. And while we seldom actually see them, an astounding 70% of Americans believe in angels, with half these people having witnessed an "angelic presence in their lives.[3]" Most people who've experienced angels say that they came out of nowhere and suddenly pulled, pushed or lifted them to safety. Another type of presence is when people are prevented from going somewhere or doing something through a sudden block—like when an unexpected phone call causes one to miss a train, and so on. Similarly, angels sometimes provide vehicles for positive outcomes, a kind of divinely-inspired serendipity. Through such interventions, harm is prevented, blessings are delivered, and lives which seemingly would otherwise have been extinguished go on. My own grandfather searched desperately for an important legal document after the death of my grandmother. He looked throughout the house for days, then fell asleep in tears, praying for help. When he awoke, the document lay neatly between the pages of the Bible he'd read just the night before. If almost half of the population has felt angels in such ways, perhaps it is because we humans actually need a fair bit of help managing our lives. In Islam, belief in angels is a requirement of faith, and angels are viewed as essential instruments of God. Yet, ironically, even cultures and faith-groups which have abandoned worship in God still believe in angels, and angels are one of the most common and universally accepted subjects for T-shirts, calendars, posters, novels, television shows, and even college courses. In short, it seems that we need to feel angels in our lives, and to believe in the awesome force and benevolence of what dwells just beyond our boundaries.

In fact, angels are intrinsic to an individual's fate, and thus the Qur'an includes detailed stories of how angels are sent down to assist in particular tasks. An angel announced to Prophet Abraham the birth of his son; and to Mary, the Mother of Jesus, about the birth of Jesus; two angels warned Prophet Lot about the impending doom of his community, and instructed him on escaping; and the Angel Gabriel related the last revelations from God to the Prophet Muhammad. In particular, the Qur'an includes a very detailed story of how Prophet Moses accompanies a man or angel (only God knows his true identity) who is described as, *"one of Our servants, on whom We had bestowed Mercy from Ourselves and whom We had taught knowledge from Our own Presence."* (18:65) Moses watches him as he performs God's business on earth, in a way which is apparently incomprehensible. Within a relatively short period of time, this "servant of God" scuttles a perfectly good boat, kills a seemingly innocent young boy, and rebuilds the proprietary wall of an ungenerous man (18:65-82). He then explains to Moses, who is understandably confounded by these actions, that an evil king is seizing all naval traffic and would have killed the sailors had they not been prevented from sailing; the young boy would have grown to be a rebellious son, and in his place, the parents will be given a more dutiful child; and the treasure which lay beneath the wall would now be inaccessible to the unkind man until the rightful owners, two orphans, reached the age of maturity and found it. In this way, the servant's actions—though hard to comprehend on the surface—were, in fact, manifestations of *"a mercy and favour from thy Lord"* (18:82). It's only that we, as human beings, are very limited in our ability to fully understand the mechanics, as it were, of divine interventions.

What we do understand about angels, however, actually reflects the scriptures quite well. Angels are considered ancient beings, older than man (Qur'an 38:71; Job 38:4-7). Winged and lacking material bodies, they neither eat nor drink (Qur'an 35:1, 51:25-28; Isaiah 6:2-8). And though they are frequently wrongly represented as either females or effeminate males, angels are actually non-gendered (53:27, 43:16-19, Matt 22:30), though they are able to take on human and other forms (Qur'an 19:17; Gen 18). Unlike us, angels fulfill their obligations to God tirelessly (42:5, 43:9, 66:6, 69:17, etc.; Isaiah 6:1-3, Gen 21:17-20, etc.). And their duty at the boundaries of life and faith is likened to that of soldiers: for they are *"in succession"* (13:11) and *"rank upon rank"* (89:22); they *"guard and protect man"* (13:11, 50:17, 82:10); and God *"commands"* them (13:11, 16:2, 19:64, 79:3-5). Fittingly, at the end of time, angels will guard both the entrance of hell (66:6, 74:31) and the perimeter of heaven: *"The Day they see the angels, no joy will there be to the sinners that Day: The angels will say: 'There is a barrier forbidden to you altogether!'"* (25:22) In this way, all of the boundaries set by God will be upheld. The most essential attribute of angels, however, is that they are able to move between the material and spiritual world on errands of mercy (16:2, 41:30, 79:3-5, etc.; 2 Pet 2:11,

Psalm 103:20-21, etc.). In essence, then, angels are able to cross bound-aries we cannot, permeating and penetrating all realms of existence: *"We descend not but by command of thy Lord: to Him belongs what is before us and what is behind us, and what is between"* (19:64). As a result, angels are per-haps one of the strongest symbols of monotheistic faith, for as they tran-scend boundaries themselves, so do they transcend the boundaries of faith which separate Jews, Christians, and Muslims. And equally, as they are best in the worship of One God, they may hold one of the strongest hopes for prolific interfaith dialogue which may unite us all towards peace and mutual understanding one day.

My mother believed in her guardian angel with devotion, and com-monly spoke about how the angel eased her path on a given day. I was personally never too sure about angels until the winter of 1977, when my father took our family to Hawaii on a business trip. Exercising my inde-pendence, I looked for ways to get away from everyone, so I ventured alone to a mall one day, by bus. I remember clearly getting off the bus to cross the road—a six-lane divided highway—to reach the mall on the oth-er side. I recall specifically looking to my left and checking for oncom-ing traffic—three lanes clear, no problem. And then, in a moment of dis-traction at my new surroundings, I began walking across the narrow divider while still looking left. Inside an instant which seemed to last for hours, I heard the sound of traffic in my right ear and turned to see that I had actually stepped out into oncoming traffic. I was about four or five steps into the inside lane, with traffic advancing three lanes wide at about 70 km/hr. I remember seeing the horrified face of the driver facing me from about two car lengths away, and the solid block of traffic, bumper-to-bumper, in each lane. "So this is how it ends," I thought slowly, "When you don't expect it." And then, in one moment, I fell hard onto the grass from a bit of a height, with my knees buckled under. I immediately turned to look at the road only to see more of the same—six lanes of furious traffic speeding by. I sat on the ground for quite a long time, maybe 20 or 30 minutes, unable to move, asking myself what just happened. One moment, I looked in the eyes of the man who was about to hit me. The next, I was sitting on the grass beyond the road, even beyond the side-walk. There was nothing in between—no steps, no walking, no running across the street. As I walked about the mall later that day, I felt disconnected with everything I saw and touched. I knew that, without a doubt, I had just been part of something quite different from the world around me. And for reasons that only God knows, I had been saved by an angel that day, though I was hardly even trying to protect myself or my faith in those years.

Thus, in similar ways, in all our lives, God provides invisible forces to assist us (9:26, 9:40, 33:9), despite our imperfections, so that we may live another day, be better than we are today, and be spared from difficulties we can hardly even imagine. God does this to show Himself to us, and to make clear His purpose, which is simply that, *"He may complete His favours on us, and we may consent to be guided"* (2:150). Yes, God has built walls around us, but these are an essential blessing, protecting and defining our existence as believers, giving us the best opportunity for long-term success. Yes, He has instructed us to defend and grow our souls in this life, but He has also mercifully directed us to learn, to understand, and to choose, so that we may be properly supported in our efforts to be righteous. And, yes, God has commanded us to comply with His directives, but out of boundless compassion, He has provided us with clear commandments and the assistance of angels so that we can do just that. Thus do our obligations to secure our belief in God become the best way by which we can truly and permanently secure our souls. In essence, then, our duty as guardians of faith is very straightforward: we need only to live contentedly inside the boundaries God has set forth for us in this life in order to see, one day, eternity stretching so far beyond these walls.

THE INSTRUMENT OF TRUTH – PART ONE – THE REVELATION

As a child of the West, I was encouraged to develop a so-called "rational" approach to everything. Religion was an optional, even illogical pursuit, I was told, a sort of private indulgence not really required by "modern" life. Trained in the sciences, I set off for university, anxious to look for the causes of everything—from environmental problems, to the problems inside me. The Bible, with its lovely stories, held a vagueness which left me grasping for real truth. In time, my sense of religion became increasingly personal and disconnected from those around me. Searching for a "bigger God," I struggled to stay on the honour roll through tests on Darwinian evolution. If this was science, maybe it wasn't for me, I concluded. Yet like permanent lenses stuck to my eyes, my "scientific attitude" kept intruding into my emerging spirituality, making me cynical, suspicious, and unsettled.

This same analytical nature was still with me when I first found the Holy Qur'an. Yet what I soon discovered is that the Qur'an is *the* most powerful proof that "Science and religion lead to the same truth," as Lemaitre (Big Bang Theory) said.

For an age-old example, consider the story of Jonah and the whale—a Bible favourite I loved as a child. Honestly, I always thought it was more of a fable, God's way of showing us how powerless man is. But I have now come to trust the Qur'an so much as an independent source, that as a new Muslim, I felt compelled to rediscover the story, and to search a little more deeply.

"Then the big Fish did swallow him, and he had done acts worthy of blame."
(37:142-144)

In 1771, a man named Marshall Jenkins was swallowed by a whale and lived. In 1892, James Bartley fell in the water while whaling and was swallowed. Two days later, his shipmates found the whale, killed it, and rescued him unconscious, as documented in the Princeton Theological Review, October, 1928. Thus, the story of Jonah being swallowed is certainly possible scientifically, if scientific proof is what we are seeking.

"But We cast him forth on the naked shore in a state of sickness, And We caused to grow, over him, a spreading plant of the gourd kind." (37:145-146)

The bitter gourd is a medicinal plant which is particularly effective in treating skin infections, burns, and bites. Even its leaves have antibacterial properties. Recently, scientists have discovered that it is one of the most powerful weapons against *Entamoeba Histolytica*, a parasite which lives in the intestinal tract of animals. Assuming Jonah survived life in the whale's digestive system, the bitter gourd would have been the perfect remedy.

Yet it's too easy to argue that the story of Jonah isn't a "scientific miracle." After all, the bitter gourd was a known cure for over a thousand years prior to the Qur'an, and the point about being swallowed could still be mainly symbolic. At the very least, however, the Qur'an is remarkably accurate from a medical point of view—after all, the parasite itself wasn't established for certain until the advent of microscopes.

Honey is another old remedy from the earliest days of recorded history. Yet the Qur'an is highly specific about the use of bees:

"There issues from within their bodies a drink of varying colours, wherein is healing for men." (16:69)

What is this liquid of different colours? Honey is usually simply shades of gold, from light yellow to dark amber. This could hardly be called different colours. Yet apitherapy, the medicinal application of bees, actually identifies five separate substances which issue from the body of bees to heal man:

Honey: Gold to amber in colour, honey mixes with chemicals issuing from a wound to convert enzymes in the honey to hydrogen peroxide, disinfecting wounds and burns.

Propolis: Yellow to dark brown in colour, this "hive sealant" is useful as a natural kind of "penicillin," to reduce cancer and various infections.

Royal Jelly: White in colour, this "queen's food" is a very strong antiviral and antibacterial which rejuvenates the skin and body.

Bee venom: Clear, to yellow, to brown, direct stings or dry venom combat degenerative diseases, including asthma, arthritis, and especially Multiple Sclerosis, as the venom contains Melittin, 100 times more powerful than hydrocortisone.

Pollen: Of varying colours, from yellow to green and blue, this perfect protein food has not even been fully analysed yet, but has already been determined to increase strength and stamina by 40-50%, as well as being able to fight many cancers.

And so, once again, the Qur'an is, at the very least, incredibly accurate medically. It's also a clear blessing, even for the sceptical reader, recommending remedies for man's most common ailments—infections, cancer, and degeneration—to alleviate pain and suffering on this earth. Yet this is only another example among a considerable number of scientific truths in the Qur'an.

By now, for instance, many people understand that there are invisible barriers which prevent salt water from mixing with fresh water around the world. Scientists have found these pycnoclines, underwater slopes separating salt water from the water around it. Interestingly, the barrier is clearly explained in the Qur'an:

> *"It is He Who has let free the two bodies of flowing water: One palatable and sweet, and the other salt and bitter; yet has He made a barrier between them, a partition that is forbidden to be passed."* (25:53)

> *"He made a separating bar between the two bodies of flowing water."* (27:61)

Of course, a hardened cynic could argue that this is a rather predictable truth, perhaps. After all, since the world's waters aren't all half-salty, the barrier could be assumed to exist, couldn't it?

In fact, the kind of proof which true sceptics need, as Bible analyst Jay Smith explains, is for information to be revealed in Holy Books which could not be guessed, assumed, or known before as folklore or folk medicine. In addition, this information should be verifiable by modern scientific instruments. Sceptics actually claim that if such evidence could be found in Holy Books, it would be proof of authenticity, and of the authorship of God. As Muslims, we should invite these sceptics to spend a little time with us. Maybe we could start by asking them a few questions.

The first question would be, what were you doing in March of 2003? In March 2003, at the University of Leicester in England, scientists confirmed that there are huge roots under mountains, which extend deeply into the earth's mantle. These downward obstructions create gripping points for horizontal movement; otherwise, the crust of the earth would move sideways in response to the flow of the mantle beneath it. In fact, if a mountain is about 800m above ground, it can have a root as much as 60,000m below ground! Some mountains have enormous roots 50 miles below the surface! Yet the language of the Qur'an is very specific on this subject:

> *"We have set on the earth mountains standing firm, lest it should shake with them."* (21:31 & 16:15 & 31:10)

> *"With the mountains as pegs"* (78:7)

And so, scientists confirmed in 2003 what the Qur'an described very particularly over 14 centuries ago, that mountains act like pegs to stabilize the earth's crust. Surely no one could ever guess—in the seventh century or now—that huge mountains are even bigger below ground than they are above ground.

A second question we would ask those sceptics is, what were you doing in July of 2003? On July 17th, 2003, in the prestigious scientific journal, *Nature*, researchers announced that they had found evidence that supernovas—huge stars—belch out spectacular quantities of cosmic dust. This special kind of dust is made up of particles which scientists say look just like "cigarette smoke." This smoke apparently provides small grains which helps young stars to form and is the first building block of planets. It's interesting to note that the dust is visible only at -257C, by the world's most powerful wave camera, attached to the James Clerk Maxwell Telescope in Hawaii—which is why it has only recently been noticed. Yet the Qur'an explains how this *"smoke"* formed planets, in a chapter aptly called *"Fusillat,"* or *"explained in detail"*:

> *"Moreover He comprehended in His design the sky, and it had been (as) smoke: He said to it and to the earth: 'Come ye together, willingly or unwillingly.'"* (41:11)

Even a sceptic should be able to admit that this is rather specific information which could hardly have been guessed over a thousand years ago.

We can ask our sceptics another question, too, going back a little further in time to September, 2002. Ironically, this was the one-year commemoration of 9-11, a very stressful time around the world. Yet while the hardship seemed enveloping, an incredible mercy was actually unfolding at the very same time, in another confirmation of God's message. At Stanford University, in September 2002, scientists Andrei Linde and Renata Kallosh determined that the universe will eventually collapse. Of course, right now, the universe is expanding; the moon, for example, is moving away two inches every year. That's interesting in itself because the Qur'an actually tells us about the expansion of the universe very clearly:

"So verily I call to witness the planets - that recede." (81:15)

Anyhow, after this period of expansion is completed, in about 10-20 billion years, the universe will apparently start collapsing. It will begin to contract, like folding up, with stars falling in towards a kind of centre, eventually collapsing to a very small, single point the size of a single proton. This is an amazing finding, which has been made possible only recently using the Hubble telescope. Yet without any such modern instruments, the Qur'an provides the same information about the end of time:

"When the stars fall" (81:2)

"When the sun (with its spacious light) is folded up" (81:1)

There is clearly no way this information could have been known 1400 years ago, and it is not anything which anyone would normally guess or assume. Our universe, which we have for all of this century assumed to be expanding, will eventually *"fold up"* in a complete collapse, just as the Qur'an tells us.

Reading the Qur'an in earnest, the world certainly starts to look both infinitely simpler and more divine. And looking at the world more carefully, the Qur'an becomes infinitely more complex and more miraculous.

THE INSTRUMENT OF TRUTH – PART TWO –
THE CONFIRMATION

T he Holy Qur'an is really unique. Like the Bible and Torah, it presents truth on many levels—explaining everything from the light in our souls, to the life beyond this one. But unlike other Holy Books, the Qur'an gives very detailed information about the material world, too—about space, oceans, earth, man, mountains, animals, plants, and more, as well as specifics about the physics of the beginning and end of time as we know it. Its scientific accuracy can literally take the reader's breath away, and send shivers down even the most cynical spine. Simply and elegantly, it presents truth as a mercy to all mankind—a confirmation, in this day and age, that God is real.

"Who has made the earth firm to live in…" (27:61)

Science is in complete agreement that Earth had a soft phase and became firm. In the very earliest days of its history, our planet was so hot that it was a molten mass of liquid iron.

"And We sent down Iron" (57:25)

Over time, Earth cooled and hardened, and the Earth's crust formed. How could anyone have any idea about the composition of the Earth's core, or its geologic history, in the 7th century, given that countless modern instruments were required for all of these "discoveries"?

"For among rocks there are some from which rivers gush forth; others there are which when split asunder send forth water; and others which sink for fear of God." (2:74)

Modern-day geology agrees that there are three kinds of rocks. The first, igneous rocks, have rivers of lava which gush forth, and they form when the magma hardens. The second kind, metamorphic rocks, form when pressure compresses fluids inside intergranular voids—so if you split them at that level, water could be extracted. The third kind, sedimentary rocks, form when sediments sink to the bottom of rivers, lakes, and oceans. Consider the staggering differences to the naked eye between sapphires and sand, or between diamonds and granite. Without a powerful microscope, how could anyone guess that rocks contain water, or that there really are only three types of rocks in the entire world?

"Allah has created every animal from water." (24:45)

"It is He Who has created man from water." (25:54)

"We made from water every living thing." (21:30)

In fact, every living thing *is* made from water. In humans, water comprises about 70% of body weight, on average. Blood alone is 90% water. In animals, the water ratio is usually 50-80%, and in insects, it is generally 70-90%. In turn, fresh plants are 75-95% water on average. Yet this is clearly not the sort of thing which would be easy to infer, is it? Staring at the carcass of a cow on the desert floor, or a rotting root vegetable, or a dead bee, could anyone have guessed, 14 centuries ago, that three quarters or more of each of these masses consisted of water?

"By the (Steeds) that run, with panting (breath), and raise the dust in clouds." (100:1-4)

It is a pivotal concept of modern meteorology that clouds need dust to form rain. Dust is required to act as "condensation nuclei," allowing the droplets of water to attach themselves until the particle is heavy enough to fall as rain. In fact, in the 20th century, scientists discovered they could raise dust in clouds deliberately, in a process called "cloud seeding," to make it rain. For hundreds of years before then, people only dreamed of being able to "make it rain"—while the Qur'an held the truth.

"Like the depths of darkness in a vast deep ocean, overwhelmed with billow topped by billow… depths of darkness, one above another." (24:40)

In actuality, there are five distinct layers in the ocean. The top epipelagic layer allows visible light and plants. Below is the mesopelagic layer, where bioluminescent creatures provide the only light. Continuing deeper, the bathypelagic layer has dimly lit creatures, mostly black and red. Lower still is the abyssopelagic layer, where there is no light. Finally, below 6000 feet, is the hadalpelagic layer, with no light at all, yet an incredible array of new species—90% of all ocean life forms—the largest ecological region in the world. How could anyone guess such separate layers, distinguished by their levels of darkness, without the equipment to descend to these depths?

And in the seventh century, who other than God could have known that the moon had once been split?

> *"The moon is cleft asunder."* (54:1)

Of course, this story is of particular relevance in the life of the Prophet Muhammad (PBUH), yet like most of the Qur'an, it has meaning on multiple levels. In March 1999, barely three years ago, NASA's Lunar Prospector analysed the moon's core. From this evidence, scientists concluded that the moon was formed when a large object the size of Mars hit the earth in a collision about 4.5 billion years ago, and the moon was split from the earth. Yet the Qur'an very unambiguously tells us the same thing it took modern science 1400 years to determine.

> *"God is He Who created seven Firmaments."* (65:12, 2:29, 41:12, 78:12)

The seven firmaments are generally acknowledged to be the seven layers of the atmosphere: the troposphere, stratosphere, mesosphere, thermosphere, exosphere, ionosphere, and magnetosphere. Again, these are 20th century findings, impossible to guess with the naked eye. Of course, some sceptics may argue that the firmaments actually don't represent the different layers of the atmosphere, so it's worth looking at a related quote:

> *"By the firmament which gives the returning rain"* (86:11)

It is a scientific fact that rain is produced through a water cycle, by which water evaporates from the earth and is returned as rain, again and again. As the Qur'an describes, the source of the rain is a single firmament. In fact, it is: the top point of the water cycle involves only one firmament, the troposphere. This is really an incredible level of accuracy, and further confirmation that the firmaments really are the layers of the atmosphere.

"He completed them as seven firmaments in two Days" (41:12)

Billions of years ago, there was a primordial atmosphere which was very thick, about 80 times what it is now, at about 800F. During the collision which split the moon from the earth, most of this primordial atmosphere was ejected. Interestingly, this is what allowed the development of a thin atmosphere which is just the right density for us to live. Thus, the earth's atmosphere, in its seven layers, seems to have had two major stages of formation—two "days," so to speak. Is modern science on the verge of confirming the Qur'anic account of Genesis?

"[There are] winds which scatter broadcasts" (51:1)

Solar wind disrupts electrical transmissions and negatively affects radio signals, radar, sonar, ship-to-shore communications, airplane navigation, global positioning satellites, Skylab, and more. In fact, solar wind is such a disturbance to electronic broadcasts that warnings about solar storms are sent out by the authorities to ships, flight agencies, the military, communications networks, etc. Since electronics and solar wind are recent "discoveries," how can we explain the precision of the Qur'an?

"By the Sky with (its) numerous Paths" (51:7)

The current theory is that space is folded at the sub-atomic level, and there are very tiny paths, called Einstein-Rosen bridges, between separate places in the universe. These so-called "wormholes" are extremely small—about 10 (-35)m in width—perhaps just big enough to allow light and electrical signals to get through. Is it possible that, once again, the Qur'an is predicting modern discoveries?

In closing, it's worth asking one more question to the sceptics of this world. What were you doing on February 28th 2003? That day was the 50-year anniversary of the discovery of DNA, the material fabric of all living things. DNA is made up of two strands, like a twisted ladder. Each strand is comprised of sequences of special proteins, paired with specific proteins on the other strand. Adenine is always paired with Thiamine, and Cytosine is always paired with Guanine, so the pairs on the ladder are AT, CG, TA, GC, and so on. When a human, plant, or animal cell is growing, each strand splits and replicates its missing pair. Then two new pairs are made. Then each new pair splits, and replicates, etc. That is how all biological life happens. In other words, the living world is based on pairs of strings which repeat, and repeat. It's actually a very simple structure, and one of the discoverers, James Watson's, first reaction was to say, "It's so beautiful!" Yet we should hardly be surprised at the beauty, as it is from the hand of God:

Beautiful pairs....

> *"We have put forth every kind of beautiful growth in pairs."* (22:5, 50:7) *"He created you in pairs"* (35:11) *"Glory to God, Who created in pairs all things that the earth produces."* (36:36) *"Who has created pairs in all things,"* (43:11) *"And of every thing God has created pairs: That you may receive instruction"* (51:49) *"Have We not created you in pairs?"* (78:8)

That repeat and repeat with beautiful precision....

> *"Glory to God, who originates creation, then repeats it"* (27:64) *"See they not how Allah originates creation, then repeats it"* (29:19) *"It is Allah Who begins (the process of) creation; then repeats it"* (30:11) *"It is He Who begins (the process of) creation; then repeats it"* (30:27)

The Qur'an puts strong emphasis on this fundamental fact of life—pairs and repetition. Yet this was made evident to us through modern science barely 50 years ago.

Certainly, the Qur'an is an invitation to study science. The world increasingly needs scientists of faith to look for confirmations of God's message in our world, to relate it to others, and perhaps to change the life of one, one hundred, or one thousand people towards belief. For as Galileo said, "Nature is a book written by God." Even more fundamentally, the Qur'an is a mercy and comfort for all believers:

> *"Verily there has come to you a convincing proof from your Lord, and we have sent unto you a light that is manifest"* (4:174) *"Isn't the Qur'an enough as a sign?"* (29:51)

Surely even the deepest sceptic cannot deny the position of honour of the Holy Qur'an among the instruments of truth—microscope and telescope, reason and Revelation. *"You will certainly know the truth of it after awhile"* (38:88).

COMMON GROUND – PART ONE –
THE OPENED BIBLE

W ho knows what each day will bring? One afternoon in 1947, a young shepherd threw rocks into caves along the Dead Sea, as always. But this time, instead of an echo, he heard shattering clay. Unknowingly, he changed world history, for the caves revealed countless earthen pots—a pre-Christian library of up to 870 manuscripts now called the "Dead Sea Scrolls," carbon-dated to as far back as 200 years before Jesus, Peace Be Upon Him.[4] The parallels to the Bible are striking: for example, the "Great Isaiah Scroll" (Cave 1) is almost verbatim the "Book of Isaiah," though it predates by 1000 years the oldest surviving manuscript of Isaiah, the "Codex" of the 9th century CE. As Dr. W. Fields, of the Sea Scroll Foundation says, "Jesus could have read from this scroll"—though no one is suggesting he did.[5] So while experts struggle to assemble bits of parchment, most are overlooking the key truth. Let's face it: non-Muslims generally reject the Qur'an for two reasons. First, they believe it is an unoriginal text largely copied from existing scriptures—so-called *"tales of the ancients"* (46:12). Second, they don't believe Muhammad, Peace and Blessings Be Upon Him, was a prophet of God. To deaf ears, Muslims ask, "Why shouldn't God's message be the same from one time to another?" Yet here is a truly momentous event, for the Bible itself repeats old scriptures! As it remains valid nonetheless, one of the most persistent arguments against the Qur'an is shattered like clay. And suddenly, seemingly insurmountable barriers between the People of the Book begin to vanish, stretching out the common ground beneath us, like mountains dissolving: *"You think the mountains are firmly fixed, but on Judgement Day, they will pass away as clouds pass away."* (27:88)

Yet one argument endures, as non-Muslims continue to doubt the authenticity of Prophet Muhammad, and writers in all camps are passionate about whether or not he is mentioned in the Bible. One website actually instructs Christian clergy on how to counter Muslim arguments that he is.[6] In turn, Muslims cite the recovered "Gospel of Barnabas," which mentions "Muhammad" by name. However, the Gospel of Barnabas has been subjected to repeated accusations that it may be a medieval forgery. So if we want to help Christians and Jews understand Prophet Muhammad, we should keep to a source they consider valid—the Bible itself.

1. Deuteronomy 18: 18 – 19 refers to a prophet "like Moses": *"I will raise up for them (the Israelites) a prophet like you from among their brethren (brothers); and I will put My words in his mouth, and he shall speak to them all that I command him."* Muhammad is very similar to Moses: both had a non-miraculous birth; were rejected then accepted; endured migration; were leaders; fought battles; enjoyed victories over enemies; were married with families; experienced common deaths; and had revelations written down during their lifetimes. Additionally, the brethren of the Israelites (descended from Isaac) are the Ismaelites (e.g. Genesis 16:12 and 25:18).

2. John 14: 16 – 17 describes a *"comforter"* sent after Jesus: *"And I (Jesus) will ask the Father, and He shall give you another comforter*, that he may abide with you forever."* And in John 16: 7, Jesus adds, *"It is better for you that I go away because if I do not go, the comforter* will not come to you. But if I go away, then I will send him to you. And when he comes, he will prove to the people of the world that they are wrong about sin and about what is right, and about God's judgement."* The critical analyses of these lines consume thousands of pages. It seems the original Aramaic was translated into Greek, Syriac, and Hebrew, producing alternate spellings of the word *"comforter"* as paraclete, paracletos, paraclyte, periklytos, paraklytos, paraqleita, or paraqleyta, resulting in different meanings: "praised one," "character witness," "helper," "comforter" or "Spirit"— the last being the accepted standard.[7] Some also mention "paraklytos" translates as "Ahmad" in Greek, and "Muhammad" means "praised one." Additionally, the description suits because Prophet Muhammad promoted stricter adherence to the scriptures. Critically, the Anchor Bible[8] states "paraclete" was never intended as "Holy Spirit." Rather, it was "an independent salvific (saviour) figure later confused with the Holy Spirit." In other words, a prophet was expected after Jesus, in the original version.

3. Compare this with Isaiah 9:6: *"For unto us a child is born, unto us a son is given; and the government shall be upon his shoulder. And his name shall be called Wonderful (Wise), Counsellor..."* Again, the suggestion is of a wise

helper who will govern, as did the Prophet Muhammad. The shoulder reference is linked by some writers to his shoulder birthmark.

4.   Jeremiah 28:9 announces a prophet of peace: *"The prophet who prophesies of peace, when the word of the prophet will come to pass, then the prophet will be known, that the Lord has truly sent him."* Even Christian writers admit that Jesus did not bring peace, and the word "Islam" means peace; the implication is that the Prophet of Peace will eventually be accepted by everyone.

5.   John 1: 20 – 21 describes an interesting conversation between John the Baptist (Yahya) and Jewish authorities in Jerusalem: *"And he (John) confessed and he denied not, but confessed, 'I am not The Messiah (Christ).' And they asked him, 'What then? Are you Elias (Elijah)?' And he said, 'I am not.' 'Are you That Prophet?' And he answered, 'No.'"* Admittedly, John is describing three separate people, Jesus, Elias, and a Prophet who will presumably come after Jesus.

6.   In Deuteronomy 33: 1 – 2, reflects on three major prophets: *"The Lord came from Sinai, and dawned like the sun from Seir upon us; He shone forth on his people from Mount Paran. Ten thousands angels were with him, a flaming fire at his right hand."* God spoke to Moses and sent down the Torah at Sinai, Jesus received the revelation at Seir/Sair (near Jerusalem), and Muhammad is from Paran, a mountain range near Mecca. (The wilderness of Paran is also where Ishmael settled, Genesis 21:21.) The fire in the right hand and thousands of holy ones easily refers to the army of 10,000 Muslims by which he took Mecca in 630 CE—a historically documented event. Quite tentatively, Christian literature generally assigns these references to Jesus throughout his life.

7.   Isaiah 29: 12 announces an illiterate prophet: *"And the book is delivered to him that is not learned, saying 'Read this, I ask thee,' And he says, 'I cannot, for I am not learned.'"* It is an historical fact that Prophet Muhammad was illiterate. Opponents vaguely argue this refers to a "false prophet."

8.   Isaiah 11: 1 – 2 advises of a great prophet descended from Ishmael: *"And there shall come forth a rod out of the stem of Jesse, and a branch shall grow out of his roots. And the Spirit of the Lord shall rest on him, the spirit of wisdom and understanding, the spirit of counsel and right, the spirit of knowledge and the fear of the Lord."* Christian writers admit "Jesse" is a contraction of "Ishmael," yet they suggest this refers to Jesus even though the Bible links Jesus to the "root of David" (Revelation 5: 5

– 6) and Isaiah further describes this unnamed prophet as one who brings in a kingdom of peace (Isaiah 11: 6 – 9), as the Prophet Muhammad is proven to have done historically.

9. Isaiah 21: 7 predicts a prophet to come after Jesus: *"And he saw a chariot with a couple of horsemen, a chariot of asses (donkeys), and a chariot of camels."* Jesus is recognized as the rider on donkeys (John 12:14), and another rider comes later on camels. Opponents curiously argue this is not a reference to the Prophet Muhammad, but to a prophecy that has not yet been fulfilled.

10. In Psalms 69: 4 - 21, there is an interesting lament: *"Those who hate me for no reason are more numerous than the hairs of my head. My enemies tell lies against me...When I was hungry, they gave me poison..."* It is historically documented that the Prophet Muhammad was poisoned on his travels, eventually causing his death, and the opponents to Islam alluded to here are still numerous today.

11. In Isaiah 41: 2 – 4, invites reflection on the Prophet's military mission: *"Who was it who brought the conqueror from the East, and makes him triumphant wherever he goes? Who gives him victory over kings and nations? … Who was it that made this happened? Who has determined the course of history?"* Bible footnotes insist that this refers to the Emperor of Persia, but it is well-documented that Muhammad's military victories were unique in reach, speed, and success.

12. The reference repeats in Isaiah 46: 10 – 11: *"Long ago, I (God) foretold what would happen. I said that My plans would never fail, that I would do everything I intended to do. I am calling a man to come from the East. He will swoop down like a hawk and accomplish what I have planned."* Based on this and the quote just above, one would have to admit that the Emperor of Persia was a messenger of God who came to conclude God's plan for mankind. But since even Christians never suggest that the emperor was any sort of prophet, in fact, the reference clearly suggests Prophet Muhammad.

13. More detail about this mysterious "man from the east" is given in Revelation 19: 11 – 12: *"I saw heaven open, and there was a white horse. Its rider is called "Faithful" and "True." With justice, he judges and fights his battles. His eyes were like a flame of fire, and he wore many crowns on his head. He had a name written on him, but no one except himself knows what it is."* This quote is particularly revealing, for Prophet Muhammad

was called Al-Amin, "truthful one," even by his enemies. Not only that, but as he fought battles, brought justice, and conquered many lands, he effectively did wear many crowns. And, critically, he was the first person ever to be called "Muhammad"—a unique name which no one knew at the time.

14. In Isaiah 28: 11 - 13, Jesus warns the Israelites about a new kind of prophet: *"If you won't listen to me, then God will use foreigners speaking some strange-sounding language to teach you a lesson. He offered rest and comfort to you all, but you refused to listen to Him. That is why the Lord is going to teach you letter by letter, line by line, lesson by lesson."* Unequivocally, the Qur'an presents verses out of the order of revelation as an enduring record that the message came in individual lines and lessons: *"We have revealed it in stages,"* (17:106) and *"By degrees, We will teach the message so you will not forget."* (87:6). With regards to the reference to a "strange-sounding language," Arabic would certainly sound strange to the Israelites. Most definitely, this quote is evidence of a strong reference to the Prophet Muhammad and the Qur'an.

Of course, critics of the Prophet Muhammad, Islam, and the Holy Qur'an may discount the significance of one or another of the Bible passages quoted, but the totality is hard to ignore. The logical conclusion for any reader with an open heart must be that the Bible makes at least some reference to Prophet Muhammad, so that his arrival as a servant of God had long been predicted in the history of mankind. Consider, too, the miracle of how God's early message about the Prophet Muhammad has been preserved through incredible circumstances: the Dead Sea Scrolls were mishandled at first and sold randomly—for example, the "Great Isaiah Scroll" was purchased by a cobbler in Bethlehem for only $64! And the Bible itself has been translated and reissued countless times, at an obvious risk to the accuracy of the original message: *"How can you say, 'We are wise for we have the Law of the Lord' when actually the lying pen of the scribes has handled it falsely."*(Jeremiah 8:8) So the Dead Sea Scrolls have become like a precious long-dormant seed for all the People of the Book, idle for millennia, finally blossoming to validate both the Holy Bible and the Holy Qur'an for whomever required such verification. In a world climate desperate for a dialogue of peace, it seems tremendously symbolic that once again, a young shepherd would offer a startling focus for hope—and we would all be witnesses, as always, to the awesome power and mercy of God.

COMMON GROUND – PART TWO –
THE CORNER STONE

G rowing up as a Christian, I had no idea Muslims worshipped the same God I did. Dressed differently, speaking languages I couldn't understand, Muslims seemed like a world apart from everything I was. It wasn't until I met a Muslim that I learned the astounding truth: Muslims believe in heaven, hell, angels, and the momentous people I was familiar with—Adam, Noah, Abraham, Moses, and Jesus. Ultimately, it is not conflict that separates us, but common ignorance of the fact that like an echo, God's word has been sent to many places and times, to be heard by everyone.

Not surprisingly, then, the Bible contains "Islamic" ideas. Consider these expressions about Judgement Day from the Dead Sea Scrolls (DSS)[9] the Bible[10], and the Qur'an.[11] Certainly, if the Bible is not invalidated by this kind of redundancy, then neither is the Qur'an. In fact, in the second example, the Qur'anic version is actually closer to the DSS than the Bible is! And in all cases, meaning is obviously preserved between examples since shared ideas mean a shared God—it's that simple.

1. Isaiah 9:19 (DSS) *Even people shall be fuel for the fire.*
   Isaiah 9:19 (NIV) *The people will be fuel for the fire.*
   Qur'an 66:6 *…a fire whose fuel is men and stones…*
2. Isaiah 9:19 (DSS) *Each man shall eat the flesh of his own arm.*
   Isaiah 9:19 (NIV) *Each will feed on the flesh of his own offspring.*
   Qur'an 25:27 *The wrongdoer will bite at his hands.*
3. Isaiah 13:13 (DSS) *The earth shall tremble out of its place.*
   Isaiah 13:13 (NIV) *The earth will shake from its place.*
   Qur'an 56:4: *The earth shall be shaken to its depths.*
4. Isaiah 24:18 (DSS) *The windows from the highest are opened…*
   Isaiah 24:18 (NIV) *The floodgates of heaven are open…*
   Qur'an 25:15, 69:16, 73:18, 82:1 *The sky (heaven) will be rent asunder…*

5. Isaiah 34:4 (DSS) *The heavens shall be rolled up like a book.*
    Isaiah 34:4 (NIV) *And the sky, rolled up like a scroll.*
    Qur'an: 21:104 *The heavens will be rolled up like a scroll.*

Dissenters might argue that Prophet Muhammad had scholars cite the Bible to him. But how could great theologians fluent in Aramaic, Syriac, Greek and Hebrew go along unnoticed on each battle, journey, prayer group, speech, and family moment for 23 years, just to whisper Arabic translations of selected lines to a man who could neither read nor write? Also, he risked a lot with this kind of redundancy—after all, enemies were at every turn, trying to overthrow his growing popularity. With a minimum of research, authorities could have formally accused him of copying existing scriptures. In a place and time where oratory was the highest art, he would have been swiftly discredited.

Yet listeners felt the Prophet had something important to say: they felt moved when they heard him, and they felt connected with God when they thought about, and acted on, the message. His prose was unique, eloquent to the highest degree, and in superb literary Arabic. In fact, even contemporary non-Muslim scholars agree about the masterful linguistic art of the Qur'an. In short, it could hardly be the product of piecemeal translations strung together on a battlefield. Additionally, history concurs that Prophet Muhammad enjoyed limited earthly gain—he suffered bankruptcy, in modern terms, and led battles when he was already at retirement age, so to speak. He received death threats, and was offered bribes just to keep quiet. At the very least, if he were trying to create the Qur'an strictly for personal glory, why didn't he direct at least some of the praise towards himself instead of God? It is because the words did not come *from* him, but *through* him. Prophet Muhammad was one in a *"series of messengers"* (5:19)—the last, actually. Thus, his message was faithfully foreshadowed in the Bible.

6. Matthew 5:9 says, *"Blessed are the peacemakers, for they shall be called the children of God."* Islam, by definition, is the religion of peace, though others argue this refers to Jesus.

7. In Matthew 21: 43, Jesus said, *"And so I tell you, the Kingdom of God will be taken from you and given to a people who will produce the proper fruits."*

This suggests that blessings will be given to a new group, after the Israelites, who will maintain stricter adherence to the scriptures.

8. Genesis 49:10 is specific: *"The sceptre shall not depart from Judah nor a lawgiver from between his feet until Shiloh come, and unto him shall the gathering of the people be."* So, scriptural leadership leaves the Children of Israel for a large community known as Shiloh (peace).

9. Similarly, Haggai 2:9 states, *"The latter glory of this house will be greater than the former,' says the Lord of Hosts, 'And in this place I will give peace,' declares the Lord of Hosts."* Again, a community of "peace" greatly honours the revelations after the initial glory of the Israelites.

10. In Genesis 21: 18 – 21, God promises Hagar regarding her son, *"I will make a great nation out of his descendants"* and states, *"God was with the boy as he grew up. He lived in the wilderness of Paran…"* This is a clear sign that Ishmael and his descendants would be blessed. And in Genesis 12: 2 – 3, God speaks to Abraham: *"And I will make thee a great nation, and I will bless thee, and make thy name great. And thou shall be a blessing. And I will bless them that bless thee. And in thee, shall all the families of the earth be blessed."* Surely, a sweeping and promise about families, made before the birth of the two boys, must apply to both Isaac and Ishmael.

11. This point is clarified in Psalms 69:8: *"I am become a stranger to my brethren, and an alien unto my mother's children,"* a fitting lament for Ishmael's exclusion in the eyes of so many.

12. This point is also addressed in Isaiah 54:1: *"O barren one, though thou did not bear; break forth into singing and cry aloud, thou that did not travail with child. For more are the children of the desolate than the children of the married wife."* This may refer to Sarah, who receives glad tidings of a child after being barren; if so, it openly suggests that the children of the desolate—i.e. the children of Hagar, whom Prophet Abraham was instructed to abandon in the desert—will be more numerous and/or more important ultimately.

13. The idea continues in Isaiah 62: 2 – 4: *"You will be called by a new name, a name given by the Lord himself. You will be like a beautiful crown for the Lord. No longer will you be called forsaken, nor your land be called, 'The Deserted Wife.' Your new name will be, "God is pleased."* Again, the

implication is that the nation of this deserted wife, Hagar, will be blessed by God.

14. In Isaiah 65: 12 – 16, God speaks to the Israelites: *"You chose to disobey me and do evil. And so I tell you that those who worship and obey me will have plenty to eat and drink, but you will be hungry and thirsty...I will give a new name to those who obey me."* In the Qur'an, the name "Islam" is given directly by God, upon perfecting man's understanding of submission.

15. In Isaiah 65: 17, God says: *"Behold, I will create a new government (new earth) and a new religion (new heavens), and the former shall not be remembered nor come to mind."* Can this be a clear statement about the coming of Islam, which presented a new style of rule and worship?

16. Isaiah 21:13: *"The burden is upon Arabia. In the forests of Arabia, you will lodge...The bowmen are the bravest men of Kedar, but few of them will be left."* Significantly, Arabia will carry the "burden" of the revelation. Few warriors will be left, again suggesting the advent of "peace."

By far the most intriguing mention of Islam in the Bible concerns references to a "cornerstone," the subject of extensive Biblical research. Hundreds of pages argue that Jesus or the Apostle Peter is "the cornerstone," but the reader should consider the following and draw his or her own conclusions.

17. In Luke 20: 17 – 18, Jesus invites serious consideration of the "cornerstone": *"What does this text mean, the stone that the builders rejected has become the cornerstone? Everyone who falls on that stone will be broken to pieces, and it will crush anyone on whom it falls?'"*

18. In Matthew 21: 42 – 44: *"Jesus said to them (the Israelites), 'Did you ever read in the scriptures, The stone which the builders rejected, the same is become the head of the corner. This is the Lord's doing, and it is marvellous in our eyes.'"*

19. In 1 Peter 2:7: *"For it stands in scripture, "See I am laying in Zion a stone, a cornerstone chosen and precious. Whoever believes in him will not be put to shame...But to those who do not believe, the stone that the builders rejected has become the very head of the corner, a stone that makes them stumble and a rock that makes them fall."*

20. In Psalms 118:22: *"The stone the builders rejected has become the chief cornerstone. This is the Lord's doing. It is marvellous in our eyes."*

21. In Mark 12: 10 – 11: *"Jesus said to them, 'The stone that the builders rejected has become the cornerstone. This was the Lord's doing, and it is amazing in our eyes.'"*

22. In Isaiah 28:16: *"Therefore, says the Lord, 'See, I am laying in Zion a foundation stone, a tested stone, a precious cornerstone, a sure foundation. Everyone who trusts will not panic."*

For all of recorded time, only one place worldwide has been singularly distinguished by its *"cornerstone"*: the Ka'ba. We can probably never know if the precious black stone was "rejected by builders" of a great Jewish temple or others at some point. Definitively, however, the stone was put precisely and deliberately on the eastern corner of the square-shaped Ka'ba, and no other site on earth is designated so uniquely as the *"cornerstone."* Interestingly, the Bible concurs that before Jesus, Mecca was a place for pilgrims, *"Who passing through the valley of Baca [Mecca] make it a well."* (Psalm 84:6) Symbolically, the cornerstone becoming the "head" may confirm that the responsibility for honouring the revelations will be given to a community associated with the cornerstone.

So the question is no longer, "Are there references to Islam in the Bible?" but rather, "Why wouldn't there be?" Couldn't we simply share One God and one core revelation? Of course, the Qur'an does not repeat the Bible exactly, as it *"reveals much of what was hidden in the Book, and passes over much that is now unnecessary"* (5:15). Similarly, portions of the Dead Sea Scrolls are not in the Bible. So each of God's messages to mankind is unique, yet linked—until the last of the revelations, the Holy Qur'an: *"Without doubt, it (the Qur'an) is announced in the revealed Books of former peoples."* (26:196) The redundancy between God's messages is intentional—like the repetition within the scriptures themselves, as stories and instructions are repeated to *"make it easy to understand and remember"* (54:17, 54:22, 54:32, 54:40). This concordance is both an act of God, and a gift from God, as well as a clear witness to the authenticity of Prophet Muhammad. Surely, it is an invitation for Christians and Jews to read—not reject—the Qur'an: *"O, People of the Book! You have no ground to stand upon unless you stand fast by the Torah and the Gospel, and all the revelation that has come to you from your Lord."* (5:68). And so it is, for the revelation *is* our common ground.

ON THE PERFECTING OF A PROPHET

I t is one of the articles of faith of Islam to believe in the Prophet Muhammad (Peace and Blessings Be Upon Him). So when anyone casts a shadow on his character, such as in the well-publicized comments by the American Reverend Falwell in 2002, the Muslim world feels deeply antagonized. Yet while the Reverend's remarks were extreme in their negativity, many non-Muslims really question the Prophet of Islam—who is he, and why do Muslims embrace him so completely? When I first came to Islam from Christianity almost two years ago, I asked myself this question, too. Muslims believed in him purely from their hearts. I admired them, but I was still captive of a secular, overly rational mindset. If I were going to accept the Prophet fully, it would have to "make sense" logically.

Muslim friends told me about his hard work, his impeccable character, and his innumerable virtues. Ironically, the more they spoke of his perfection, the more I resisted. It reminded me too much of the fervour of Christians regarding Jesus (PBUH). Risk comes with excessive praise—inadvertently, a wonderful prophet can be raised to a status higher than a mortal man. Like many current and former Christians, I would not believe that Jesus was God, and I was scared of language which elevated any prophet too highly.

So every time I read about the Prophet, I prayed for protection from my own misconceptions, my own cultural prejudices. Then one day, I came upon a lovely story about the infant Prophet being nursed by a Bedouin. While he lived with the tribe, they enjoyed bountiful harvests and animals full of milk. The Bedouins soon became convinced this particular baby was very special. I had seen God looking out for the children in my life and providing for them inexplicably at particularly difficult times. So, by the grace of God, the Bedouin's story opened a door for me.

Slowly, with more reading, the walls around my heart began to disintegrate. Polygamy was acceptable among Muslims, Jews, Christians, and polytheists at the time. But the Prophet had many wives, and non-Muslims eagerly cited this as evidence of perversion. What was the rational truth? First, he was loyal to one wife for 20 years, until her death, though she was his elder by 15 years. After her death, he married two women within a few years—one the elderly, destitute widow of an old friend, and the other the beloved daughter of his best friend and staunchest supporter. The latter, the lovely Aisha (may God be pleased with her) was a bright, beautiful, young woman he had known since her birth. She was one of the first converts to Islam and remained one of his most loyal confidantes throughout his life, as well as being a gifted historian. Having the option to marry only her, why wouldn't he have done so? She was surely everything he could desire, physically, emotionally, intellectually, and spiritually, and he chose her company on his deathbed. Yet he married others later, relative strangers, women from different cultures, age groups, physical attributes, and social positions—most bringing several children to add to his responsibilities, and most destined to a life of destitution as widows without the mercy of his offer. His marriages formed alliances between previously disparate peoples—Egyptian Copts, Jews, warring Arab tribes, and Blacks—and shattered the roots of racism and social repression. Simultaneously, his home became the first school of Islam, as his wives and their children became ambassadors among their own peoples, thereby increasing both the acceptance and the reach of Islam. It's simply illogical to think that a man in his 50s and 60s, with a perfect young wife already, would seek to complicate his life by adding more than 20 or 30 people to his household, including many offspring of other men, just to satisfy his sexual needs. Clearly, his complex home life was part of his calling and in no way reflected deviance on his part.

The image of the Prophet as a warrior was another point of contention which I found myself debating with my own Christian relatives. For after extensive reading, my conclusion was that he was simply a man with an opinion far different from the prevalent viewpoint, and this is never easy in any place at any time. He fought to defend himself and his community, and to protect his right and others' rights to profess their faith. He did it superbly, but excellence is hardly something to hold against someone. A simple and factual look at his choices tells it best. He could have been at home quietly with a few children and grandchildren, in comfort and peace. Instead, he was on the battlefield with rocks strapped to his stomach to fade the feeling of hunger, washing his body with sand. He did not become rich, nor did he retire to a leisurely life. In fact, he continued to live a very basic, frugal life, even when he became the head of state, enduring poverty, exhaustion, harassment, and continual threats from all corners. Further, he did not become the object of worship for anyone—proof is in the fact that Muslims celebrate his birth, death, and calling simply as days of reflection and prayer. The Muslim high holidays relate strictly to the message of Islam—the submission to one God—and not to the man. If he were really a megalomaniac, as those strongly opposed to Islam argue, why didn't he "invent" verses of the Qur'an to compel Muslims to recognize him as better than all prophets and make himself the object of all prayers. Instead, he is respectfully referred to in the Qur'an as a beautiful example of mankind, an illiterate among his own people, and a simple messenger. The message is always clear—all praise is due to God, not the Prophet.

Yet in a further assault on his character, non-Muslims then and now insist that Prophet Muhammad was fed all his information by other people and simply "rehearsed tales of the ancients." Yet this is illogical. First of all, the Prophet spent most of his time prior to his calling with salesmen, not scholars. These caravan merchants knew "a little about a lot," having travelled extensively, but they could hardly be expected to know worldly subjects deeply. Most of them were illiterate themselves, with an education suited strictly to trade. Yet the Qur'an contains extensive details about past communities and religious doctrines, and about geological and human history. The depth of the knowledge conveyed is too great to be simply hearsay at a fireside chat among tradesmen. This knowledge requires full-time scholarship to acquire even today, never mind 1300 years ago when there were few texts and scientific instruments, and even fewer translations. When do his opponents suppose he would have acquired so much knowledge anyhow? This would have required daily conversations with sages in the middle of numerous battles, an incredibly busy family life, countless daily prayers, and his own mission to deliver the message to others. Yet he was never seen with any mortal teacher, and even his enemies have never suggested that he had one.

In fact, some fervent opponents insist that Muhammad was delusional—receiving inspiration from his own insanity. But if this were true, how could he simultaneously administer a massive, complex household with many wives and children, an intricate administration composed of alliances between peoples of different religious, socio-cultural, political, and economic backgrounds, and also strategize the stability of the Islamic empire for both the present and the future? The Prophet's military and political savvy are enshrined in the historical record, in volumes upon volumes published by Muslims and non-Muslims alike. And the basic reality is that he cannot have been insane and infinitely pragmatic at the same time. Besides, if his only goal had been to manipulate people, why didn't he have more commonly accepted tactics? Magic, for example, is easy to learn. Yet the Prophet's record, even as quoted by non-believers, is devoid of cheap illusions.

And what of the "new knowledge" contained in the Qur'an—the scientific revelations about the rotation of the earth, speed of light, layers of the atmosphere, creation of stars, separation of the oceans, types of rocks, origin of rain, gender of plants, composition of human tissue, formation of the embryo, origin of iron, and so on? Of all the sacred books around the world, only the Qur'an contains verifiable scientific data. What mortal source could have imparted such things to the Prophet? None. And to what end? Since these facts could not be verified until very recently, what benefit were they in convincing anyone in his time? None. If the Prophet intended to persuade people with some sort of self-contrived document, why put in a lot of material that wouldn't make sense to anyone for another 1000 years or more?

Truthfully, if he simply hoped for personal gain, for an easier life for himself, he would have been better off to just keep quiet and forget about the Qur'an completely. I see how my own life would be a lot smoother with my relatives if I hadn't converted to Islam. The Prophet Muhammad had already lost his father, mother, and guardian grandfather. Why wouldn't he want to please and protect the only family he had left, his beloved uncle, and adhere to polytheism? Why wouldn't he have wanted to simply retire comfortably in Meccan society as a prosperous husband, good father, and prominent member of the community?

The fact is that the Prophet Muhammad was a hard-working, brilliant, courageous, and spiritually profound man who gave everything he had in this life to argue the faith of Islam amid tremendous opposition, sacrificing his wealth, his family, his health, and his personal comfort. His only purpose was to convince anyone who would listen to worship one God, not himself—and the sum total of his words and actions proves nothing less than how anxious the Prophet was to convey the divine Message and rescue everybody from the potential tragedy of dying in a state of unbelief: *"There has come to you (O people) a Messenger from among yourselves; extremely grievous to him is your suffering, ardently anxious is he over you, and for the believers, full of pity and compassion."* (9:128) In less time than most people spend getting a basic education, he engineered the first welfare system in the world; installed a national health policy of cleanliness, good diet, and preventative care that is still valid today; abolished slavery; eliminated female infanticide and gender discrimination in family life and inheritance; overthrew racism; inclined millions upon millions of potent, passionate people towards sexual conservatism; and convinced entire nations and generations after them to abstain from alcohol. What's more, he is personally responsible for the fact that over a billion people around the world pray daily in constant remembrance of one God. With painstaking precision, he related a divine message, some of which—the scientific truths—meant no sense to anyone at the time. The Prophet was competent in all fields of existence and achieved more than almost anyone—some would say anyone—who has ever lived. What's more, his accomplishments are historical facts easily substantiated by any person with the inclination to read, in any library around the world.

Clearly, Prophet Muhammad achieved genuine perfection by being the ultimate model for all mankind, and his moral and spiritual worth is not a mere abstraction but a dynamic and vibrant reality. His unique and honourable character consistently and truly reflected the Qur'anic teachings: *"Indeed, in the Messenger of God, you have a beautiful pattern of conduct."* (33:21) And his profound belief and devotional practices exemplified a sublime simplicity which is so easily applicable to the lives of each and every believer, regardless of his or her place of origin—or time in history. Thus, we can understand why Muslims embrace the Prophet Muhammad so completely—because his life has been and will always be the light which makes the path to what is right more visible and more achievable.

JESUS – THE BAREFOOT MESSENGER

Honestly, if I had had to give up Jesus (PBUH) to become a Muslim, I don't think I could have done it. When I was very poor but somehow managed, I don't know how many times I called to mind the story of Jesus feeding the masses miraculously from only a basket full of bread and fish, and I felt grateful and hopeful. When I thought of a simple man who walked about barefoot and unpretentious, telling people to love their neighbours and do the right thing, I was always sure that Jesus was real, and good. But still, there was a "Jesus problem" all around me. My French Roman Catholic upbringing was full of stories of cloths stained with the blood of Jesus and weeping statues. Sometimes, I was supposed to pray to images of an innocent little baby in a manger—other times to a murdered figure hanging by his hands and feet. And I wondered more than once if communion wasn't a little bit odd—eating the flesh and blood of Jesus, or in other words, God, as I was told. I often found myself wishing that the whole world would go away and I could be alone with Jesus, in a quiet, private conversation, and he would explain clearly what I had come to suspect—that his legacy had gotten quite out of hand, much to his dismay. Thankfully, the Holy Qur'an eventually came into my life bringing with it the blessing of this exact interpretation. And quite frankly, though there is much more to authenticate the Qur'an than this, it would have been enough for me.

In fact, there are a lot of Christians, Muslims, and Jews asking themselves the simple question, "What did Jesus really say?" Countless books have been written on the subject, and a consortium of 75 Christian scholars from around the world, known collectively as the "Jesus Seminar," have spent almost 20 years coming up with an answer. Shockingly, they have concluded that what Jesus really said is no more than 18% of the words attributed to him in the Bible. That makes the task of unearthing the real truth about Jesus even more daunting. Many researchers have tried to pin down "the historical Jesus," and a lot has been written about how Saul of Tarsus ("Paul") seemingly negated some of Jesus's clearest instructions about circumcision, prohibited meat, etc. But no doubt the greatest controversy of all—one which divides not only Jews and Muslims from Christians, but also Christians from each other—is whether or not Jesus can be considered to be God, as both the "Son" and the "Father," and how the Holy Spirit fits into everything to yield the concept of "the Trinity." So many discussions between Muslims and Christians tragically break on the subject of Jesus's sonship—but perhaps, in fact, we are really not so very far apart after all.

The question which must be answered first and foremost is, did Jesus ever consider himself to be "the Father"? In other words, did Jesus ever ask people to worship him as God? If he did, then a whole lot of Bible quotes don't make much sense:

- *Matt 4:10: Jesus tells his followers to worship only God.*
- *Matt 10:32-33: Jesus says that he will be a witness before God on the Day of Judgement: "Whoever acknowledges me before men, I will also acknowledge him before my Father in heaven. But whoever disowns me before men, I will disown him before my Father in heaven."*
- *Matt 15:9: Jesus warns his followers against worshipping him!" 'These people honour me with their lips, but their hearts are far from me. They worship me in vain; their teachings are but rules taught by men."*
- *Matt 23:9 Jesus tells his followers that God is not on earth: "Call no man your father upon the earth: for One is your Father, which is in heaven."*
- *Matt 24:36/Mark 13:32: Jesus doesn't know when Judgement Day is because only God knows.*
- *Matt 26:39: Jesus falls on his face (prostrates), prays and submits to God saying that life/matters are "Not as I will but as You will."*
- *Mark 10:18: Jesus says, "Why do you call me good? None is good but God alone."*
- *Mark 12:29: Jesus says, "The Lord our God is One God."*
- *Luke 23:34: Jesus asks God's forgiveness for his followers.*
- *Luke 23:46: Jesus submits himself completely, in public, saying, "Father, into Thy hands I commend my spirit."*
- *John 1: 18 & 5:37: Jesus tells his listeners, who are standing right in front of him, that none of them has ever seen or heard God.*
- *John 5:41: Jesus says, "I do not accept praise from men."*

- *John 8:28: Jesus says, "I do nothing on my own, only what the Father has taught me."*
- *John 8:29: Jesus says submits to God completely, saying he "only does what pleases Him."*
- *John 8:50: Jesus says, "I am not seeking glory for myself, but there is One Who seeks it, and He is the judge."*
- *John 14:28: Jesus says, "My Father (God) is greater than me."*
- *John 14:81: Jesus explains to his followers that he submits to God (and also implies that people may wrongly understand him): "But the world must learn that I love the Father and that I do exactly what my Father has commanded me."*
- *John 17:3: John directly states that God and Jesus are separate: "That they might know Thee, the only true God, and Jesus Christ, whom You have sent."*
- *John 20:17: Jesus tells Mary Magdelene that he will ascend to "my father and your father—my God and your God."*
- *Numbers 23:19: The Old Testament states that, "God is not a man, that he should lie, nor a son of man, that he should change his purpose."*

In fact, it seems clear that Jesus submitted himself to God and consistently encouraged his followers to do the same. It's just as the Qur'an informs: *"Assuredly they have disbelieved who say: God is the Messiah, son of Mary"* (5:72), but the Messiah himself proclaimed: *"Worship God, my Lord and your Lord."* (5:72) The Qur'an also tells us that it is blasphemy to state that God is Jesus (5:72) and on the Day of Judgement, Jesus will be called to answer for the manner in which so many of his followers worship him, and he will explicitly state that he never encouraged them to worship any other than God alone (5:116).

Further, in John 17:20-23, Jesus says, *"I pray also for those who will believe in me through their message, that all of them may be one, Father, just as you are in me and I am in you… that they may be one as we are one."* Clearly, then, when Jesus says that he is one with God, he cannot mean it literally. For if he did, then he would also be praying that all individuals in the world might be combined into one, which is absurd except in the symbolic sense of a single faith community. And if the idea that Jesus is literally God is not from Jesus, then it must be a human idea, apparently stemming from man's desire to believe that we are sinless thanks to Jesus's death. Critically, since man has the potential for limitless evil, then Jesus's death must be an "infinite sacrifice"—much more significant than the death of a single man, even one as noble and elevated as the Prophet Jesus. The Christian Doctrine of Atonement, in other words, requires a really, really big Jesus— for only one as large as God Himself might account for the forgiveness of all sins, no matter how great, in all people, no matter how numerous.

But did Jesus ever suggest that his own death was enough to erase all the sins of mankind? If he did, then the Bible is highly contradictory for several verses state exactly the opposite—that is, that submission to God and good deeds which will please God are the only key to salvation:

- *James 4: 7-10: "Submit yourselves therefore to God. Resist the devil, and he will flee from you. Draw nigh to God, and he will draw nigh to you. Cleanse your hands, you sinners, and purify your hearts."*
- *James 1:12: "Blessed is the man who perseveres under trial, because when he has stood the test, he will receive the crown of life that God has promised to those who love him."*
- *James 1:22: "Do not merely listen to the word, and so deceive yourselves. Do what it says."*
- *James 2:24: "You see that a person is justified by what he does and not by faith alone."*
- *James 2:26: "As the body without the spirit is dead, so faith without deeds is dead."*
- *Matt 18:3: "And he said: Whoever humbles himself like a child is the greatest in the kingdom of heaven."*
- *Matt 6:33: "Seek first his kingdom and righteousness, and these things will be given to you as well".*
- *Matt 7:11: "How much more will your Father in heaven give good gifts to those who ask Him!"*
- *Matt 17:20: "If you have faith as small as a mustard seed, you can say to this mountain, 'Move from here to there' and it will move."*
- *Mark 11:24: "Whatever you ask for in prayer, believe you have received it, and it will be yours."*
- *1 Pet 5:6-7: "Humble yourselves therefore under the mighty hand of God, that he may exalt you in due time, casting all your care upon Him, for He cares for you."*

–   *Prov 3:5-6: "Trust in the Lord with all your heart; and lean not unto
    your own understanding. In all your ways acknowledge Him, and He
    will direct your paths."*

As well, countless Bible references consider Jesus to be a prophet
only (Deut 18:15, Deut 18:18, Acts 3:22-23, Acts 7:37, Matt 14: 5, Matt
21:11, Matt 21:46, Luke 7:16, Luke 7:39, Luke 13:33, Luke 24:19, John
3:2, John 4:19, John 6:14, John 7:40, John 9:17, Heb 3:1, etc.)—and he is
even referred to as a teacher (rabbi) (John 1:38, John 1:49, John 3:2, John
6:25, John 20:16, etc.). So if Jesus's death is not enough of a sacrifice to
erase all sins, then are humans responsible for their own salvation? This
argument is at the core of the biggest Christian debate, having already
split the Christians into sects. The whole Protestant movement, in fact,
started because some Christians rightly insisted that man 'earns' his way
to heaven through good works, a belief which is still generally upheld by
Mormons, Lutherans, Episcopelians, Methodists, Presbyterians, and others. That's in sharp contrast to Catholics, for example, who believe that
good works are not required for salvation—only faith in Jesus as God. It's
actually amazing that Christians can even consider themselves unified
given such a profound rift. The simplicity of salvation which does not
depend on effort has been dubbed "carnal Christianity," for it really does
take the pressure off the average church-goer. Yet the simple truth is that
Jesus was sent as *"an example for the Children of Israel."* (43:59) His death
brought him closer to God, for he *"will be held in honour in this world and
in the hereafter, and he will be in the company of the righteous, those nearest to God"*
(3:45). Yet the death of Jesus or of any prophet does not bring any one of
us closer to God automatically—only if we follow their blessed example
and adhere to the message of the revelations.

So, did Jesus ever consider himself to be the "son of God," in the
literal sense? To answer the question, it's necessary to first look at the use
of this idiom in the Bible:

–   *John 17:12: A "son of destruction" is someone who is doomed.*
–   *Luke 16:8 and Luke 20:34: "Sons of this world" ("sons of this age")
    are people alive at the time.*
–   *Luke 10:6: A "son of peace" is a peace-loving, non-violent person.*
–   *Matt 9:15 and Mark 2:19: "Sons of the bridegroom" are wedding guests.*
–   *Matt 23:15: A "son of hell" is someone who deserves to go to hell.*

- *Mark 3:17: "Sons of thunder" are violent men.*
- *Zech 4:14: "Sons of oil" are priests or anointed ones.*
- *Lam 3:13: "Sons of a quiver" are arrows.*
- *Ephes 2:2: "Sons of disobedience" are people of bad character.*
- *Job 5:7: "Sons of the burning coal" are sparks.*
- *Job 41:28: A "son of a bow" is an arrow.*
- *Gen 5:32: A "son of 500 years" is someone who is very old.*
- *Gen 15:3: A "son of my house" is one's own son.*
- *Deut 25:2: A "son of stripes" is someone one who deserves a beating.*
- *Heb 7:5: "Sons of Levi" are priests.*
- *Judges 19:22, 1 Sam 2:12 and 1 Sam 25:17: "Sons of Belial" are wicked men.*
- *1 Sam 20:31: A "son of death" is someone who must die.*
- *1 Kings 4:30, Gen 29:1 and Ezek 25:4: "Sons of the east" are the wisest easterners.*
- *1 Kings 20:35: "Sons of the prophets" are disciples.*
- *11 Kings 14:14: "Sons of pledging" are hostages.*
- *Exod 12:5: A "son of one year" is a one-year old male.*
- *2 Chron 25:13: "Sons of the band" are soldiers.*
- *Ps 29:1: "Sons of the mighty" are heroes.*
- *Ps 89:22: A "son of wickedness" is an evil person.*
- *Is 14:12: A "son of the morning" is Lucifer (Satan), who is as a fallen star.*
- *Is 21:10: A "son of the floor" is threshed (fallen) grain.*
- *Is 56:6: "Sons of the stranger" are Gentiles.*
- *Lam 4:2: "Sons of Zion" are the people of Jerusalem.*
- *1 Thess 5:5: "Sons of light" ("sons of day") are those who are righteous.*

Clearly, the expression "son of" is a very common phrase which is used with figurative rather than literal intent. The Qur'an uses this sort of literary device, too, wherein a *"son of the road"* is a traveller (2:177); the uncle of Prophet Muhammad is called *"the father of a flame"* (111:1); *"the mother of the Book"* (3:7; 13:39; 43:3) is a heavenly scripture, and so on. Further, the actual term "son of God" is used many times in the Bible to refer to someone other than Jesus:

- *Matt 5:9 and Luke 6:35: Peacemakers (the pious/righteous) are sons of God.*
- *Heb 7:1-3: Melchisedec is the son of God.*

- *Gen 6:2: All males are sons of God.*
- *Gen 14:18: The King of Salem (Melchisedec) is the son of God.*
- *Exod 4:22, Jer 31:9, Hos 11:1: Israel is God's son, God's first-born son.*
- *Jer 31:9, Jer 31:20: Ephraim is the son of God, and God is the father of Israel.*
- *Psalm 2:7, 2 Sam 7:14: King David is the son of God.*
- *Psalm 82:6: Kings and rulers are sons of God.*
- *Job 1:6 and Job 2:1: Angels are sons of God*
- *Romans 8:14, John 3: 1-2, Deut 14:1, Matt 5:16, Matt 7:11, Matt 5:44, Isaiah 64:8. Mal 2:10, 2 Cor 6:18, Gal 3:26, Heb 2:10: Believers are sons of God.*

Further, it's interesting to note that with only one exception (from Romans), all of the references to Jesus as the son of God (which might be intended as non-literal anyway) are from the Gospels—that is, from the chapters by Matthew, Mark, Luke, and John:

- John 3:18, John 5:24-25, John 9:35, John 10:36, John 19:67, John 20:31, Luke 1:35, Luke 3:38, Luke 4:41. Luke 8:28, Mark 1:1, Mark 3:11, Mark 9:7, Mark 14:62, Mark 15:37, Matt, 3:17, Matt 8:29, Matt 14:33, Matt 16:16, Matt 26:64, Matt 27:41, Matt 27:54, Romans 1:4: *Jesus is the son of God.*

For centuries, those who have upheld the idea that Jesus was the literal son of God have argued that the references to Jesus are simply more numerous and impressive than the other uses of "son of God"—but the actual counts simply don't support this conclusion. It's also a well-known fact of the Bible that the Gospels of Matthew, Mark, and Luke are synoptic—essentially just repetitions or versions of the same information; this means that there are actually fewer than a half-dozen references to Jesus as the "son of God" in each gospel, and these are simply being repeated by the different story-tellers. In addition, the Jesus Seminar, Christian scholars themselves, have concluded that most of the gospels are actually not authentically from Jesus, though they purport to be. Finally, the one reference to Jesus as the "son of God" in Romans is actually from Paul, and not from Jesus.

So if we eliminate duplicate or questionable references and we look at the very common use of the phrase in other references, we're left with the essential truth that "son of God" is used to denote Jesus in the same way that it is used elsewhere—that is, as potent, figurative language. Jesus was sent by God and inspired by him: *"We sent him with clear signs and strengthened him with the Holy Spirit"* (2:87, 2:253). And Jesus was, without a doubt, unique, created just by the will of God and not by any mortal means (3:59). But Jesus was not literally the son of God. In fact, the Qur'an warns those who say that God has begotten a son: *"No knowledge have they of such a thing. It is a grievous thing that issues from their mouths."* (18:4-5)

So if Jesus wasn't the literal son of God, and he never suggested that he was God either, then what is the Trinity, and why did I get baptized and cross myself for decades in the "name of the Father, the Son, and the Holy Ghost?" Webster's dictionary defines it as "a threefold consubstantial personality in one divine being or substance—the union of one God, Son, and Holy Spirit as three infinite persons." First, few people can understand what this means. Supporters simply answer that it's not against reason, but beyond it, being a mystery rather than a contradiction. The doctrine requires faith—some would say blind faith—more than anything else, arguably something best left to mystics and scholars. For almost two millennia, then, the average Christian has been convinced that, "If you try to understand the Trinity, you will lose your mind, but if you don't believe it, you will lose your soul."

Yet the truth is that the first Christians did not have a concept of the Trinity, as evident in the Dead Sea Scrolls and over 300 years of Bible history following Jesus's death. There is, in fact, no direct mention of the Trinity in the Bible, and theologians agree that the Trinity is a manmade idea which did not exist during the life of Jesus or the Apostolic age and actually does not appear in Christianity until the fourth century.[12] This is really a startling finding which should be publicized widely, yet is not, except in the Qur'an, which states bluntly: *"They blaspheme who say: God is one of three in a trinity"* (5:72-75); *"Don't say three—it is better for you. God has no son. Jesus worships God,"* (4:171) *and "God will raise Jesus and clear him of this falsehood and blasphemy"* (3:55). Clearly, God is not the author of confusion.

So if the Bible never said anything about a Trinity, and Jesus never said he was God or the literal "son of God," then the Qur'anic and Biblical versions of Jesus's life might actually be one and the same. And if that's the case, how did we ever get into the mess we are in today, with our ideological trenches dug so deep that we can hardly hear each other screaming—or preaching?

THESE LAST FEW DAYS

On February 9th, 2003, the *Sunday Telegraph* ran the headline, "The End of the Universe is Cancelled," announcing that dark energy in the cosmos will make the universe expand forever. Oddly enough, the world was already supposed to be over, according to *Sun Magazine*[13] because "ancient" scrolls just discovered set the end date for January 2001. In May 2002, as if to clarify things, tabloids reported that the Vatican was writing a guide for surviving the end of the world. The infamous joke—"World ends at 8. News at 11."—couldn't be far off, for society systematically tries to rationalize, sensationalize or trivialize the end of time, to keep from really thinking about it. It is, after all, *"the great news about which they cannot agree"* (Qur'an 78:2-3). Belief in the Last Day is central to Jews, Christians, and Muslims, but only a minority among the general population see it as serious front page news. For the secular majority, it seems there are only two perspectives— believe it's not going to happen for billions of years, and don't change your behaviour at all, or try to figure out when the end is coming, and *maybe* plan to change sometime.

Eschatology—the study of the end of time—relies on four sources: revelations, science, traditions, and experiences. In their respective scriptures, Muslims, Jews and Christians agree on many features of the Last Day itself: Jesus returns; the present world is destroyed; the moment is announced with a trumpet sound; all people alive at the time die; dead bodies are resurrected; God judges between people; there are levels of reward; wrongdoers are punished by fire; and the righteous are given a peaceful and permanent life in heaven. (The main point of disagreement is in the assurance of salvation, which only Christians believe to be automatic with the acceptance of Jesus (PBUH)).

In *The Physics of Judgment Day* (2002), Dr. H.Y. Khan discusses the importance of science in helping some people confirm their belief in the Last Day. In 2003, for example, using the Hubble Telescope, scientists found conclusively that "dark energy" and "exotic dark matter" in the cosmos—which actually makes up to 90% of "everything" (known matter like planets, people, etc. comprise less than 10%)—is "pulling" the universe apart ever faster, like a powerful anti-gravity force. The yellow G2 star we affectionately call "the sun" will become more luminous, causing temperatures on earth to rise excessively, boiling away the oceans; gravitational shifts will create massive earthquakes which will crumble mountains, and the atmosphere will be in turmoil as the sun collapses and falls, along with other stars and planets. Finally, matter will get rolled up into black holes, leaving only a featureless void. Curiously, some scientists speculate that through "quantum tunnelling," all matter in these black holes may turn to iron before disappearing, since this element has the least binding energy.[14] Thus, science agrees completely with the Qur'an's description of that fateful time: *the sky will be ripped open* (25:25; 73:18, 77:9, 78:19, 82:1, 84:1); *the earth will move and shake* (56:4, 69:14, 84:4, 99:1, 99:2); *the mountains will be flattened and scattered* (18:47, 27:88; 52:10, 56:5, 69:14, 70:9, 77:10, 78:20, 81:3, 84:3, 101:5); *the oceans will boil and bubble over* (81:6, 82:3); *the sky will be filled with a kind of smoke* (44:10); and *the sun and stars will become dark, scattered, and fall* (52:9, 77:8, 81:1, 81:2, 82:2). In fact, the Qur'an also singles out *"iron"* as especially important among elements: *"And We sent down iron."* (57:25). Maurice Bucaille, respected Christian author of *The Bible, the Qur'an and Science*, states that there is not a single scientific error in the Qur'an.

With regards to traditions and trusted interpretations, Islam has numerous "hadith" (sayings) of the Prophet Muhammad (PBUH), which help to clarify matters of faith. From the highly respected hadith collection of *Sahih Muslim*, one can conclude that Muslims, Jews and Christians believe in many of the same signs of the coming of the Day of Judgment: great turmoil, violence and bloodshed, perhaps even between brothers; senseless murder; moral degradation and confusion, where what is evil seems good and what is good seems evil; growth in materialism and inflation; the scarcity of wise people and scholars; rule by people who are foolish and corrupt; the rejection of piety and religious adherence; the appearance of false messiahs; and the contraction of time. Interestingly, hadith also predict that as Judgment Day approaches, a "mountain of gold" will be uncovered in the Euphrates (oil?) which will bring death to all those who try to seek profit from it. Is the current situation in the Middle East an evolving sign? Only God knows.

Examining common experiences, it's easy to find definitive proof that *"the signs have started already"* (47:18). The daily news is full of senseless violence, as children are raped and murdered, and random attacks kill innocent families as they go about their day. In countless court cases around the world, wealthy and powerful people escape prison for the same crimes which send common folk to jail or to their death because it is possible to buy and sell justice. Failures in the legal system are rampant as repeat offenders go free on the street because we are "confused" about what righteousness really means. The corruption of public office has become such an accepted standard that people hardly care to vote in democratic elections anymore. And moral degradation has increasingly become the lifeblood of television and popular movies. Consider the following other examples from the Qur'an that the signs of the Last Day are all around us right now:

"Every mother with sucking baby will forget her babe, and every pregnant mother will drop her load unformed." (22:2) In Canada, 32 out of 1000 live births are aborted[15] and in the USA, one million teen girls get pregnant every year, two-thirds resulting in abortions (planned or spontaneous). Almost 213,000 children were neglected in 1993, a 300% increase from the previous five years, and among young Canadians aged 15 – 24, 33% are victims of parental neglect.[16]

"Everyone will be as in a drunken state, but not drunk." (22:2). As of 2000, 32.8% of Canadians had used illicit drugs in their lives[17], and there were 200 million illicit drug users worldwide in 2001.[18] In 2002, 19.5 million Americans used illegal drugs in an average month.[19]

"Friends will be foes to one another, except the righteous." (43:67) In 2002, there was an overwhelming volume of "intimate violence": 60% of sexually assaulted women knew their attacker; 20% of children murdered knew their assailant; 40% of workplace violence victims knew their offenders; and 44% of murder victims knew the perpetrator.[20]

"No father can avail his son nor son avail his father." (31:33) *"Fear a day when a man shall flee his brother, mother, father, wife, and children."* (80:34 - 6) Almost 22% of American households are fatherless, and father absence creates the most serious social issues: 63% of youth suicides, 90% of home-

less or runaway youth, 80% rapists, 71% of high school dropouts, and 85% of youth in penitentiaries.[21] And in Canada, 65% of children in single par-ent families headed by women are poor.[22]

So our communities are just as God promised, providing a model for us: *"We will make them taste the lesser punishment before the severer punishment."* (32:21) And additional evidence that the signs have begun is that our lives currently operate under some of the same conditions as the Last Day:

On Judgment Day, "no soul will be able to avail another." (2:48)

Every day, "no bearer of burdens can bear the burdens of another." (6:164)

On Judgment Day, "no intercession will be accepted." (2:48)

Every day, "you have no intercessor besides God." (32:04)

On Judgment Day, "no soul will speak except by God's leave." (11:105)

Every day, "it is God who has made for man a tongue and a pair of lips" (90:9) and "taught man intelligent speech." (55:4)

On Judgement Day, "not a thing will be hidden from God." (40:16)

Every day, "nothing is hidden from the Lord so much as the weight of an atom on earth or in heaven." (10:61)

In this way, examples from our lives (30:28) confirm that what we are promised is true (51:5). And as a similar pledge has been made to all People of the Book, it is inaccurate for non-Muslims to regard the Islamic view of God as fearful and threatening. For these warnings are signs by which we may receive guidance in order to be saved, a true witness to God's attributes of mercy and benevolence.

To those who have cosmic angst and prefer to think in terms of billions of years, we can ask, "Why would the universe last forever?" One scientist explains: The universe either has a purpose, or it does not. If it has no purpose, then it is absurd. If it has a purpose, and that purpose is not achieved, then the universe is futile. If it has a purpose, and that purpose is achieved, then further continuation is pointless. In other words, an eternal universe would be absurd, futile, or pointless. Therefore, the universe cannot be eternal. (Holt, 2004) Even according to a scientific and strictly logical viewpoint, then, there *will* be a Last Day. The answer to the question, "Is the universe going to end?" is "Yes."

For those who want the latest prediction, we can advise going to the grocery store newsstands—the end is apparently coming any day via alien invasions, apocalyptic plagues, geological glitches, and bizarre cosmic alignments. In fact, extensive libraries of hundreds of date setters are available in print and online, with the years 1000 and 2000 being especially popular. Without a doubt, some predict more than others—Jehovah's Witnesses have a total of 15 failed dates so far, a record of sorts. And others add more dates every month—with over 30 separate predictions between now and 2076 already. If there's anything to learn from all of this, it's that we can't seem to get it right. As the Qur'an states, *"People cannot anticipate its term"* (15:5, 16:61), for *"knowledge of the Day and Hour is only with God."* (7:187) And the Bible delivers a similar message, *"But of that Day and Hour no one knows."* (Matthew 24:35-36). Thus, it is clear and excessive arrogance to assume we can "guess" what God has already told us we cannot. The answer to the question, "When is the world going to end?" is "Nobody knows." And the Qur'an warns us that when the end is coming, it is only the confused people who will be asking, *"When will be the Hour of Judgment?"* (51:12)

So the only worthwhile question left is, "Are you ready?" While it is possible to dispute the differences between scriptures and traditions among People of the Book, and even among those of the same faith, the overriding point is that the warnings and descriptions about the Day of Judgment are presented as incentives for obedient living. Science and experience help us reach conclusions about the correctness of scriptures and traditions, but only our convictions can save us. Ask yourself, "If I were to face God today, to account for my words, my actions, my intentions, and my life, would I stand a chance of being rewarded?" Consider your answer carefully. For when that Day comes, it will be too late to suddenly start believing: *"Faith will not benefit a soul who did not believe before."* (6:158) Then, with every fibre of your being, strive for the best ways to spend these last few days.

RESURRECTION

We all make mistakes in this life. Some people tell us that's how we learn. Some people tell us we're wrong and we should have been more careful. But it's so easy to do things we shouldn't, isn't it? It happens to each of us every day—and it happens so quickly. One wrong turn on the road and we can injure someone. One moment of anger and we can do something we will spend a lifetime trying to forget. One unthinking stroke of the keyboard, or of the fist, or of our mouths, and an action is begun which can be difficult—or even impossible—to erase. It's easy to get down on ourselves for all the ways in which we make all kinds of errors in our daily lives, by which jobs are lost, homes and families are broken, and for which we spend days or years of our lives in a state of shame and agony. Sure, after a small mistake, it may be pretty easy to pick yourself up and dust yourself off, as they say, and keep moving. But after a big mistake, it's a great deal harder. So just where can we get the strength to go past the really difficult points in our lives? When we feel that our lives are in ruins, how is it that we can ever feel joy or hope again?

Easter is the perfect time to think about this idea, actually. For Christians, this marks the moment of the resurrection of Jesus (peace be upon him). And while Muslims do not associate the resurrection of Jesus with any particular date on the calendar, there is a shared belief that Jesus was lifted from his life on this earth and returned to God at a critical point when things were actually not very easy for him at all. He was rescued from his difficulties and brought to everlasting safety and comfort with the Creator. How much we all wish, on our hardest days, that someone would just lift us up from our lives, pull us right out of our situation, and take us home to safety. But, in fact, the resurrection of Jesus was hardly something that could be expected to happen to everyone, for Prophet Jesus was special, above ordinary humans. We, on the other hand, are regular people, put on this earth to worship God, and our resurrection is not assured until Judgement Day. In the meantime, we are simply *"toiling, painfully toiling"* (84:6) in this life—some days, more painfully than others. And being suddenly rescued and taken home to God is not an option in our control.

Yet, we need to remember that God created us into these difficulties for a reason. It's essentially the way by which we each prove ourselves, because as humans, we are limited by design—and it's how we try to rise above those limitations that will make a difference in the end, when we will all be judged before our Creator. There are many, many related examples from the lives of the prophets, each of whom passed through strenuous trials and taught his people to be constant in turning to God for help in securing happiness and prosperity in this life and the next. For example, God tested Prophet Solomon, and when he was successful, God made him a powerful king, with even the winds under his dominion, as he *"Enjoyed, indeed, a near approach to Us, and a beautiful place of final return"* (38:40). As for Prophet David, Solomon's father, he was called to arbitrate between two disputing brothers who approached him to settle a business matter between them. In rendering quick judgment before sufficiently listening to both litigants, David came to understand that God had tested him, and he sought and received forgiveness, as the Qur'an again echoes the message of divine mercy: *"David gathered that We had tried him: he asked forgiveness of his Lord, fell down, bowing in prostration, and turned to God in repentance. So We forgave him this lapse: he enjoyed, indeed, a near approach to Us, and a beautiful place of final return."* (38:24-25) Even Prophet Moses tasted the tragedy and trial of committing an act he would regret. Prior to his actual mission, he accidentally killed someone while mediating an altercation between two local residents: *"Moses struck him with his fist and made an end of him. He said: "This is a work of evil (Satan), for he is an enemy that manifestly misleads. O my Lord! I have indeed wronged my soul! Do then forgive me!"* (28:15-16) Thus, Moses turned to God in repentance and, ever-mercifully, he was later worthy enough in the judgment of God to be personally given the Holy Commandments. And so it is that the prophets become the supreme example for us about how our only hope is to seek the limitless shelter and compassion of God, and to keep striving to the best of our abilities, even after—or despite—our failings.

In fact, God promises forgiveness to anyone who turns to Him sincerely: *"God promises you His forgiveness and bounties. And God cares for all things and knows all things."* (2:268) For He is patient with our faults and our shortcomings, forgiving us even when we inevitably make different mistakes as our lives go on: *"God blots out sins and forgives again and again"* (4:43, 4:99, 22:60). The advice is clear: even when we are in error, God is the only one Who can really help us: *"If anyone does evil or wrongs his own soul, but afterwards seeks God's forgiveness, He will find God Oft-Forgiving and Most Merciful"* (4:110), as *"God forgives what is past"* (5:95), and *"He is the Lord of Forgiveness."* (74:56) Surely there could be no clearer message than this, and the examples from the scriptures are abundant that forgiveness is available to all of us: *"if the thief repents after his crime, and amends his conduct, God turns to him in forgiveness; for God is Oft-forgiving, Most Merciful."* (5:39) For as long as it is our intention to improve ourselves, and we are really trying to commit fewer errors, we will be received in God's mercy every time. Our first duty, then, is simply to *"be quick in the race for forgiveness from your Lord."* (3:133).

And that is the essence, quite simply, of how each one of us can be resurrected in our own lives, like a phoenix rising from the ashes of despair and destruction to live another day, with the hope of a better life. *"Even after men give up all hope, God scatters mercy far and wide."* (42:28) God's mercy becomes the new ground under which each of us stands every day, from the very moment that we decide to try to arise from even the darkest times in our lives and call out to God through our sadness and fears, saying, *"I hope that my Lord will guide me ever closer than this to the right path."* (18:24) God promises to hear our prayers, and to shower us with His blessings. And thus, the tears we cry to Our Lord, through all those periods of deepest despair, will become like the rain which *"gives life to the earth after its death."* (16:65). For in the ultimate act of benevolence from our Creator, our failings will help us to develop sincere and profound humility, as we realize that we are helpless without His mercy. And through such submission, we will have the best chance to achieve our ultimate resurrection, when we are welcomed to our home of peace and security, with God. As always, the Qur'an says it best, in a beautiful verse from the chapter about Prophet Noah, who once carried so many to safety and security himself: *"Ask for forgiveness from your Lord, for He is Oft-forgiving…*

Don't you understand that He produced you from the earth, growing gradually, and in the end, He will return you to the earth and raise you forth at the resurrection?" (71:10-18)

And if God is ready to be so merciful towards us and to forgive us, then surely we can learn to forgive, too, for the advice is clear as to how we should treat each other: *"Overlook any human faults with gracious forgiveness"* (15:85)—and how we should treat ourselves: *"Patiently persevere and ask forgiveness for thy faults,"* (40:55) and *"hope that God will remove your ills and admit you to Gardens"* (26:82-83). For in doing this, we will be acknowledging that we can overcome our feelings of shame, loss, sorrow, hatred, frustration, humiliation, anger, embarrassment, and regret—simply because the awareness of God's mercy in our lives is enough of a reward. It's also an acknowledgment that even though we are very worried about how we will ever go on from here, how we will ever cope with what lies ahead of us as we try to rebuild our lives, we still can feel an emerging sense of peace and hope because *"God is enough for a protector, and God is enough for a Helper"* (4:45). In a way, it's the ultimate test of ego, to see if we can rise above our discomfort and simply be thankful to God for a second chance, and to see if we can find a way to care a little less about the past, and a lot more about the future—most especially, about our eternal future.

And so it seems that suffering can actually teach us a lot: *"Before thee [Muhammad], We sent messengers to many nations, and We afflicted the nations with suffering and adversity, that they might learn humility."* (6:42, 7:94). In fact, history is full of examples of righteous people who suffered or watched their families or communities go through horrific experiences. Among those are some of the prophets themselves. Prophet Moses had to flee his homeland to escape religious persecution, appealing to God in humility: *"O my Lord! Forgive me and my brother! Admit us to Thy mercy! For Thou art the Most Merciful of those who show mercy!"* (7:151). *"So God forgave him: for He is the Oft-Forgiving, Most Merciful."* (28:16) In turn, Prophet Muhammad was forced into exile during part of his mission, continually turning to God in complete submission: *"Glory to God, Who is highest above all, exalted and great beyond measure…Though you may not understand it all, He is always patient, and most forgiving."* (17:43-44) Prophet Job was inflicted with pain and disease for many years, releasing himself into God's mercy: *"He cried to his Lord, 'Truly distress has seized me, but Thou art the Most*

Merciful of those that are merciful.'"(21:83-84). And Prophet Joseph, who was unfairly imprisoned at the prime of his life, still held his burden in patience and was willing to admit his own imperfections and his utter reliance on God's benevolence: *"Nor do I absolve my own self of blame: the human soul is certainly prone to evil, unless my Lord do bestow His Mercy. But surely my Lord is Oft-forgiving, Most Merciful."* (12:53)

Tragically, most of the suffering we experience in this life is something we inflict on ourselves each and every day, whenever we make poor choices. And our human failings simply mean that pain of all kinds will be pretty well inevitable throughout our lives. These difficulties will be as individual as we are, for they form part of our fate, and they are given to us to test if we are willing to admit that everything comes from God, and thus only God—not this material life, and not we, ourselves—can ever provide real relief from our suffering: *"God puts no burden on any person beyond what He has given him. After a difficulty, God will soon grant relief."* (65:7) Therefore, through a deepening belief in God, we can turn our cries over our own misery into cries of surrender to our Creator, *"Who listens to the distressed soul when it calls on Him, and Who relieves its suffering"* (27:62). In doing this, we will convert our pain into salvation as we surrender to faith, and we will have the new hope of living our entire futures, from that point forward, according to God's will for us. God knows us well and understands that it's going to be very hard for us to turn our lives around: *"Seek assistance through patience and prayer. And most surely it is a hard thing except for the humble ones."* (2:45) Yet if we are able to do just that, in an open admission that we are nothing, and we will never be or do anything, without God's help, then a great reward is promised to us in the end: *"Surely as to those who believe and do good and humble themselves to their Lord, these are the devotees of the Garden, and in it they will abide."* (11:23) It's all part of our realization, ultimately, that our real home is not our big house in the suburbs, our apartment downtown, our condominium uptown, or even the shelter or the jail cell where we might find ourselves for a time in this life. Our real home is with God.

CHAPTER V

Nourishing Faith: Practice

"And Paradise will be brought near for the God-revering, pious; not (any longer) is it far. 'This is what was promised for you – for everyone who was penitent, careful in keeping his duties (to God), who felt awe of the All-Merciful without seeing Him, and has come with a heart contrite and devout. Now enter it in peace (secure from any trouble or distress). This is the Day of immortality.' Therein will be for them everything that they desire, and in Our Presence there is yet more." (50:31-35)

* * *

"He who amongst you sees something abominable should modify it with the help of his hand; and if he has not strength enough to do it, then he should do it with his tongue, and if he has not strength enough to do it, then he should abhor it from his heart, and that is the least of faith." (Sahih Muslim, from *Kitab Al-Iman* 'The Book of Faith,' Hadith 79)

A LIFE OF PRAYER

The first Thursday of May is observed as National Day of Prayer in the United States. In Canada, there is a similar event, World Religion Day, held yearly the third Sunday of January. It seems that religion needs to be put on national calendars for the general public, apparently having the same status as "Women's Day," "Earth Day," "Ground Hog Day," or even "National Secretary's Day." Admittedly, it's a valiant effort on the part of politicians to hold religion as something to be remembered. But what God asks of us is not a day—but a lifetime—of prayer.

What does it mean to engage in a lifetime of prayer? It means that we should acquire and maintain a "prayer habit" each day of our lives. I remember when my mother, who is Christian, first visited me following my conversion to Islam. She was struck by the frequency of prayers in our home. We would just get supper started, it seemed, and it was time to pray. We would finish supper, and excuse ourselves for prayer again. Wasn't it a lot of work to pray like this all the time, she asked? Her intention was good—she really was trying to understand my new faith, and my new life. But in her voice was the trace of a common sentiment—that it couldn't possibly be very much fun to do something which is so demanding.

In fact, it is difficult to keep up the prayer habit. I remember when I first heard the story of one of the companions of the Prophet Muhammad, Abbad Ibn Bishr, who kept praying with an arrow struck through him. Yet, somehow, I find it hard to pray in the quiet and safety of my own home sometimes, in full health. The children are rushing around. Supper is late. I am tired from working outside my home each day. There is a bill to worry about, and a big day ahead tomorrow. And outside the home, it's even harder. There's often no place to pray. And even when there is, there may be no proper place to wash before prayers. So why do we pray at all, if it's so hard to do? Simply put: it's because a life without prayer is even harder.

The blessings of prayer are surprisingly numerous. Of course, there are the benefits in the afterlife—and these are the most important of all. Sadly, though, these are hard for most people to understand, unless they have already chosen to be strong believers. In fact, many people around the world have sort of given up talking and thinking about Judgement Day altogether. For the average person, it seems that the afterlife is what they will do after they retire. So the real question most people want answered, before they will even consider a habit of prayer, is 'What benefit will prayer bring me in this life?'

First of all, there are astounding health benefits, which are well documented by leading medical researchers. In brief, prayer helps to induce the 'relaxation response,' which leads to a drop in blood pressure and heart rate, and a reduction in stress hormones, like cortisol.[1] Additionally, it increases alpha and theta waves in the brain, thereby reducing anxiety and making us feel good about ourselves.[2] It also increases the levels of interleukin-6, a blood protein which promotes the healthy functioning of the immune system, and it can alter the rate of growth of yeast and other organisms, as tested in laboratories.[3] Of course, Islamic prayers also flex muscles and improve circulation through stretching and deep breathing, in particular through prostration, which places the head below the heart, like many yoga positions also do. In fact, while scientists are not completely certain of all of the physiological responses to prayer, they have no doubts about the fact that prayer does cause a number of significant effects in the body, and that these are always beneficial. Dr. Dale Matthews, of Georgetown University, says, "If prayer were available in pill form, no pharmacy could stock enough of it."

Independent studies found that hypertension is about 40% lower among those who study religious books and attend services.[4] Elderly patients with a strong religious faith are 14 times less likely to die after surgery than those without faith, and the risk of dying for those over 64 years of age is 46% lower for those who attend religious functions.[5] At Georgetown University, 75% of current studies in the field confirm that those who with an active religious life live healthier and longer, and they have a speedier recovery from depression, alcoholism, hip surgery, drug addiction, stroke, arthritis, heart attacks, and bypass surgery. At Dartmouth University, religious belief was found to be the best predictor of survival among 232 heart patients. In turn, the US Office of Technological Assessment reports that "religiosity" has a 92% benefit on mental health.

Secondly, perhaps what is even more striking about prayer is that even praying for others offers huge benefits. In 1988, in the first study of its kind, at San Francisco General Hospital, scientists concluded that on 6/26 outcomes (such as the need for antibiotics), the individuals who were prayed for by others recovered much better than those who didn't. The US Office of Technological Assessment reports that "intercessory prayers" (prayers for others) have a very positive effect on health. At Duke University, patients recovering from angioplasty did better if they received intercessory prayers than if they didn't. And at Baptist Memorial University, intercessory prayers, both before and after surgery, improved the recovery rate of patients. Dr. Krucoff (of Duke University) conducted a study of 750 patients with life-threatening diseases at nine independent medical centres throughout the US; the patients who received intercessory prayers showed a remarkable 50 – 100% fewer complications after surgery.[6] In another study, AIDS patients who were prayed for were 70% less likely to develop complications.[7] And in the Annals of Internal Medicine, 23 studies of over 2774 patients revealed that intercessory prayers had a positive effect in 57% of cases. Additionally, in May 2003, a survey revealed that 30% of Americans report "remarkable healing" from their own or others' prayers.

In fact, it should come as no surprise that scientists have discovered what prayerful people know intuitively: prayer helps. Fundamentally, prayer helps because one perfect God made prayer a blessing for us, not just an obligation—something that will not only improve us in the next life, but also improve our health and happiness in this life. Think about what all the magazines at the grocery-store check-outs are preaching these days: self-care. Self-care, in fact, is the buzz word of the decade. The magazines tell you to take some time for yourself each day, read a little, watch what you eat and keep your body clean, exercise a little, join a spiritual community, learn to feel happy about yourself and your life, and try to volunteer to help others somehow. These are such obvious things that one has to wonder why it takes teams of scientists hundreds of thousands of dollars to tell us these things. Yet prayer does all this for us—and more.

A website based on the book "Christian Prayer for Dummies," has interesting statistics with regards to the daily prayers of Americans: 95% thank God; 76% ask forgiveness; 67% praise the attributes of God; 61% ask for specifics; 47% remain silent; 52% pray several times a day; 37% pray only once a day; 21% pray with their families; and 33% pray in a prayer group. Another website helps Christians learn how to pray[8] as it seems that many have forgotten, and there are great inconsistencies in the prayers of ordinary people. It advises Christians to do the following, three times daily, for at least 10 minutes each time: give God glory, ask that His will be done (i.e. submit to God); ask for what they need rather than want; ask for the forgiveness of their own sins and the sins of others; ask for help resisting the devil; and give God glory again. This all sounds strangely familiar, doesn't it?

So while some Christians are to be commended for working hard to regain the ability to pray properly, the mercy of Islam is that our prayers have been clearly defined for us from the outset, and have never changed or been forgotten. Five times daily, we perform the prayer ritual, glorifying God, submitting, asking for our needs, pleading for forgiveness, asking for strength in resisting the devil, and glorifying God again. It is really the perfect agenda.

To those who say that they simply haven't the time to pray each day, we can ask only one question. How long will it take you to accomplish your goals without God's help? You can submit a hundred resumes for a new job and have them all lost or ignored, while God's hand can easily move one resume to the right position. Think of the Prophet Moses (PBUH), who was able to split the water in an instant to walk his people safely across, with God's help; yet when God was upset with the people of Moses, they lost 40 years wandering in the desert. The few minutes each day you spend praying can really save you months and years of effort. For as Ghandi said, "Properly understood and applied, prayer is the most potent instrument of action."

What will happen if you don't pray? It will be hard to notice any difference at first. Like a first cigarette, the effect seems negligible. But you will know that in smoking that first cigarette, you have begun a habit which will kill you eventually—not after one or two or even a thousand cigarettes, but sometime later, and you will never know when. Missing prayers is similar. At first, you may not notice a change. Slowly, though, you will become more careless with the prayer habit, and more neglectful. In this state, you will be more and more tempted to miss further prayers. Eventually, your prayer habit will be completely compromised, or disappear. In the end, this will kill a lot of opportunities for you in this life, and all of your opportunities in the next life.

What will happen if you pray? You will feel better, and you will help those around you to feel better, too. You will improve your opportunities for success in this life, and you will ensure your best chance for success in the next life, for *"regular prayers are enjoined on all the believers."* (4:103) You will also be providing a wonderful model for prayer for believers around the world, as Islamic prayers are beautiful, consistent, and all-encompassing. In fact, prayer may also be one of the most productive points for dialogue between all of the People of the Book, the real bridge which joins believers towards one God. I once drove past a Muslim man praying at the intersection of three major on-ramps to Toronto's busiest airport. In the middle of a hectic day and tens of thousands of cars, perhaps even on his first day in a new country, he placed his prayer mat by the side of the road, and took time to honour God. This is the image of Islam the world should see. This is the life of prayer the world should know.

VIGILANCE

As the "New Year" starts, most Muslims are still reflecting on Ramadan just passed. A common western tradition is the "New Year's resolution," in which one vows to exercise self-control over a specific weakness such as candy or smoking. But as one who has "crossed over" from one set of values to another, I have found the commitment to Ramadan is far beyond any "New Year's resolution" I ever took. The glorious Qur'an prescribes fasting for us so that we may learn "self-restraint." The miracle is that self-restraint is about much more than skipping lunch. Continual, practiced self-restraint is at the very root of one of the key attributes of a believer: vigilance.

What is vigilance? It is the condition of watchfulness and guardedness that acts as a personal warning system to keep us away from anything that can weaken our faith. By the grace of God, we have been sent clear signs of how erosion can slowly change even the hardest substances on earth. Rocks stronger than any human can slowly deteriorate, one handful of sand at a time, through the gradual action of natural forces like water and wind… until a shoreline completely changes. The melting of glaciers is another sign for us—by the slightest shift in the earth's temperature, the ice starts to melt away, eventually changing the geography of the entire world.

In human lives, erosion happens in the social sphere, when we slowly compromise our values and our beliefs. A Muslim boy from my son's school told him last week that it was not necessary to wash before prayers—only preferable. Perhaps next, the idea may creep in that one or more of the daily prayers is not necessary, only preferable. It's like the *hijab* (head scarf) for women. Is it wrong to leave it off completely or to let hair show out the front or down the back? Only God can judge us in the end. But one thing is certain: once we expose ourselves a bit, it becomes easier to expose ourselves more over time. And it's certainly far easier to loosen the scarf and let it slide down the shoulders than to put one on in the first place. For unless we clearly hold to our boundaries, they will recede naturally as time passes. The signs are all around us.

We are all at risk from this kind of erosion. No man or woman wakes up one morning and thinks, "I will ruin my family today." It begins slowly with just an improper glance or the breath of a fragrance, and temptation is born. And no teen ever thinks, "I will become an alcoholic." Rather, it starts with just "one sip" from a friend's drink or one party "because a friend is going." And what of the male or female Muslim who works in a non-Muslim society? Day after day, there is mixing and prayer times can't always be accommodated. After years of this, how strong will belief— or practice—be? Clearly, as soon as vigilance is weak, erosion sets in. How else can we explain how millions of good people of the Book around the world eat pork through a "forgotten" prohibition?

Are any of us strong enough to resist this kind of slipping? How many of us flip channels on the television and settle on shows we know are inappropriate if only for a minute. *Haram* (prohibited) topics and images fill our senses and are hard to "shake" once they set themselves on our retinas and eardrums. So instead of having the scriptures in our heads as we drive from A to B, we are humming the top 10. And how simple it is for our children to copy the entertainers who mock everyone just for a laugh! How easily we—and our families—begin to attend to marketing ploys which aim to make us yearn for the "ornaments" of this life. In such a way, our thoughts are slowly replaced by useless ramblings and distractions, and our time is slowly eroded—time which is so precious, every second a gift, and maybe the last.

For communities and nations, vigilance is an even bigger challenge. Our voices are often quiet on important issues which will affect humanity forever. We are usually busy struggling with our own existence, and it is hard to challenge the status quo. But what happens when we remain silent? Did you know that if the prohibition on pork had been adhered to worldwide, we might well be without key products that are presently destroying the earth? It's true: nitroglycerine (for manufacturing explosives) and some of the worse causes of pollution in this century (rubber, plastics, insecticides, herbicides, dyes, strong adhesives and antifreeze, for instance) were all invented using fatty acids from pigs. And while many of these products are manufactured synthetically now, they might

not exist at all if pig carcasses had never been touched. Was the prohibition on pork in the holy books a warning to us individually and collectively? Only God knows.

In fact, there is so much we don't know that it becomes very complex to guard ourselves and remain vigilant. For example, many common medicines use fatty acids from pork while some are completely
synthetic. But can we be sure which is going into our bodies? Common
problem pharmaceuticals include many cosmetics, estrogen and proges-
terone (in birth control pills), insulin (for diabetes), oxytocin (for induc-
ing childbirth), cortisone and corticosteroids (for skin and other ailments), and TSH (for defective thyroids), to name just a few. Should we
check everything when we are prescribed medicine? Yes, we should.
Isn't this a lot of work? Yes, it is. Guarding faith takes constant effort—
but recovering a lost faith is even harder. And without a doubt, we need
to install believers in all spheres of human activity and development—
medicine, education, science, technology, and social systems—to be able
to articulate clear visions for this ever-changing world and to give each
one of us a chance—no matter where we live or work—to be in the company of careful and judicious people.

In essence, vigilance is really about developing and guarding personal boundaries. Through Ramadan, we learn to recognize our bodies as
"gates" through which we can allow or prevent the passage of anything.
We all know the feeling that follows the fast everyday—each time we put
something in our mouths after sundown, we can't help but quickly ask
ourselves if it is ok to do so. This reflex is the key operating mechanism for
vigilance. Each time something comes to any of our senses, we should
question if it is good for us or not. If we do this each and every time, we
will be safe and we will be in God's favour, as this is His clear promise to
us. If we remain watchful over ourselves, God will keep watch over us.

HYPOCRITES

T he poets who write merely for the sake of writing, who like to hear their own words bouncing off the thin veneer of the social constructs they have created for themselves, and who obscure the true breadth and depth of the matters they are referring to, are like souls lost in a maze of formless valleys: "And the poets, it is those straying in evil who follow them. Do you not see that they wander distracted in every valley? And that they say what they practise not?" (26:224-226) As they drift like tumbleweed through endless trends, playing with words, following every vain thought and whim, letting themselves be pulled along by their ever-changing desires, leading their readers and listeners to waft right along with them, they are actually deprived of all authenticity in their opinions, words, and actions—becoming simple manufacturers and packagers of a false reality to which countless others become pointlessly committed, and thereby terribly lost.

Without a doubt, the media today feeds the established anti-Islamic prejudice of many westerners. And as Muslims, we are concerned that some observers in the West will increasingly view Islam as a religion to be despised—apparently full of terrorists and hypocrites, as evidenced among the growing ranks of the highly visible, yet sometimes seemingly contradictory, religious representatives who grace our front pages and news programs every day. Yet, actually, it is not our public image in the media which we must guard most of all. Rather, it is our own daily representation to others. For in the simple beginnings of hypocrisy inside each and every one of us germinates the single biggest threat to our faith.

The history of the world, of course, is full of giants of hypocrisy—and they have come from all religious persuasions. The People of the Book easily recognize Judas, who proclaimed loyalty to Jesus, then betrayed him. There are also some questions around the Apostle Paul, a Jew originally called "Saul" who converted to Christianity and then spread the doctrine of Jesus to the masses. At times, he accused the other Apostles that they "walked not uprightly according to the truth of the Gospel," (Galatians 2:14), then insisted that "those who labour under the law of God are under a *curse"* (Galatians 3:10) and that *"God's covenant is decaying"* (Hebrews 8:13). "Saint Paul," after whom my father was named, went on to lay the foundation of modern Christian orthodoxy by "smoothing" over the original religion of Jesus to make it "easier" and more attractive for the masses.

To tell the truth, I was a bit suspicious of religious hypocrisy in some of the practices of my youth. For example, I could never understand why the little candles inside my Roman Catholic church were differently priced for different saints. Saint Patrick might cost $2, but Saint Francis cost $5. It turns out that, in fact, that the history of many great Christian saints is unfortunately infected with stories of countless hypocrites. Constantine "The Great" (reigning Roman Emperor, 285-337), who was heralded in history books as a "model of Christian virtue and holiness," actually murdered two of his brothers-in-law, his son, and his wife, among others. "Saint Augustine" (354-430), whom I learned to pray to as a young Catholic myself, actually advocated killing anyone who refused to convert to Christianity and thought women were of no use except for bearing children. "Saint Thomas" (1225-1274) supported slavery adamantly, killed anyone suspected of being a heretic, and hated women vehemently, believing they were mostly all witches. In fact, his writings inspired the great witch hunts of later centuries by which countless innocent women were killed, sometimes for simply having repeated stillbirths. For her part, Saint Theresa, after whom my mother was named, apparently practised bizarre rituals of self-chastisement, including piercing her breasts with needles and rolling in broken glass.

But does anyone really lose faith when a character who is "larger than life" falls from grace? Not likely. Hitler was a devout Christian and so was Mussolini, but Christians didn't abandon the church "en masse" either during or after their rule. The actions of the Irish Republican Army hardly represent Catholics worldwide, and each new attack of terror is just that and only that—it doesn't cause the average Catholic around the world to see his or her faith as a religion of violence. And so it is with Saddam's family and the questions being raised about their religious sincerity. There is no risk of contagious apostasy here.

The real risk is when the hypocrites are not so famous and not so distant. In fact, the closer they get to our lives, the more their hypocrisy threatens us. The Catholic Church, for example, has been rocked with so-called "sex scandals" in which priests have been found guilty of assaulting young students in their care at boarding schools across Canada. Those affected by these experiences, many of them Native Canadians whose families were "pressured" into converting to Christianity at the time, are cynical about the church as a result and have turned away from monotheism. Many families in my home province of Quebec know someone who was touched by such events as the number of victims in that province alone is estimated at over 6000, mainly poor children housed in church orphanages between 1940 and 1960. In the first six months of 2002 alone, 174 Catholic priests were forced out of their jobs in the US due to allegations of sexual misconduct, as the "Crisis in the Catholic Church" begins to overwhelm the legal system. All this has done much to seed scepticism into the otherwise fervently Roman Catholic populations of the Canadian and American northeast, one family and one neighbourhood at a time. After all, these are not ancient historical figures in an unreal time; these are contemporary religious people seen at churches and schools around the country, violating core values of the faith, acting out their hypocrisy on a grand scale.

In the lives of our cities and communities, there are many more examples of hypocrisy. There are Christians who attend church every Sunday and grow up to be murderers. There are Muslims who send their children to Qu'ran schools, yet beat their wives almost daily. And there are Jews who go to temple every Sabbath, then rape young girls in moments of drunken passion. There are countless Christians who say "Praise Jesus," and in the same breath, gossip viciously about their neighbours or co-workers, just as there are Jews wishing each other *"Shalom"* (peace), and lying in their everyday business practices. So, too, there are Muslims who say, *"Insha Allah,"* (God willing) every few words, yet backbite their own family members. All over the world, in every faith, there are men who fornicate though they ritually practice prayers. And all over the world, there are women who raise money for charity, then spend thousands of dollars on personal jewellery. These acts of hypocrisy, both large and small, are committed regularly by so many nameless believers that we hardly stop to consider them sometimes. Yet the impact is systemic and invasive.

How many men finish a prayer and within minutes, yell at their wife about a bill paid late? A woman who is weakened by years of this may begin to neglect her own prayers and question the integrity of her husband's worship. And what kind of image will this inspire in their children, as they notice the conflict between theory and practice of the faith? How many women read holy books while their husbands are at work, then pressure the husband for a better house or appliances on his return home? A man who is subjected to this for years may well begin to doubt his wife's capacity to understand the religion. And what kind of message does it send to children, as greed and materialism contrast the message of sufficiency and gratitude God inspires? Slowly, but slowly, we begin to erode the beliefs of those around us who are closest to us and depend on us for support in our faith. For each of our acts of hypocrisy has the power to cast another into doubt.

The circle of doubt can spread horribly quickly. The average non-Muslim is probably more affected in his opinion about Islam when he sees each one of us go about our public lives than when he sees Saddam hoarding gold. Everyone expects politicians—in all faiths and cultures—to be ethically challenged. This is hardly worth anyone's attention. But real people carry real messages. So when a Muslim husband and wife go shopping and he walks far ahead of her and speaks to her in a demeaning tone, he conveys a clear message that Islam disgraces women—and this is both his lie and his grievous sin. When a covered woman looks judgmentally at what another woman wears, be she Muslim or not, she sends the message that Muslims assume an air of superiority, though humility is supposed to be our most distinguishing feature. The woman who calls herself Muslim yet tries to make herself attractive outside the house, and the Muslim man who goes to a dance club or bar after work, are both sending the message that Muslims—in fact—are not much different than everyone, having all of the same weaknesses and no viable alternatives to degenerative societies. And when Muslim families are "too busy" to join a public school endeavour or wider neighbourhood project, they send the message that Islam is an insular, rather than a universal, religion.

We believe in asceticism, but we really practice controlled materialism—seeking to understand the Prophet's simple life, we still think about the new minivan. We hope that our spouses will be pious and sincere, but we still watch the music videos in passing. We wish peace on everyone in our everyday greetings, but we still rail at each other in daily, weekly battles over issues which have absolutely nothing to do with faith-building. We go to classes and groups to learn about the traps and tests of this world, but we still waste hours every day. Worse of all, we do all these things in full public view of non-Muslims so that slowly, but steadily, our beautiful religion becomes vulnerable to misunderstanding on a massive scale. Yet God warns us clearly to act in accordance with what we are called to do, as exemplified through the stories of previous civilizations. For instance, Prophet Jethro (Shu'ayb) implored his people to discard their false values and guard against corruption and deception: *"I do not wish to forbid you from something and then do it myself. Rather, I only wish to set things right so far as I am able."* (11:88) And Prophet Muhammad himself described the three main characteristics of a hypocrite: *"When he speaks, he lies; when he gives his word, he breaks it; and when he is given a trust, he is unfaithful"*.[9]

As Muslims, we all understand that the penalty for giving the wrong information about Islam is very serious. We may think that this means misquoting a verse number from the Qu'ran or being unclear about the chronology of some event in the Prophet's life. But giving wrong information because we set a bad example is much more common, and the global dimension of this type of hypocrisy is staggering. For example, the Prophet Muhammad installed the first welfare system in the world, and Zakat is a pillar of Islam, yet youth in wealthy Muslim countries race their Mercedes through the desert for sport while their Muslim brothers and sisters not so far away die of starvation and disease. There are leaders of Muslim countries who make it impossible for covered women to attend schools and make the whole world think that Islam is regressive. And there are leaders of other Muslim countries who force all women to cover, and make the whole world believe that Islam is repressive.

Of course, Muslims aren't the only ones to be guilty of large-scale hypocrisy. There are countless Christian families discharging their guilt by contributing $30 monthly to foster one child in Christian Africa where malaria kills more than 3000 children a day, while countless TV evangelists compete for better Nielsen ratings in delivering the "word of God." If the important thing is for people to hear the message, why should it matter who gets to tell it? Is the word of the commercial sponsors equally important? Wealthy Americans prosper only a few dozen miles from devastatingly poor Mexican villages, and rich western pre-teens wear clothing produced in forced-labour manufacturing plants by children their own age who think about where the next meal will be, instead of the next party, as they earn an average of fifty cents an hour—less than a Western teen will spend on a pack of gum. And there are "modern" Jewish families in suburban America driving their only child between prestigious schools and expensive after-school activities while their Orthodox counterparts a few blocks away in urban America live five children to a bedroom struggling for a sustainable, devotional life in a secular culture. Meanwhile, so-called "stars" earn million-dollar salaries per sports game, concert or movie, while over one million black children in countless American cities live below the "deep" poverty line—with annual family incomes below $7000.

In the end, it is not enough to have faith. We must truly become what we believe. For all the People of the Book, there is only one protection against hypocrisy: effort. It is easier to watch TV than to watch over our children's emerging values. It is easier to say the first thing that comes into our mouths than to control our words. It is easier to read the sales flyers than holy books. Always, it is easier to "go with the flow" and "just relax" than it is to exercise self-restraint, sound judgement, and diligent practice. The Quakers, a conservative Christian sect, have historically refused to take oaths in a court of law because they believe in always being truthful, and that there is not one truth for every day and one for the courts. Their vigilance against hypocrisy is distinctively heroic. The point is that everyone can do what is easy. But the question is, can we do what is right?

As Muslims, we are uniquely blessed with a clear record of the word of God which has been left untouched by the ever-changing self-interests of historical and political figures—through time, our Qu'ran is intact. Thus, we have a clear set of prescriptions for our actions, and the singularly perfect model of the Prophet Muhammad, who thankfully lived a relatively long life as a real person—knowing birth, life, illness, work, war, love, frustration, hunger, fear, sorrow, faith, marriage, children, pain, death, and God. Through his example, we know that it is possible to experience all of life without any hypocrisy whatsoever. What are we waiting for?

ON SHARING TRUTH

As a covered woman in this culture, I am noticed as a Muslim, though my husband, walking alone, is not. Head covers are much talked about. My mother, still a Christian, keeps hoping I am just a "hobby Muslim" and I will take off my hijab sometime soon. But there are images of covered women from my own past which give me comfort—not from Turkey, Pakistan, or the Middle East, where I have never yet been, but from right here in Canada.

First, there were the amazing Catholic nuns who led the convent school I attended for eight years. My best memories of childhood are their beautiful faces, completely ringed in black flowing cloth, and the lovely flapping of clean, long robes up and down the hallways, like the sound of soft, huge wings. They spoke in whispers and they smelled wonderful—like fresh laundry in the wind. I often dreamt of living with them, and I hid on the library shelves after classes just to be in their light a little longer every day.

To this day, there remain countless nuns around the world—more than 85,000 in the US alone. They cover themselves completely in loose, dark garments, including their hair and neck. They have only a small ring of white around the face, to highlight their cleanliness and purity. The dress of these Christian sisters sets them apart from others, much like Muslim dress sets us apart. Like us, it represents their constant devotion to one God.

In the Bible, Corinthians 11, Christians are told, *"Every woman who prays or speaks with her head uncovered dishonours her head."* The nuns are engaged in continuous worship through every aspect of their lives—breathing, learning, and living in the name of God—so they believe they should cover at all times. In fact, many Christian women throughout the Western world have now concluded the same thing and are beginning to cover their heads every day. Web-based support groups and information for covering Christian women are becoming more and more prevalent on the Internet—yet strangely, these are hardly mentioned when American television discusses Muslim women as being visibly marginalized and oppressed by their "outdated" clothing.

Not only Christians but Jewish women, too, are covered. In fact, in Jewish law, women who are or have been married (including widows and divorcees) are required to cover their hair. Rabbinic law prohibits any blessings or prayers from being recited in the presence of an uncovered woman since her hair is considered "nudity." Traditionally, a Jewish woman who did not cover was deemed an adulteress or prostitute, and the veil was a sign of a woman's self-respect. The same was true for a man's beard, which could never be cut according to Jewish law. Yet now, only a handful of Orthodox Jews around the world adhere to these regulations, the popular majority seemingly oblivious to them.

Actually, in a peculiar sort of way, the Muslim woman's head covering can be seen to represent the source of misunderstanding between the three religions of the Book. It isn't really about the scarf at all. Rather, it's about theory and practice. Simply put, *more* Muslims adhere to *more* of their rules *more* of the time and *more* strictly than Christians or Jews. Thus, Muslims are labeled ultra-conservative and even "fundamentalist," a word which has become increasingly politicized. In actual fact, if Christians and Jews were to follow their own ordinances, we would all look, act, and feel a lot more similar than different.

Take the example of some other Christian women who are covering dutifully even to this day. The Amish and the Mennonites sprang from the "Anabaptist" movement—Christians who rebelled against the status quo in Europe in the 16th century, and now number over three million worldwide. Though many attempts were made to wipe them out through persecution and genocide, they survived in pockets around the world, many of them settling and still thriving in the west, particularly in Pennsylvania. Their conservative life does not permit any displays of pride (such as fancy furnishings or even buttons) and strictly forbids lying, alcohol, modern conveniences such as kitchen appliances, and the media. Men grow beards and are forbidden to wear gold. Men and women guard their chastity and piety at all costs. They refuse to collect social assistance of any kind because they do not believe in "begging." And they will not be photographed nor will they display pictures in their houses because they believe they should never try to make images of God's work. Men and women must pray and work separately, and they all wear plain, loose suits with long sleeves. Women must cover their heads at all times, with both an inside "bonnet" covering which is on at all times, and an outside covering. Their dress sets them apart from the masses, as they want God to recognize that they consecrate every moment of their lives.

Another sub-group of Christians, the Quakers, have also settled in their own western communities after expulsion from 16th century Europe, and exceed 300,000. Quakers believe that all people are equal, regardless of colour or gender, and that everyone has the light of God inside them. They believe in peace and simple living so they prohibit television and the media, alcohol, sports, and hobbies which detract from religious studies. They reject the "details" of the Bible as being unimportant, and focus on the deeper revelations and making every action an act of worship. Clothes is always for decency and never for pride, so their women cover at all times, with plain head coverings, as even ribbons or colours are judged to be ostentatious. The women and men wear loose, long clothing, and both sexes guard their chastity and their faith carefully. No one member has authority over the others, as all are equal in the eyes of God. Again, their dress style is intended to distinguish them as they seek to be a "Holy Nation" in God's eyes.

Of course, we never hear much about these kinds of parallels on the news when the media is so eager to point out all the ways in which Muslims are different from everyone else. And there are more examples, too. Among the Jews, the sexes must be separated for prayers, as they are in Islam, and like Muslims, Jewish men are not allowed to have sexual relations with their menstruating wives, while menstruating Jewish women are not allowed into the synagogue for prayers. And as regards polygamy, long heard as a public cry against Islam though it is seldom practiced by Muslims in our times, Old Testament and Rabbinic writings state that it is legal so that it was practised widely by European Jews until the 16th century, and it is still practised among some sects of Yemeni Jews, as well as some Orthodox Jews in Israel, who allow a maximum of four wives.

The fast is another instance of clear similarities. Fasting is prescribed to all Jews, following the teachings of Moses. Traditionally, some special months of fasting were upheld, in particular the ninth month, and the most important fast on the yearly Day of Atonement continues to this time. Bible fasts for Christians prescribe abstention—not just from food and drink, but also from certain pleasures, and encourages particular acts of charity and justice. Additionally, fasting was prescribed to Christians to strengthen certain prayers at times of difficulties. The Bible mentions the importance of intention and dedicating yourself to prayer during fast times to avoid putting on the "sad face of a hypocrite," as told in the Gospel of Matthew.

With regards to prayers, Christians were advised to wash their feet before prayer to clear away sins, and Exodus advises both Jews and Christians to use water in daily processes of ritual purification. To this day, Jewish Temple Priests rinse their hands three times before prayers, and all worshipers are instructed to wash before prayers and put on clean clothes. In Joshua, Moses is told to take off his shoes for prayer because the prayer ground must be clean as he prepares to meet God. And Orthodox Christians today still routinely prostrate in congregational prayers as a symbol of humility and submission to God.

And so we are labeled as being so different in our practices when in fact, the word of God has been sent to others who simply seem to have forgotten it or chosen to "adjust" their religion for the "changing times." Our covered women are not the only covered women, and we are not the only people who prostrate, fast, perform ritual purification, try to main-tain purity in our sexual relations and our family lives, or abstain from alco-hol and the poor influences of the media. There are others on this earth with the genuine intention to live pious and devoted lives in a secular world, who continue to defend their ways despite overwhelming forces. Like other conservative religious groups in the west, we must become firmly established amid a sea of opposition to yield thriving communities which preserve, model, and disseminate faith-based values. It is an integral part of our covenant with God to invite people to belief. May it become an inte-gral part of our lives, then, to build on what we share with other believ-ers, rather than on what divides us.

ABSTAINING FROM ALCOHOL

Like all converts to Islam, I am sometimes haunted by my past and always in awe of the mercy of God. By the grace of Allah, many people reading this have probably never tried alcohol themselves. For like all the prohibitions in Islam, this is one of God's mercies on believers. Yet for me, some of the most painful memories relate to alcohol. Actually, I was never one of those people who drank uncontrollably and then did hugely embarrassing things. I was what was called a "good drinker"—and that's what makes it even more frightening.

I started early, as I was offered wine with family dinners, and I watched my parents consume three to five drinks of alcohol every weekday—more on weekends. A large bottle of alcohol lasted two or three days in my home—less if friends dropped by. In fact, the Canadian national average age for trying alcohol is 12 years of age, and about 73% of Canadians over age 12 drink alcohol. Only 3-4% are visibly dependent; the rest are "normal" people—going to jobs and coming home to their families. However, they just can't function for any length of time without alcohol. They "miss" a drink if they don't have it—and they make every effort to plan weekly routines around it. They talk about brands, plan visits to bars, clubs, and parties, and may even make their own. They don't feel "right" until they've had a drink—and if they can't get any, they become depressed or aggressive. Over the months and years, they tend to use it like prayer to meditate on the best and worse moments of their lives.

My family was very typical of Canadian families. On average, Canadians consume 7.6 litres of alcohol per person per year. The industry itself reports sales in 2001 of over 14.5 billion cases (12 X 750 ml bottles). Every single one—every one—of my relations drinks alcohol, and I sadly have several close relatives who have crashed cars, lost their jobs or families, or embarrassed themselves in public—all under the influence of alcohol. Did you know that in a typical year in Canada, more than 6500 people die in alcohol-related accidents, and more than 81,000 people are hospitalized? Among all injured drivers in Canada, over 77% have alcohol in their bloodstream.

What is the big attraction anyhow? Alcohol doesn't taste as good as people say it does. It's often too spicy, sweet, dry, or bitter—depending on what kind of alcohol—and it can burn your throat when it goes down. Most people actually "mix" it with pop or juice to hide the taste. It makes you gain weight through useless calories and lethargy. Drink a lot and you will vomit, sometimes for two or three days. Drink even more, and you may go blind or die. And once you start, it's hard to stop. People who drink know all of these things, but still they drink. My Muslim friends often ask me, "Why do people drink if they know that there are all these dangers and problems with it?" This question bothered me enough in the past to make me stop drinking for years at a time. My family's response was no big surprise—they accused me then, like now, of "not being very much fun." This concept of "fun," in fact, is at the very heart of the issue.

First, "fun" is what you do to "let go" of "the stresses of the week." For drinkers of any caliber, life is divided into work days and non-work days. On work days, drinking must be limited—drink too much and your breath and skin smell tart in the morning, detectable to any other drinker, such as an employer. But on weekends, drinking is unlimited. This leads to the birth of a national phenomenon—the race to weekends. People will talk about the coming weekend beginning on Wednesdays. Then, on Mondays and Tuesdays, they talk about the previous weekend. And so, the life of the average Canadian quickly becomes a monotony of alternating days, five plus two, five plus two. The only concept of "future" and "hope" is the hope for what will happen during future weekends. The main bond between members becomes the alcohol itself as discussions of which beer is better, which bar is better, and which party was the best fill lives quickly and easily and the weeks pass by. Horrible jobs with little meaning are tolerated because "it's almost Friday," and it isn't important anymore to think about how time in this life should really be spent. Any occasion is cause for an alcohol-driven celebration, and many capable people who have the potential to really benefit this world are "dulled" into submission by the monotony of this pointless social and economic cycle.

Second, fun is what happens when you "don't take life too seriously." I personally can't count the number of times I have been told to just "relax." It seems that *not* taking life seriously is a fervent goal of the majority of people. They believe that life is meant for pleasure; some will actually tell you that "God gave them the gift of this life strictly for their enjoyment." In fact, if you begin to think too deeply about the meaning of life, you quickly become a social outcast in this culture. Dare to suggest that someone should slow down their drinking and you will find yourself socially adrift. You may think that's alright—after all, who needs friends who drink alcohol all the time? However, the reality is that you will have almost an impossible time finding friends who don't drink alcohol in this culture. Only 12% of all Canadians over age 12 report that they abstain from alcohol, and many of these are youth and elders. As an adult, you will have to content yourself with being alone, and without a strong faith, it is almost impossible to bear the loneliness. Sadly, eventually, one submits to the culture instead of God.

Third, "fun" means acting without due care for consequences. Every week, all over this country, people apologize to loved ones for inexcusable behaviours they committed when they were drunk—fornication, domestic violence, gambling and financial recklessness, dangerous driving, immoral business practices—and so on. It's a "perfect excuse" because other drinkers understand, so you are likely to be forgiven. Ultimately, acting carefully becomes quite unimportant. More than 60% of Canadians report problems from their own or someone else's drinking, and alcohol abuse costs Canada over 2.7% of its gross domestic product annually. That's over 18.5 billion dollars a year—money that certainly could be better spent. Beyond the inexcusable acts committed under the influence of alcohol, there are the unforgettable ones—telling loved ones hurtful things, divulging long-held family secrets, becoming sexually explicit, acting in embarrassing way with employers, and so on. The reason is that alcohol brings a sense of slowness and confusion—a lot like what you feel just as you wake up in the morning and are still half dreaming. Typically, problem behaviours happen often over a lifetime until life feels "out of control" so that it becomes easier to continue drinking to "numb" the spiritual pain. And so, many give up the power of their will, given to them by God, and begin to believe in what is sometimes called "the Gospel of now"—having no faith in the hereafter and little faith in their ability to control and change their lives for the better, they live only for today.

As believers, we hold the biggest truth of all—belief in the afterlife. Without it, time, pleasure and reward are measured completely differently. If time is defined only by what is on the calendar this week, why should I care about my spiritual condition at the time of my death? If community is counted only as whoever will accept me in this life, why do I need to care if my life is acceptable to my Maker? If now is all that matters, what is the point of improving myself? Clearly, alcohol creates a powerful distortion—subtle yet persistent throughout the user's life— that the meaning of life is negotiated here and now on this earth alone. Alcohol users suffer what researchers call "reward deficiency syndrome" –they want instant gratification at all times. So how can they be expected to believe in—or even understand—the afterlife. Thus, alcohol robs users of the belief which is the key to understanding the purpose of our lives. And in shielding believers from alcohol, God protects our faith.

Many times I walked away from a party by myself on a cold night, disgusted with everyone I knew, staring up at the night sky, feeling completely alone. Thanks to God for the angels that kept me safe through a difficult, dangerous life. Truthfully, I wish I had known then that somewhere throughout the world, in thousands of vibrant communities, over a billion people abstained from alcohol deliberately. Muslims have a duty to tell everyone that they don't drink *because* of their faith. Someone, somewhere, some day will hear the message as the voice of his own soul, and perhaps change for the better. We all come from God at the start. God willing, we will all be with Him in the end.

THE PROHIBITION ON PORK

Growing up as a young French Canadian in Quebec, I was exposed to pork as part of my diet from a very early age. In fact, pork is the most important meat in French Canadian cooking—it is baked, fried, boiled, ground, salted, smoked, and subjected to every kind of preparation process imaginable. French Canadian meals typically centre on bacon, ham, pork sausages, pork chops, tourtiere (pork pie), cretons (cooked, cold pork spread for sandwiches), and various pastries based on lard (pork fat). Many times I heard my mother tell the story of how I could eat a half pound of bacon to myself from the age of 2! But my culture is not alone in this. In Asian cultures, pork remains the meat of choice. And in the southern United States, for example, pork remains a very popular food—you can even buy pork brains in a can.

The Qur'an clearly tells us that the meat of the pig is unclean for us to eat. In fact, the Torah and the Bible contain the same warning. In Isaiah (65:2-4 and 66:17), God warns believers not to eat pork; Deuteronomy (14:8) reads, *"None of their flesh must you eat and carcass you must not touch."* And Leviticus (Chapter 2, verse 8) states, *"They are unclean for you."*

When I became a Muslim, I had to immediately stop eating pork. I have to admit that I missed bacon at first, and my children complained that I wasn't cooking ham anymore—one of their favourite meals. I stopped eating pork because I respected the rules of my new faith, Islam, and I understood the meat of this animal to be *haram* (prohibited). Still, I was left with a lingering curiosity about the reason for such a prohibition. As God will protect believers, I assumed there must be something quite horrible about pork. So I set out to discover what it might be. What I found out shocked and disgusted me beyond all expectations.

First of all, pigs are scavengers. This means that they will eat anything—dead animals, excrement, garbage, other pigs, everything. As a result, they have a very high parasite to body weight ratio—in other words, they are infested with all kinds of internal and external parasites, most of which they can pass along to humans:

- *Primitive Neuroectodermal Tumours (PNET)*: Pork parasites can cause brain tumours in children, according to the *Journal of Paediatric and Perinatal Epidemiology*[10]. Children raised on pig farms have 12 times the risk of having this problem than other children.
- *Nipah Virus:* This is a deadly form of encephalitis (swelling of the brain). An outbreak in Borneo in 1999 caused 100 deaths and led to the forced slaughter of over 1 million pigs.
- *Clostridium Perfringens Type C:* According to the *New England Journal of Medicine*[11], this potentially deadly disease is spread by eating infected pigs; tragically, the disease is even more deadly if the patient is malnourished, such as in poor or war-torn countries.
- *Hepatitis E:* Pork is a "reservoir" of this deadly virus, especially in warm climates, according to the *Mayo Clinic Pro.*[12]
- *Porcine Endogenous Retrovirus (PERV):* This extremely deadly virus is found naturally in the heart, spleen and kidney of pigs, according to the *Lancet*[13]
- *Trichinosis:* This common worm-like parasite is found in all kinds of animals which are prohibited to eat, such as pigs, dogs, rats, and other carnivores. When the worm eggs are swallowed, stomach acid dissolves the hard casing and releases worms into the stomach; the worms can then travel through the stomach lining into the arteries and muscles and anything from a minor fever to death. According to some statistics, up to 1 in 6 Canadians may be carrying Trichonosis, many with no symptoms, as a result of having eaten pork in the past.
- *Taenia Solium:* Commonly known as "tapeworms," these creatures live in the flesh of pigs and infect the intestines of humans, where they can cause the growth of football-size cysts which put pressure on other internal organs, ultimately causing death. These long worms can grow as long as 12 inches, living inside the intestines. In California, in August, 1997, one unfortunate 10-year old boy was actually found to have a tapeworm in his brain.
- *Influenza:* Pigs harbour the influenza virus naturally, so they incubate it in the summer. As a result, ingesting pieces of pig lungs (as in pork sausages) can increase the likelihood of getting the flu in the winter.

- *Excessive Histamine, Imidazole, and Growth Hormones:* Pigs have these chemicals in larger proportions than most animals, and these have been related to inflammation in the tendons and cartilage of humans, possible causing arthritis and rheumatism.

Ingestion is not the only way humans can come into contact with porcine diseases. *The Saturday Evening Post*[14] reports that pig skin has been used in human skin grafts in China for centuries, as a treatment for burns. And many diabetics throughout Canada inadvertently inject daily with insulin drawn from pigs. In a frightening new development, CNN.com[15] reports a number of laboratories experimenting with growing "miniature pigs" for the purposes of turning them into organ and tissue donors for humans. Yet even a primary researcher on this project, Julia Greenstein, will only say that the pigs "don't *appear* to be capable of infecting" humans. According to the highly respected journal, *The Independent*[16], the truth is devastating: "PERV can pass into human cells easily, and such transplant procedures could easily introduce infectious agents from animals into human populations."

What many people don't realize is that there are other common, hidden sources of pig material on the grocery shelves, such as *rennet.* Rennet is a chemical which coagulates milk and it is commonly used in the manufacturing of cheese. The active ingredient in rennet is the enzyme chymosine, which is found in the stomach lining of new baby calves and lambs. (The enzyme helps them digest their mother's milk, and so it is not found in adult animals.) Of course, eating mashed bits of slaughtered baby animals is not halal (permissible) in the least. But what makes matters even more serious is that many times, the enzyme pepsin is substituted for chymosin when making the rennet—and pepsin comes the blood of adult cows or pigs! In fact, the original recipe for Pepsi-cola included pepsin (that's how it got its name) which came from pig blood. Thankfully, Pepsi does not contain pepsin anymore.

Another hidden source of pork materials is *gelatin.* Gelatin is a chemical which stiffens liquids, and it is commonly used in make up, face and hand creams, vitamins, Jello, cake mixes, cereal bars, frosted cereals, ice cream, frozen yogurt, some plain or fruit yogurts, gummy bears, some chocolates, certain kinds of candies, and other products. It is manufactured from collagen, which comes from animal carcasses. Of course, eating carcasses is *haram* (prohibited). But even worse than this, the gelatin manufactured in the US—Canada's primary supplier—is entirely made from pig skin! Ironically, American and European gelatin manufacturers are locked in a public relations war: Europe's gelatin comes from cow carcasses and skins and may carry Mad Cow Disease; while US gelatin, made from pigs, has the "potential for contamination" from parasites.[17] In addition, pig-based gelatin may cause terrible "immunological reactions with the common children's vaccine for measles, mumps and rubella," so children who receive the vaccine and eat pork may become very ill.

A further problem is that the diseases pigs carry are hard to avoid even with proper cooking, as many of the viruses are resistant to heat. And since the diseases mainly start in the stomach or intestines, an infected person will have contaminated excrement. Without proper hand-washing, this material can get into someone else's food easily enough, especially in a restaurant where a cook is infected. With an incubation time of up to 45 days, it is often hard to detect, trace, or prevent the spread of some very lethal illnesses.

Obviously, I don't miss bacon anymore, and I regret ever eating it. My revulsion at having eaten such a dirty food is surpassed by another horror—how the religion of my youth, a "religion of the Book," could have strayed so far from such a basic rule. I have met so-called Muslims, for example, who do not practise at all—they never pray, they do not go to the mosque, they will not fast, and they may even drink alcohol. But they will still refuse to eat pork. The same is true for many non-practising Jews—even those who know very little about their own religion will avoid pork completely. Yet nowadays, many Christians are genuinely surprised when you tell them that the Prophet Jesus prohibited such a thing. Actually, they aren't eating pork to defy God's word—they simply seem to have collectively either forgotten the rule—or never known. And for some reason, the prohibition is not commonly discussed. In fact, they have eaten it for so long now—generations—that stopping would require a massive amount of awareness and determination.

Ironically, the so-called "Bible belt" in the US also coincides with the agricultural belt, and pig farmers have become a significant political force. The "pork lobby" is a massive political network made up of regional and national groups of pork farmers across Canada and the US. They form "Pork Advocacy Coalitions" which spend millions of political dollars each year to "advocate and enhance the swine industry's viability and profitability through monitoring, informing and affecting issues of concern to the industry." The disclosed list of political contributions by the National Pork Producers Council is extensive[18], and many of the bigger contributions are kept secret.

Among both producers and consumers, there is a tendency to either ignore or trivialize the parasite problem. For example, one website sells a "Biosecurity Product Calculator" which pig farmers can use to measure the disease risk their pigs might pose to the public, to establish a "safe" margin of risk to consumers. One of my very close relatives had a large Taenia Solium worm living inside her intestines as a child growing up in Quebec. It made her very hungry so that she "ate for two people" every day without gaining weight. She still jokes that she missed it when it was finally removed because she put on 20 pounds when her "helper" was gone! Apparently, it took numerous attempts to get it out because if even one small piece was left, it kept regenerating. When it was finally successfully extracted, its full length was 10 -12 inches. That is actually a lot like having a snake living inside a human body.

The only way to be safe is to try to avoid all possible sources of contamination—obvious and hidden pork products. Be sure to read the labels carefully when you buy cheese, yogurt, chocolates, candies, cereal bars, and other processed foods. One brand of yogurt may have gelatin, while another may be safe. Even inside a single brand, one flavour may be gelatin-free, while another may not be. Alternately, try to shop in vegetarian supply stores—these shops are extremely careful to keep out any animal product. If you want more information about this important topic, try www.jamiais-lamia.org/halalharam.htm to learn more about hidden haram (prohibited) foods. Or, try www.mercola.com, a site which is hosted by a medical doctor who recommends that absolutely everyone abstain from pork.

As always, the essential truth about life is where it always has been—in the scriptures. They tell us that it is important to be clean inside and out—and it's just not possible to eat pork and stay clean. The Qur'an and Bible also tell us to honour all of God's gifts and show our gratitude—yet eating pork can waste or destroy the very gift of our lives. Fundamentally, the Qur'an also tells us to read so that we can understand. God willing, we can all follow these instructions to honour our duties and our faith, and to help our children, and their children, to do the same.

CHAPTER VI

Clear Signs Around Us

"Those who remember God standing and sitting and lying on their sides and reflect on the creation of the heavens and the earth: 'Our Lord! You have not created this in vain! Glory be to You; save us then from the chastisement of the fire.'" (3:191)

* * *

"A Muslim never gives a fellow Muslim a better gift than wisdom through which God increases him in guidance or turns him away from harmful behavior." (From the hadith collection of Al-Bayhaqi)

REASON TO BELIEVE

I grew up as a Christian thanks largely to my mother and other relatives, for my father was an atheist. A close brush with death in his teens left him hospitalized for two years, but rather than "finding God" in the miracle of his survival, he became disaffected and cynical. Every day at dinner, he professed that life was pointless, God had never existed, and only stupid people believed otherwise. His views weren't that unique, actually. As a product of the 20th century western world, he learned about psychology and evolution from popular magazines, and his life became defined in terms of his ego and his origins as an ape. As the miracle of Genesis became displaced with "scientific explanations," he reflected a general feeling that informed people no longer believed in miracles.

In fact, the prevailing western viewpoint is still that scientific explanations are necessarily correct, and religious belief is irrational or the result of psychological or educational deficits. The unwritten assumption is that if scientists favour atheism, then atheism must be scientific. Students of faith attending public schools find themselves increasingly unable to relate to a science program which promotes the idea that man is closer to gorillas than to God. But it hasn't always been that way. Prior to the 1870s, atheism was restricted to a few intellectuals, and science and religion were assumed to work together. The list of western scientists of faith is immense, including such notables as Joule (thermodynamics): "Order is infinitely manifested in the universe governed by the will of God"; Isaac Newton: "Creation is the only scientific explanation"; Faraday (physics): "Because one God created the world, all of nature must be interconnected"; Lord Kelvin (physics): "If you think strongly enough, you will be forced by science to the belief in God"; Boyle (chemistry): "From a knowledge of His work, we shall know Him"; Pasteur (microbiology): "The more I study nature, the more I stand amazed at the work of the Creator"; and Einstein: "The pursuit of science leads to a religious feeling." Consistent with these sentiments, religious lobby groups in the US are fighting to get God back into the science curriculum. In fact, in Kansas, Kentucky, Alabama, and Nebraska, evolution may now be taught only as a theory, along with cre-ationist views.[1] And in growing numbers, young scientists are expressing their views that evolution alone "cannot fully account for the world we observe".[2]

Of course, for those of us who already believe, the best quotes about the connection between religion and science come from the holy books. The Bible says *"You have ordered everything with measure, number, and weight"* (Wisdom 11:20), and the Qur'an states, *"It is Allah who has given order and proportion, and who has measured everything"* (65:3). But what about the five million Canadians who are atheist or have no religious affiliation (Statistics Canada, 2001), or the 220 million people worldwide who classify them-selves as atheists (adherents.com)? What might make them believe in God? Would they think things over, for example, if some astounding scientif-ic revelation pointed directly to God? Or would they still insist, as the Qur'an tells us, in meeting *"angels face to face,"* or in finding *"a ladder to the skies"?* (17:90)

Well, if ever there was a discovery to startle even the most cynical mind, the findings about "Phi" are it. What is "Phi"? It is a mathematical constant, the so-called "golden" number—1.61803398875... It's actually necessary to explore the math before the miracle. At its simplest, if you seg-ment a line so one side is 1 unit long, and the other side is 1.61803398875... units long, you will have "the golden ratio" (golden proportion, golden mean, golden section, or divine proportion). If you make a rectangle 1 unit high from two parallel lines 1.61803398875 units long, you will cre-ate a "golden rectangle." You can then segment the golden rectangle into smaller squares and golden rectangles, all with the same golden ratio, continuing infinitely towards the middle. And if you draw a line which touches the edges of each golden rectangle symmetrically going towards the middle, you will create a "golden spiral." For thousands of years, peo-ple have known about the visual appeal of shapes based on the ratio, so these proportions were used in building the Parthenon and the Pyramids. But the mathematics of the ratio have made progress since the Greeks and Egyptians, particularly with the work of the famed 12th century Italian mathematician, Fibonacci, who was inspired by the writings of Al-Khwarizmi, the Muslim "father of algebra." Fibonacci is credited with a

series of numbers (1,1,2,3,5,8,13,21,34,55,89,144, etc, each one the sum
of the previous two) which explains countless mathematical problems,
like population growth and the stock market. Fibonacci numbers have a
lot of interesting properties; the most intriguing is that the ratio of any
two consecutive Fibonacci numbers becomes the golden number itself,
as we advance in the series (5/3=1/6; 8/5=1.625; 13/8 = 1.615385, etc.).
Fibonacci himself said, "Someday these numbers will unlock the secrets
of the universe."

It seems he was right, for scientists have discovered, particularly
within the last decade, that the golden number defines the geometry and
growth rates of countless natural shapes. The golden spiral, for example,
is the shape of ocean whirlpools, the movement of water down the drain,
tornadoes, hurricanes, our solar system, the Milky Way galaxy, elephant
tusks, and ram horns; the movement of schools of fish, swarms of insects,
and flocks of birds when they disperse and regroup; the growth of ivy
leaves and the shape of unfolding bracken; growth patterns formed by
cells in cultures; the geometric molecular and atomic pattern of all solid
metals; the biomolecular assembly structure of all proteins; the path of
the peregrine falcon diving for its prey; the spacing between the arms of
most starfish; the spacing between segments of a cross-section of most
fruits, such as the pear, apple, okra, papaya, and banana; and the beautiful
shape of snail, hermit crab, and nautilus shells. The golden ratio appears
in the proportions of the parrot's beak; the growth rates of epidermal
cells in plants; the distance from Mercury to Venus compared with Venus
to Earth; the growth of quasi-crystals; segments in river branches, lightning, blood vessels, the growth of tree roots and branches of most plants,
the veins on most leaves, and the ducts and nerves in the lungs, heart,
liver, kidney, and brain; the wings of birds and flying insects; eye mark-
ings on moth wings; the growth rates of bee and rabbit populations; the
number of possible paths around a bee hive; the bodies of the dolphin
and angelfish; the segmentation of the fruit fly; the standard resistance of
circuits in series or parallel; and the critical value of the spin of black
holes. In sum, Phi is beginning to emerge as a possible "master paradigm"–a kind of generic template for the universe—and one of the greatest scientific arguments for intelligent design.

Yet there is more to convince the skeptic, for this is truly a miracle of huge proportions. In plants, the astounding finding is that almost all seed, leaf, petal, branch, and root arrangements are a function of the golden ratio derived from Fibonnaci numbers. For example, if you count the seeds on a daisy head, you will see golden spiral pairs—with 21 seeds going clockwise, and 34 seeds running counter-clockwise—both Fibonacci numbers. Pine cones also have a similar arrangement, but their golden spirals run 5 in one direction and 8 in the other, also Fibonacci numbers. Pineapple seeds are in golden spiral pairs of 8 and 13; sunflowers have seed spirals of 21 or 34 clockwise, and 34 or 55 counter-clockwise; other species of sunflowers have spiral pairs of 55 and 89, or 89 and 144, or 144 and 233; cacti and succulents have spiral pairs of 8 and 13, or 13 and 21; spruce and fir cones have 21 scales arranged in spirals of 8 turns or "windings," and pine cones have 34 scales in 13 windings. The numbers are always Fibonacci numbers. Petals tell the same story. Iris, lily and clovers have 3 petals; primrose, and buttercups have 5; the delphinium has 8; ragworts and marigolds have 13; asters have 21; sunflowers have 21 and 34, or 34 and 55, or 55 and 89; most daisies have 13, 21 or 34, while Michaelmas Daisies have 55 or 89; and all Senecio plant species have 13 or 21 petals. Every single petal arrangement is a Fibonacci number again! Continuing, leaf branching off the stem—phyllotaxis—repeats the pattern. In determining phyllotaxis, count one leaf, then count how many turns around the stem (P) and how many leaves you encounter (Q) until you get to a leaf which is vertically directly above the first leaf counted. The "divergence ratios" (P/Q) of common plants are amazing, as both numerators and denominators are Fibonacci numbers: elm, linden and grasses, 1/2; beech, hazel, blackberry, and sedges, 1/3; apple, cherry, oak, holly, plum, and common groundsel, 2/5; poplar, rose, pear, willow, and plantains, 3/8; leeks, 5/13; leeks, almonds, and pussy willows, 5/13; cabbage, aster, and hawkweeds, 3/8. In fact, 92% of plants studied so far have "Fibonacci phyllotaxis," and actual occurrences are certainly higher considering the mathematics of plant growth became a field of study only in the 1990s. Not surprisingly, the literature is filled with comments like, "Why does 'Mother Nature' like using Phi so much?"—for the Qur'an warns us that disbelievers will simply say, *"What means God by all this similitude?"* (59:21)

In turn, the golden ratio is found abundantly in humans, accounting for virtually every relationship between parts of the face—for example the distance between forehead and nose, and nose and chin—as well as in the spacing of the finger bones, hand, and forearm between various joints. Fibonacci numbers dictate the number of bones in the sternum, vertebral column, cranium, upper limb skeleton, hand and wrist. And the golden spiral is evidenced in fingerprints, the growth of the foetus, and the shape of the cochlea (ear). Most critically, the DNA helix displays Phi twice: the cross-section of DNA is a golden spiral, and the length of one complete revolution is 34 angstroms, while the width of the helix is 21 angstrom—a perfect golden ratio of 34:21.

It seems, then, that despite Freud and Darwin, we are finding out what Pasteur predicted a century ago: "A little science takes you away from God, but more of it takes you to Him." Startling new discoveries reveal more about the simplicity than the complexity of the universe, for there is an all-encompassing harmony of design. Now God is back in academic circles as scientists openly discuss how Phi keeps popping up so frequently. The finding of this kind of self-similarity in the universe defies "rational" explanation and points to the most basic questions, as Stephen Hawking puts it: "What is it that breathes fire into the equations and makes a universe for them to describe?...Why does the universe go to all the bother of existing?" The Qur'an best answers these questions, for it tells us, *"many are the similitudes which Allah propounds to men, so that they may reflect"* (59:21). So science is strengthening—not shattering—the miracles now, giving even the most resolved atheist a reason to reconsider, and perhaps even a reason to believe. Pity my father has long since passed away.

THE SMALLEST MERCIES

Sometimes, you can feel grateful for the smallest things. I was once thankful for a single potato. I was pregnant with my first child, in an uncertain marriage, when I tracked down an old friend of my mother's, a woman who had moved to a run-down, one-room boathouse on an island, her nine children now scattered all over the world. She had no phone and hadn't been expecting anyone that day. With tears in our eyes, meeting again after almost 20 years, we shared her lunch— one large, soft, delicious baked potato—and talked about life. She spoke about watching the first yellow crocus break the ground every April, and being thankful for the incredible beauty of spring. For my mother and her generation, and even most of her own family, this woman had become eccentric, and an outcast. But I felt myself enveloped by her vision of the world as a sanctuary of small mercies. Unknown to me at the time, our views were distinctly Islamic. For in becoming grateful for every sign of beauty, comfort, or hope, we learn to recognize God's light on our path.

It's funny how we will thank a waiter for bringing us a glass of water, but we often won't thank our spouses or children for the same thing. It's a question of frequency and familiarity, isn't it? If someone you are close to gives you something simple every day, you begin to expect it. Maybe this is what happens to all the gifts God gives us, too. We take so many things for granted—from the air we breathe, to the lungs that pull in the air, to the new day placed before us. So how much of a gift do we need to receive from God before we say thank you? We're waiting for the new job, the new baby, someone's miraculous recovery, a great exam score, or travel documents, aren't we? But a gift shouldn't have to be so big before we will notice it. Most of us have looked through a microscope at least once in our lives. Everything is suddenly so clearly visible, broken down into components which almost miraculously seem large and obvious. Perhaps if we could somehow learn to look closely enough at our own lives, we would see even the tiniest components of mercy which are showered on us every day.

Imagine someone who is underemployed, working a warehouse job, although he is a trained scientist in his own country. Months of waiting for a "good job" turn into years, and he becomes distressed at his own fate and wonders if God is punishing him. One day, he runs into an old friend who tells him about a job opening. He takes the bus to the interview, wishing he had a car. He does as well as he can, but he is flustered at some of the questions because it's been a long time since he worked in his field. He returns to the warehouse, depressed and frustrated, and wondering why his life is so horrible. When he gets home that night, he is really upset that vandals have thrown garbage near his front door, and as he cleans it up angrily, he wishes he lived somewhere else. After more than one month, the employer still hasn't called. He feels his prayers are seldom answered, and his faith slowly erodes, enveloping his family in his despair.

Let us imagine another scientist working at a warehouse. Each day, he is thankful that he can provide for his family, and thankful for the co-workers who bring him tea when he is cold. He prays that God will always guide him, and that he will be worthy of God's mercy. One day, he runs into an old friend who tells him about a job opening. That night, he prays in gratitude for the joy of seeing his old friend again, and he thanks God for the gift of hope. On the interview day, he thanks God for a late shift which allows him to attend the interview without changing his schedule, and is thankful when the bus shows up on time, allowing him to arrive without stress. During the interview, he is thankful for every question he is able to answer well, and for the sense of humour that lets him softly pass over his faults. He returns to his warehouse job, grateful that another bus is on schedule, giving him time to change and eat before his shift. He is thankful for an easy shift that night, and for the comforting memory of an interesting day. Home again, he notices that vandals have spread garbage near his front door, but he is grateful that his family is unharmed, and he cleans it quietly. He continues at the warehouse, praying in thanks for every meal he eats, every gesture of affection from his family, and every bill he is able to pay. He is grateful for all that God does, seen and unseen, to help him every day, and he sees God's light so strongly on his path that he feels deeply contented and safe, for *"God increases in guidance those who seek guidance."* (19:76) Whether he gets the new job or not, each day will continue to offer him countless things to be grateful for. And as God grants him fresh grace along the path, he will still and always be grateful for each gift he moves beyond—the old job, the former house, past friends, and earlier opportunities. What more meaning than this can any life have?

In the Holy Qur'an, there are many examples of gratitude. Mary, the mother of Jesus, withdrew from her community to birth her child—alone, hungry and thirsty. A voice told her to shake the date tree beside her for food, and to find a rivulet under the tree. She didn't complain that the ground was dirty, or that she would have preferred the warm comfort of her own home. She simply thanked God for helping and protecting her. This is the essence of gratitude—to take notice of every good we receive and attribute it to God. In turn, the Prophet Noah prayed to be delivered his community. Yet God did not just give him a boat, ready-made, or somehow transport him to a new community. The mercies came as small steps in a life of struggle. Without a doubt, Noah was grateful for the guidance to build the boat, for the physical strength that allowed him to labour each day, and for each tree turned to lumber. And what of the Prophet Muhammad, who hid from his aggressors in a cave? God did not strike them dead to protect the Prophet, but instead inspired a tiny spider to build its web across the entrance, making it look abandoned. Clearly, acts of God are not always dramatic or glamorous on the surface, but they are always exquisite below the surface, for they are perfectly appropriate for the problem—exactly enough help, at precisely the right moment, for *"if anyone puts his trust in God, sufficient is God for him."* (65:3)

If we learn to see the small mercies in every moment of our existence, to break down the large events in our lives into component parts like this, and to be thankful for everything, then we will perceive each mercy we receive to be like a sign along the path, telling us that we are still travelling in God's light. Our gratitude will become like a power source, lighting up each individual step in a continuous motion towards God, who tells us, so essentially, *"Remember me, and I will remember you."* (2:152)

We will also really begin to understand the actual basis of submission, the idea of *"Insha Allah"* (God willing), which so many of us say each day, but few of us really live in our hearts in any consistent way. For submission is about surrendering our greed, pride, ambition, and desires, and—like unspoiled children—being grateful for the simple pleasures in life, for *"if you are grateful, God is pleased with you."* (39:7)

Of course, how we are all bound together by these mercies remains a profound mystery. For example, the Prophet Moses' people were granted manna from heaven for their provisions, for which they were grateful. As a child, I saw manna once—in the mountains of Quebec—and when it falls, it strikes a broad area. So there were probably people beyond Moses' community who felt the benefits of it, though they simply saw flies falling from above—neither a sign nor a reason for gratitude. Curiously, all under the same sky, the signs don't have the same meaning for all of us. Even more elusive, sometimes it is someone's benevolence which carries the mercy from God. For example, the Prophet Joseph was separated from his family and bought by a kind Egyptian, who raised him well, and through this, God *"established him throughout the land."* (12:21) At other times, it is someone's inequity which carries it forward. For example, a woman's failed attempt to seduce the Prophet Joseph led him to be imprisoned, where he was *"turned away from their snare"* (12:34) and kept secure. Sometimes, even a simple act of nature is a way for God to send a mercy forward, like the hunger of the whale which mistakenly swallowed Prophet Jonah, delivering him safely unto the shore. Equally mysterious, the journey from one mercy to another is an obscure thing to understand—Prophet Moses received such a huge blessing, as the waters parted for his easy passage. Yet the other shore was his safe home for only a short time, before other mercies, and further guidance, took him to far and many other places—one no less important than the other.

Clearly, life is infinitely complex and our understanding is limited, but *"God always completes His light."* (61:8) The grace of the Qur'an is that it gives such fundamentally good advice: *"Call in remembrance the benefits you have received from God so that you may prosper."* (7:69) It's a simple thing to do, really: thank God for everything. For in learning to be grateful for every small mercy, you will develop a perspective on life which will make you more patient, contented, profound, and enlightened. And you will soon delight in the sheer magnitude of the benevolence of God, the All-Merciful, in the life you have been given.

The day I brought my third child home from the hospital following his birth one January day, my first marriage was already in ruins. I sat
by my living room window, feeling apprehensive at what lay ahead—soon
to be alone with three young children, thousands of miles from family.
The dear friend who had shared her potato was now long dead. I stared
out blankly at my yard, watching my two older children playing outside,
my baby sleeping in my arms, asking God for strength and belief in myself.
As my eyes drifted across the white expanse covering my yard, I suddenly spotted it: one perfect baby daffodil, bright yellow, peering through
the top of the snow. It was quite out of season, and I hadn't planted such
a thing. Yet there it was, a perfect golden miniature daffodil. I held it in
my eyes for days, and I have held it in my heart forever since. It made me
happy in a way I cannot explain, and it made me feel hopeful, and safe,
like nothing else could. For while I never saw it in my yard again, it was
a sufficient reminder on that day that God is always watching, and if we
are grateful for the small things, God provides for everything.

SUPERSTITION

For me, the hardest part about becoming a Muslim involved "small things"—not big ones. The main ideas about God and righteousness were self-evident and even the transition to the headscarf was relatively easy. But it was really hard to stop saying "Good luck" in my very public work life. Yet if one genuinely submits to God's power and believes in fate, there is no such thing as luck. Practising Christians, Jews and Muslims all agree on this point, after all. Still, I realized quickly that saying, "God bless," instead of "good luck," was risky business—you can easily become the target of criticism for being "too religious" in the secular realm. So in order to sustain myself both spiritually and financially, I found myself self-editing and saying, "All the best" instead. Yet so many people seemed unsettled, as though I hadn't really said what they needed to hear. And I was left wondering about an evident question I ignored a few years ago, when I didn't really have a religious practice myself: How did superstition manage to push God right out of the mainstream?

Superstition is defined as a belief which is not based on reason, and which usually arises out of ignorance or fear. Some suggest that superstition stems from religious feelings which are unenlightened or misdirected—a sort of displaced religious tendency. It seems that when people stop believing in God, they are willing—and needing—to believe in anything, as Pope John Paul II once stated. Superstition leads to an "excessive scrupulosity in outward observances"—people who always wear a "lucky pair of socks" for job interviews, sports stars who always eat the same "lucky meal" before a game, etc. And it causes people to have an irrational belief in the ominous significance of particular things or circumstances, like black cats and broken mirrors. It seems that in the absence of faith, people find the world to be immense, mysterious, and inherently frightening. So they struggle to empower themselves with a false sense of control, a kind of insurance—a rabbit's foot instead of a prayer. Some writers even suggest that superstition is a symptom of a fundamental psychological weakness—a combination of a visceral human fear of the unknown and a refusal of responsibility. In other words, if everything depends on the stars, or on the roll of the dice, then what can I really do to change the outcome of my life? The manifest world is indeed something to be in awe about—but without the recognition that God is the Creator, humans can easily be overcome with impotence and confusion. And it is these essential conditions which breed superstition.

The current state of popular confusion cannot be underestimated. A recent Harris Poll (2003) of Americans found that 10% of men and 16% of women believe there is heaven but no hell; 22% of men and 20% of women believe there is one God but no Satan. Fumento (1999) found that overall, in the USA, belief in astrology is at about 37% and rising yearly, having doubled since 1976, with 17% believing strongly in fortune telling. This should come as no surprise since it seems that many people are really unclear about even the most essential facts of life. Erlich and Erlich (1996) state that a sort of "antiscience mentality" prevails, and a recent poll corroborates this: for example, 85% of Americans are unaware that oxygen is derived from plants and 47% do not believe that the earth goes around the sun once a year. As Carl Sagan (1996) writes, "We have arranged things so that almost no one can understand." So in the absence of any real knowledge that One God created everything for a purpose, people have improvised a pseudo-reality in which the paranormal is in control of the universe—luck, superstition, stars, and all manner of omens and portents.

In Italy, the heart of the Catholic Church, 1.5 million people regularly consult fortune-tellers and 60 million Italians read their daily horoscopes. About 17% of the population nationwide fully embraces superstition, which has become a $450 million-dollar-a-year business in this country, to such an extent that the government is concerned about the 97% of unreported tax earnings. As a former Christian myself, I actually met a number of people who had "lucky" rosaries. The ideological conflict is staggering. The church has officially responded to these alarming trends with the Pope advising followers to read the signs from God, not the wrong kind of signs, and warning followers that Satan is inducing them to chase after charlatans. Yet the frenzy is fuelled by Italian media who turn popular astrologists and fortune-tellers into the rich and famous of their generation.

In China, authorities are becoming increasingly concerned with the apparent link between belief in fortune telling and violence; reports are that 30% of murderers used fortune-tellers regularly, and many people commit acts of violence—including on themselves—after a prediction. In Bhubanneswan, India, in 1999, a Hindu woman committed suicide after two astrologers predicted she would become a widow. Stories like these make quick headlines in the media only as a hypocritical afterthought. For it is commonplace for journalists to manipulate reality to invoke fear and a dramatic response. Systematically, the media undermine individual empowerment and fuel helplessness, thereby driving people to respond with superstition to "protect themselves" from the apparent chaos of life. Reporters choose the stories they cover, the experts they consult, and the quotes they extract for publication. Fear is their lifeblood, as it is for multinational insurance companies. Overwhelmed by seemingly random tragedies around the world, people begin to believe that it is only "luck" which keeps them alive for this day while someone else has just been mutilated. Advertisers are eager to prey on this emotion, selling all kinds of products which "guarantee" safety, good health, and happiness, when all is really in our Creator's control.

As a response to the overwhelming power of the media, India, for example, has instituted strong regulations which state that "advertisers cannot take advantage of superstition or ignorance," and that there is to be "no advertising of talismans, charms, character reading from photographs, or other such matter, as well as those which trade on the superstition of the general public." And in Hong Kong, advertising regulations state that "words playing on fear or superstition should be avoided." But can simple rules really protect people from becoming victims of their own weaknesses? Hardly. Lottery sales in the USA, for example, are conveniently not subject to FTC regulations. And Atlantic Canada, the poorest part of the country, spends $419 yearly per capita on lottery tickets, as people choose their "lucky numbers" week after week.

In fact, the lottery is not the only big profit-maker in the business of superstition. Astrologers make more than the average doctor—up to $250 for a phone consultation, $100-$200 by email, and $200-$500 online, according to web advertisements. Other sites boast inexpensive online courses to train people as tarot card readers, and it seems that obtaining credentials is fairly simple—just pay $50 US for the "Apprentice Tarot Reader Examination," and you will be issued a certificate. So if it is widely known that so little expertise is required to become a "professional" in this field, one has to wonder at the depth of confusion which leads ordinary people to pay so much for the illusion of a guarantee about the future, though only God can grant such a thing—or for some kind of advance knowledge about what will happen next, though only God knows.

The essence of superstition is actually found in the deepest psychological problems. The superstitious person may do everything in threes, carry "lucky" objects about all day, whisper "protective" incantations, or repeat ritualistic motions, fearing that any small variation will bring on an unpredictable wave of evil. The parallel between these behaviours and compulsive disorders, schizophrenia, or neurosis are striking. So why, then, is superstition being fostered globally? Across communities, Hallowe'en is promoted—yet it is nothing but a ritual steeped in superstition—the belief that if we do not appease the dead, evil will befall us. Blockbuster horror movies serve the millions who pay to be frightened. Leaving the theatre, they see the world with different eyes—like children after a campfire story—imagining negative omens around them, rendering them more helpless than ever, fueling the belief—and need—for even more superstition. A recent study of young Britons[3] found that after exposure to Harry Potter, interest in casting spells and fortune telling rose by 12%. Even the very young are being dazzled by Yugi-Oh and his colleagues—casting spells and indoctrinating superstition into the next generation.

Truthfully, if we really want to learn more about superstition, we need to look to the birds—not the black birds which superstitious people believe to be portents of death, but to five simple pigeons. The famous behavioural psychologist, B.F. Skinner, decided to test the hypothesis that superstition was nothing more than basic conditioning in response to fear. He delivered food to caged pigeons at regular intervals, and watched each bird develop an association between the chance action it was performing at the time the food was delivered, and the food itself. One bird associated food with turning two or three times counter-clockwise in his cage, and another with thrusting his head into the upper corners of the cage. A third bird understood the food service to be related to a special tossing motion with his head, and two birds developed a sort of pendulum motion. Thus, in the absence of any understanding of the real world around them (the fact that they were part of an experiment, and that food would be delivered anyhow), these five pigeons became "superstitious"—each developing and acting out complex rituals to "guarantee" the delivery of food.[4]

It was hardly Skinner's aim to make a religious point here, but inadvertently he did. For the poor birds did not understand the essence of their lives, nor the scientist who was acting as the all-powerful being in their experimental universe, sustaining their lives. Likewise, in the absence of any real understanding about God or creation, superstition takes shape, as we are quick to assign meaning to the most arbitrary aspects of our lives— the shoes we wore when we received happy news, the calendar date when something bad always happens, the astrological symbol of people we love or hate, and so on. Perhaps we are simply so desperate for signs that we are ready to "read truth" into anything. But the Holy Qur'an warns us all that God makes His signs clear (2:221), not conjectural (6:148), and we need to shun all abomination (74:5). And astrology, luck, and omens are really a case in point of how we must beware not to incline towards those who do wrong or the fire may touch us (11:113).

Once we make such erroneous associations, and once we become superstitious, we are vulnerable to spending the rest of our lives in useless pursuits—like Skinner's birds—moving our bodies and mouths arbitrarily all day long. Engaged in such pointless practices, we will lose the opportunity to do what is really important. For unlike the birds, we have the chance to use our will to seek an understanding of God. It is only once we see every event in our lives with respect to our relationship with God that everything starts to make sense. We can simply choose to ask for God's help, thank God for what we receive, and ask God for protection from whatever frightens us. It's a simple, all-encompassing act of belief, trust, and submission, just to acknowledge that all the power is with God. Luck has absolutely nothing to do with it.

ONE HELL OF A GAMBLE

When the man who would become my husband started talking to me about the eternal fire of hell, I remember being shocked and working to restrain my comments. As a sort of New-Age, Buddhist-leaning, disaffected western Christian, I had evolved past this concept of hell years ago, as had my community. To us, hell was more of a symbolic thing, pretty elusive actually, and we didn't need to worry about it too much anyhow because we weren't going there. First, we believed in Jesus, and Jesus had died to save us. Also, as Catholics, we believed in purgatory, so even if Jesus's death left us with a few sins, in a worse-case scenario, we would just end up in purgatory for awhile—to wait, like a time-out, until we were let into heaven. And we didn't need to worry about purgatory much either, because every week we confessed our sins one-by-one, and the priest forgave us. So we might only go to purgatory for a short time for the sins we were too embarrassed to reveal in the confessional. Then there was also the growing possibility of rein-carnation—a pretty appealing idea which regularly came up at dinners and on long car rides. Under all of these assumptions, we lived comfort-ably, trusting that sin was an allowable, natural error, that forgiveness was an easy guarantee, and that the Bible was just exaggerating that nasty busi-ness about fire for literary value—kind of like Dante. Yet I wanted to show respect towards my new Muslim friend, so I listened, as someone witnesses a cultural experience—at times thinking it was intellectually interesting, and at times thinking that if he stayed in Canada long enough, he would eventually smooth over his primitive view and understand what I understood. Little did I know that the exact opposite would hap-pen. For his conversations aroused a curiosity that sent me looking for proof in the scriptures—the Bible and the Qur'an—only to discover the disturbing truth. Hell is real. And the denial of hell is based on scriptural distortions and illogical assumptions—conjectures of the grandest order—

which are tragically turning even devout believers into reckless gamblers who think that hell can be erased, reduced, or avoided completely.

In fact, it helps to picture a huge room full of gambling tables. It goes down a bit from where you are standing, like a pit. The lights are turned down low, so your eyes need to adjust for awhile before you can see anything at all. The mood is intense and chaotic. This is not one of those casinos where people have come to have a few drinks and blow twenty dollars. These are really high-stakes games, where everything is on the line. The players come from all different walks of life—but they have one thing in common. They all believe that they can win a free pass to heaven. Let's have a closer look.

The first thing you will notice is that the crowd in this place is staggering—much bigger than you would have thought. In the US, Barna (2003) polls reveal that less than one-half of one percent of people expects to go to hell. When asked what hell is, less than one third believes it to be a place of eternal torment, and the majority of people (64%) expects to go to heaven anyhow. The prominent Christian writer, Wayne Jackson (2003), writes that half of Americans no longer believe in hell at all. And in Canada, decades of research reveal that belief in heaven is generally 20% stronger than belief in hell—71% versus 53% in 1985, and 78% versus 60% in 1991—as people pick and choose doctrine like vegetables at a market. In Ireland, the gap is even wider, as 85% of people believe in heaven, but only 53% believe in hell.[5] And in the US, only 45% of people believe in God[6], but 52% believe in heaven[7] —meaning, in effect, that 7% believes in eternal bliss without any consideration of God or any fear of punishment. This kind of logic can only come about when people stop referring to authentic sources, so it shouldn't surprise anyone that ordinary Britons hold friends (46%) and Princess Diana (13%) as being more inspiring than sacred texts (6%).[8] The tabloids at the casino gift shop are selling fast, it seems.

As with any kind of casino, this place includes a share of players who think they have the games figured out. These are highly educated, intelligent people who are over in one corner ranting about the alleged injustice of hell, and they are stirring up the crowd. Since hell is harsh and cruel, with no chance of remediation, they argue, it maligns the character of God and even suggests a kind of sadism. In essence, they insist that the idea of eternal punishment is impossible to reconcile with the concept of a benevolent God. The logic put forward is that if we are under constant threat of punishment, our love and trust in God will suffer; therefore, a threat of punishment must not exist. The crowd here actually includes a lot of upstanding members of prominent faiths, as well as most of the people alive today who describe themselves as materialists or modernists. There isn't much point, it seems, in reminding them in the midst of the rhetoric that strict parents still enjoy the love of their children—they can't hear you above the sound of their own voices. A lot of novice players are flocking towards these folks, too, because everyone wins at this table— no hell, no problem.

Next, you turn your sight and notice that, like other casinos, there are some tricky numbers games over in one corner. It seems the players are moving words around quickly and counting things—like balls hidden under moving cups. The first game involves the 23 occurrences of the word "hell" in the Bible. It turns out that this is a translation of three separate Greek words: "Hades," which occurs 10 times (as in Luke 16:23)— a place of non-existence, with no fire and no screams; "Tartarus," which occurs only once (in 2 Pet 2:4), as a place where fallen angels go for punishment; and "Gehenna," which occurs 12 times (as in Matt 5:22) and literally refers to a valley near Jerusalem previously used to dump criminals. Focusing their eyes on literal interpretations as the cups move quickly, players conclude that eternal punishment was never mentioned in the Bible. The next game plays with the 64 occurrences of "sheol" in the Hebrew Bible. In 32 cases, it refers to an eternal fire, and in 32 cases it does not (three times to a pit, and 29 times to the grave). Betting on these 50-50 odds, players conclude that eternal fire is doubtful and therefore nothing to worry about. The third numbers game involves the 70 occurrences of "aionios" in the Greek Bible—translated as eternal or everlasting. Since the majority of occurrences (42) are in combination with "zoe"— meaning life—players conclude that life is eternal, but not punishment. Another numbers game looks at the 504 occurrences of the word "eternity" in the English Bible; it is used 394 times as an adjective, and 110 times as a noun—once in the plural. These mixed uses—and the odd pluralization of eternity—create just enough confusion and ambiguity to dismiss eternal punishment. Yet another numbers game looks at the six schools of thought which arose within 300 years of Jesus; since only one of them believed in eternal punishment, the doctrine is rejected five to one. Ever vigilant, there's even a bunch of accountants sitting over at their own table, working to invent new numbers games for the scheduled expansion of the facility. They are seriously looking at revenues, and they agree unanimously that a scary hell is really bad for business, keeping away the patrons. After all, just look at church attendance these days. So they're thinking of a new game where people play for matchsticks and there's no dress code at all—anything goes. Like in any business, it seems, to keep up in the hell gamble these days, you've got to give people what they want—a reduced version of hell to fit the reduced version of sin.

So your eyes move around the room again and you notice a very quiet and dignified group of people playing cards and smiling inwardly—they must have an ace up their sleeve. You inquire and find out that they believe eternal life is automatic upon the acceptance of Jesus Christ, so hell is inherently negated for them (Rom 8:2). Since the only ones in hell will be those who have not accepted Jesus as their savior, these folks are generous and careful to put aside some of their winnings every hour to sponsor missionary work around the world to save others. But ask them why Jesus himself warned his own followers about sinners going to hell and implored them to do whatever actions they could to avoid hell (Matt 5:22, 5:29, 10:28, 18:8-9, 23:15, 23:33; Mark 9:44-48, etc), and they become strangely silent before deciding which one of them will politely explain the rules to you again. In that momentary hush, you will hear the soft laughter of a few people sitting among them. They're happy because with or without Jesus, they have a sure-fire win in the idea of purgatory, a kind of cleansing place which allows them to avoid hell completely. There's not much point in telling them that purgatory was invented over a thousand years after Jesus by ecumenical councils.[9] It's a hugely comforting concept, so they're not ready to give it up—and besides, it's benefited the church so much, as sinners have paid hefty cash "indulgences" to have their indiscretions forgiven and their days in purgatory reduced, turning sin into a multi-million dollar industry long before music videos were ever devised.

Finally, no casino would be complete without its share of distractions. There are television screens blasting hellish images—random destruction and murder, horrific scenes of babies with their bodies blown apart, and people on fire—while you try to concentrate on the games. If you look at the screens long enough, you can lose track of the gamble you're playing and start to think that it's a hell of a life anyway. So you stay at the casino much longer than you should. The place is also full of people walking around, trying to sell you cheap goods while you're in the middle of your turn, working hard to empty your pockets, blasting their advertising slogans: "This is one hell of a great cell phone…" "Just buy it for the hell of it…" "You'll have a hell of a time if you…" "If you don't do this, there'll be hell to pay…" "If you're feeling sore as hell, just take two of these and…" "Our product is guaranteed to last until hell freezes over…" "Our new athletic wear lets you give them hell…" "Without this tool, you won't have a hope in hell…" "When all hell breaks loose, just dial…" "If weeds scare the hell out of you, then…" "We're sure as hell you will love this set of knives…" "We're hell-bent on giving you great service…" "If your last insurance company put you through hell, then…" "Our new van is hell on wheels…" "If you're wondering what the hell you're going to do when you retire then…" "If you don't know how the hell to get a stain out, then…" "Our new wireless service lets you raise hell and…" "If you want rodents and pests to get the hell out…" And so on. The subliminal message in all of the advertising is clear: hell is everywhere, and therefore, nowhere. And then there are the promotional bits which come over the loudspeakers periodically, as carefully timed as electroshock. One set tells you that you have only one life, which was given to you for your enjoyment: "If God didn't want you to have sex and wine and limitless freedoms, He wouldn't have given you these things, right?" a deep voice suggests. "You're not going to hell, so relax." The other set of radio messages hint that recent discoveries suggest you may actually have more than one life: "Haven't you ever had that feeling of having been somewhere before?" a soft voice inquires. "If so, then you will have a chance to be punished, if necessary, and a chance to start over, if you need it, so that eventually you will end up in heaven. You're not going to hell, so relax." It doesn't seem to matter to anyone that the messages contradict each other—is it one life or many? Everyone is happy enough just to hum along the slogan as they gamble: "You're not going to hell, so relax."

Of course, this kind of business operation is hard to administer. There are countless people behind the scenes, working the lights, the music, the cash registers, and the restaurants—and mostly, there are a lot of security staff walking around trying to handle all of the obvious paradoxes and contradictions. Every shift is busy, though they are a massive crew. One security officer is dealing with the concern that at the numbers table, 32 verses are not enough to convince players that hell is real—but at the card table, two verses (2 Macc 12 and 1 Cor 3: 13-15) are enough to convince them that universal redemption is real. Someone has dared to suggest that the game may be fixed. Another officer is handling a complaint of bias: it seems that no one has trouble accepting the idea of being rewarded forever—only of being punished forever. Eternity, in other words, is being selectively applied. Across the room, an experienced officer is trying to settle a small dispute between two first-time gamblers— one who thinks that sinners will be annihilated when they die, and the other who thinks that sinners will suffer eternal torment. The officer firmly tells them both to just relax and have a drink on the house. The same officer is then suddenly called to a back table where a woman is insisting that it's odd how people deliberately use only literal interpretations of the Bible when they want to discard hell, but they deliberately use only symbolic interpretations when they want to justify the Trinity. She is forcibly removed from the game and sent to the bar for correction. Meanwhile, another officer attends to a table where someone has brought their two teenagers with them, clearly against house policy. What's more, the teens are moving between the numbers games and the card games, pestering people with their remarks. One of them apparently said, "Why do you even care if hell is eternal or not, or whether it has a fire in it or not, if you think that no one is going there anyway?" And the other teen reportedly said, "Why do all of these professors think they know what the Bible says about hell if they can't even agree on what eternity means?" So the disruptive youth are taken away to play death games at the video-arcade in the lobby.

By now, the crowd at the bar is building, and they've started telling hell jokes. "How can there be any old people in hell? After all, the Bible says there will be gnashing of teeth (Matt 25:30), but they have no teeth to gnash!" Everyone snickers. Another minor disturbance is then reported at one of the numbers games. It seems that a bunch of tourists from different countries are trying to explain to everyone, in broken English, how the counts of individual words are different in their versions of the Bible. This is obviously slowing things down a bit for the regular players, who are getting annoyed. The biggest disturbance of the night, though, is at the front door. It seems that a young woman, dressed conservatively, has somehow gotten past security. And as people enter the casino, she is handing them a flyer which asks, "If it's true that God never gets angry and God never punishes us, then how can we explain the stories of Moses, and Noah, and Lot, and all the great prophets?" Dismissing her as just another doomsday type, patrons ignore her politely as she is escorted out.

Why not step outside the casino with her for a minute and have a look around? There's a lot of activity going on here. The streets and buildings are full of hard-working people who avoid the hell-gamble entirely because they just don't think that you can win heaven that easily. They are from all different faiths, actually—people who believe that to earn God's favour, you have to restrain yourself and work righteousness in this life, and if you don't, you will be seriously at risk of going to hell. The funny thing is that a lot of these people are actually reading the very same Bible as the folks inside the casino. Yet they find proof there that hell exists as a severe chastisement from God for anyone who chooses the wrong path, even if that person believes in all of the prophets, including Jesus. And they don't have any trouble with the idea that a just and loving God could also put us to the test, and judge us harshly when we fail.

But most of the folks outside the casino have the Holy Qur'an on their favourite book list. The Qur'an does not argue the particulars of hell, but simply gives a few examples of penalties—such as boiling drinks (6:70, 14:16, 44:45, 55:44), hot smoke and horrid smells (40:72, 56:43), and terrible heat and flames (14:50, 17:97, 22:19, 23:104, 54:48, 56:42), as it paints word pictures for us in human terms so that we might begin to understand divine ideas. Then, in a clear and definitive summary, the Qur'an states that there will be *other penalties of a similar kind* (38:58)— in other words, the exact temperature of hell is hardly the point here. Neither does the Qur'an entertain a debate on eternity nor on whether we will be annihilated versus tormented for ages. Simply, it states that in hell, we will suffer humiliation (4:151, 22:57, 58:16) and chastisement (14:17, 45:10, 58:15), and those therein will be *"neither alive nor dead"* (20:74). More than anything, the Qur'an does not invite a discussion of the relative merits of hell or the "morality" of God's character, for ultimately it is not God Who has been unfair, but the sinners who have been unfair to themselves (43:76). Whether or not we personally think that hell is a good idea, or even a fair one, is truly irrelevant, for *"whatever God does is good, whether or not man can understand it,"* (Isa 55:8-9)—or, put another way, *"It may be that ... you may dislike something which is good for you"* (2:216). The fact that hell is hard for us to accept is a problem with our limitations—not God's—and the cafeteria-style religion which has resulted from our reluctance to embrace faith wholeheartedly is an error of the highest magnitude. As we pick over beliefs for the sake of comfort and convenience, and substitute the manmade "doctrine of eternal security" in place of the divine Doctrine of Eternal Punishment, we are gambling away the only real security we will ever have—that of being in the grace of God. Hell exists, whether we want to believe it or not, and the Qur'an warns that gambling of all sorts is an abomination (5:90). So is the hell gamble really something which anyone should be betting on?

A THRONE OVER WATER

A picture is worth a thousand words, isn't it? When you're trying to explain something complicated, it's important to have a visual representation. Imagine trying to communicate detailed plans for a building using only words, or attempting to teach surgery without pictures, models or demonstrations. The more complex the idea is, the more we need images to explain it. So how could we ever understand the revelations just from words? God's design for us is the most complex phenomenon of all, yet God wants us to understand it very well because that's the whole point of our existence. So, through divine wisdom, knowing our weaknesses better than we know our own, God mercifully gives us a picture to explain the meaning of life, drawn from something very basic that is all around and through us. And that is water.

First, water represents our connection to God. God created *"on a throne over water to try us, to see which one is best in conduct"* (11:7), testifying to the exalted importance of water, and we begin life in a cradle of water in the womb. As we mature, water is a metaphor for each of our responsibilities:

- To be steadfast: *"If you suffer thirst in the cause of God, God will not suffer the reward to be lost."* (9:120)
- To understand our opportunities in this life: *"God has made the ships subject to you, that they may sail through the sea."* (14:32)
- To keep the revelations as a guide: *"Rivers and roads are for you to guide yourselves."* (16:15)
- To be grateful for our blessings: *"The earth is humbled, then God sends rain to it and life increases."* (41:39)
- And to remember the Last Day: *"It is He who shows you thunder and lightning by way of fear and hope."* (13:12, 30:24)

Water and faith are inextricably linked, and throughout our lives, water—like faith—is our strength. When we are strained, we lose water through sweat or tears, and water loss in our bones is the most common sign of aging. Our hearts—the source of our intentions (33:5, etc.)—are water pumps (blood plasma is over 90% water), and dehydration causes the heart to harden and stop physiologically, whereas *"hearts soften in remembrance of God"* (39:23). In addition, water warns of the Last Day, through floods, storms, and drought: *"God will make them taste of the lesser punishment before the greater punishment."* (32:21) Ultimately, changes in water will signal the end of time, as our world will vanish *"as clouds pass away"* (27:88), and our life-giving water will *"boil with swell"* (81:6) and *"burst forth"* (82:3). Water ensures our resurrection, as rain brings life to dry vegetation (16:65 and others). And if we have proven our devotion, we will be admitted to a water-filled paradise of gardens beneath which rivers flow (2:25, etc.), lush green colours (55:64), springs (77:41, etc.), and fountains (56:18, etc.). If we have failed in this life, we will spend eternity in a place devoid of water—an eternal fire. Water defines our lives—not just here but in the hereafter.

Second, water is like the signature of God. First, consider that a sketch in a back room of the Smithsonian was recently authenticated as a Michelangelo because it used "incised lines with an edged ruler as the basis for construction"—a style used in just one other known piece.[10] Now, consider that the human body is 70% water on average over a lifespan *("Man is made from water."* (25:54)), and there is a 70% ratio of water to land on earth. Also, invisible "barriers" (pycnoclines) in the ocean prevent fresh and salt water from mixing *("Between them is a barrier they do not transgress."* (25:53, 27:61, 55:20)); and there is a barrier—a microscopic wall inside every human, animal or plant cell—which controls metabolic salt from mixing with water. If one key similarity can guarantee authorship for Michelangelo, don't these striking correspondences suggest that God made both man and his world? In addition, to protect the fresh water supply on earth, evaporation comes down again as rain, permitting life for plants (75-95% water) and animals (50-90% water): *"Every living thing is made from water."* (21:30) In fact, water is the mark of life we search for on other planets—for nothing living can survive without it. Uniquely, water is useful in all three states of matter—as a gas, liquid, and solid—whereas other substances are useful in only one or two states of matter. Water is the best solvent, so it is the ideal medium for underwater ecosystems, distributing nutrients and minerals optimally. Water is also the only liquid on earth that freezes from the top down instead of the bottom up, allowing aquatic life to survive under ice, to sustain rivers, lakes, and oceans through colder climates. In so many ways, water is uniquely essential to life, having the most unusual properties, and it is convincing evidence of divine design: *"Let man look at how God has provided water in abundance"* (80:25). In one Qur'anic parable, disbelievers are punished for stopping a thirsty camel from drinking. The story suggests that the relationship between a camel and water is blessed, and science agrees: camels can lose 40% of their weight in body water, whereas a 15% loss is lethal for any other animal; and when there is access to water, they can drink up to 100 litres in 10 minutes, swelling blood cells by 240%—while every other animals' cells burst at 150% or less. Again and again, like waves on the shore, water is offered as evidence of the divine.

Third, water is a depiction of salvation. Hydrogen and oxygen are both highly flammable, but joined together as water, they put out fires. Hot water burns deeply, yet cold water relieves burns. Mold grows in dirty water, but clean water kills it. Cold water causes frostbite, yet warm water heals the affected limbs. What other substance on earth is a cure for itself? The two opposing forces inside each water molecule reflect how good and evil oppose each other inside each one of us—and how we each have the cure for the problems we create for ourselves. For as obviously as we can distinguish between water which is hot and cold—or clean and dirty—we can choose between right and wrong.

Prophet Noah's overwhelming rain teaches that God is the best guide through difficulties. Prophet Jonah's journey over the ocean relates that when we make poor choices, God is our only hope of salvation. Prophet Job's healing water reminds us to be patient for God's help, and Prophet Joseph's fall into the well reflects the fact that our troubles can be a way for God to redirect our lives. Prophet Moses' life testifies that God can do anything, including making the impossible, possible, as he survived adrift on a river as an infant; made water spring from a rock; and parted the sea. And the rivulet offered to Mary, the mother of Jesus, as she birthed, is a good reminder that God's help can also come through the simple things all around us, if we will only ask and be thankful. Yet if we ignore God's message, water becomes a warning instead of a blessing, as terrible storms threatened Moses' people and destroyed disbelievers who rejected Prophet Salih. As only God brings rain, only God brings mercy—for water, like revelation, is *"a healing for those who believe."* (41:44)

Fourth, water is a witness to the power of God. The ocean can rock a baby to sleep, or become a tsunami lashing the shore. A strong river can shape canyons, carving passageways in the landscape, or build to furious rapids preventing all passage. A violent rainstorm can wash away a community, and deliver fresh water to another. A slow river can spill its edges to cover entire valleys, or dry to the very last drop, just as a fog thicker than smoke can fill the air one minute, then vanish without a trace. A trickle of water can build gigantic stalagtites in caves, layer upon layer, or wear away the strongest rock, piece by piece. The gentlest dew can fall at dawn, and violent hailstones at dusk. Water can make the most frightening sound of crashing thunder, or the most soothing sound of waves and fountains. And one microscopic drop of rain can split the light of the enormous sun into all of its colours, making a tiny, perfect rainbow as beautiful as any in the sky. As only God controls life, only God controls water, and we *"are not the guardians of its stores."* (15:22)

Sixth, water is a mirror of the meaning of life. Just as we look into water to see ourselves and the life below the surface all at once, when we study the revelations, we learn about this life and what is beyond it, all at the same time. In fact, anyone who looks at water long enough begins to adjust his or her sight to distinguish more of what is beneath the surface. It's the same for the revelations, which become deeper and clearer for any who make an effort to understand them. Interestingly, several hundred thousand unknown species, the highest species diversity rate per area, and the biggest mountains on earth, actually originate in the lowest ocean layers, where there is no light and we cannot see.[11] It's the same for our lives— there is so much more than we know right now, and we must learn to believe beyond what is obvious, and to *"believe in the unseen"* (2:2). In one of the most mysterious stories in the Qur'an, the Queen of Sheba imagines a pool of water and tucks up her skirt to wade in. But Prophet Solomon tells her it's only a glass surface with water beneath, or a palace, not really a pool at all—and the miracle of that moment convinces her to submit to God. The story reveals that water is a special symbol of revelation, with a meaning far deeper than our senses can ever capture.

Ultimately, water is a picture of the promise of God. Three great "pledges" in the Holy Qur'an are taken on water: *"By the firmament of the returning rain…"* (86:11); *"By the ocean with swell…"* (52:6); *"By the steeds that run and raise dust in the clouds…"* (100:1 - 4). These model the oaths we take before important testimonies, with one hand on a Holy Book, to attest we will speaking the truth. God's testimony is that the revelations are true, and water is the living book by which the promise is made. Water is a comprehensive proof for our senses, the image which succeeds where words only fail: *"If all the trees on earth were pens, and the ocean were ink, with seven oceans behind it to add to its supply, the words of God could not be exhausted."* (18:109, 31:27). Like rain, the Qur'an has been sent down in stages to support life.

In fact, there are so many parallels between the Qur'an and water that even puddles seem precious indeed, part of a magnificent masterpiece from the Greatest Designer. Water provides images which inform our hearts about the purpose of our existence, sketching for us in detail the connections between the *ayats* (proofs) of revelation and the *ayats* of nature. Each believer is an individual stream, and as God is the source of the clearest water on the highest mountain, so God is the ocean to Whom we all must return. God is our beginning and our end, and the cycle of water is really the cycle of life. Every one of our tears comes back as a raindrop someday, somewhere. There are few clearer pictures of God than this.

THE PULSE OF CREATION

Since time beyond records, humans have played games. One of these is an ancient form for a lone player clutching a bent stick. If the stick is thrown with ample force even against the wind, it returns, finding its master. It is a game man seldom tires of playing or watching, repeating the motion in ritual satisfaction and disbelief. It seems both curious and mysterious, for once something is thrown, it should keep moving in one direction. The force of our arm, after all, seems to dominate both the air and the stick, and we wilfully intend the direction of the release. But the stick, the boomerang, returns to the hand which set it aloft instead of continuing along an infinite linear journey—like an echo. We feel it's a contrast to everything we see around us, the ball rolling away, animals running from their predators, or ships heading out to space. But is it really such a different act of motion after all? For the ball, rolling with sufficient energy and without impediment or friction, would eventually circle the globe and return to us. The animal fleeing today, if able, would try to find its way back home. And the ship sent out to space would, in time, lose its fuel or its orbit and begin a slow decline, a return. Our world is absolutely full, in fact, of boomerangs—objects which set out for a journey only for a time, with a programmed return to their origins, experiencing life as an arc, a wave.

Movement which ritually rises and returns in wave forms is, ultimately, one of the defining attributes of our universe—a unifying feature—and the evidence for our senses and our minds abounds. All the particles of matter and energy which make up our world travel in waves—light, sound, electricity, magnetism, and everything else we experience—along with our own thoughts, brainwaves, and phenomena we are only beginning to uncover, such as the tiny strings which seem to articulate the dimensions of space and time. In fact, waves have become the focus of study for legions of physicists and mathematicians whose findings consistently hint that the universe is peculiarly common unto itself, remarkably similar in patterns and laws. They routinely observe, with devices designed to give man control over nature and himself, that the world strangely seems to be already controlled. For the rhythm of the universe is oddly constant, waveforms defining virtually every single part and process. So ubiquitous is the waveform, in fact, that the entire universe and all that is in it have come to be defined, even within the realm of the most materialistic science, in terms of wavelengths, half-lives, frequencies, amplitudes, ranges, periodicities, and spectra—as even sceptics are forced to admit that "nature loves the waveform." For it turns out that everything from iron to sunshine to heart cells can actually be defined by its own particular pattern, as every single atom can only emit or absorb certain wavelengths. So the wave itself has become the meeting place of Newtonian and Quantum mechanics, the basis of the ever-present scientific quest for a "Theory of Everything."

Yet a person need not be a scientist to make similar observations. The ocean is dramatically evident in every corner of the globe, the tides rising and releasing their load, waves forming every second since time immemorial. And the moon, whose orbit largely draws the earth's water into a waveform, is itself moving in an orbit which, like that of all satellites throughout the universe, will eventually decay and collapse. The stars scattered throughout the sky are no different, their lives rising to a peak of light only to begin the process of slow death a moment later, eventually to collapse on themselves, as will our own sun—whose life is patterned by constant internal seismic activity, wave upon wave of heat reverberating through its core. And day-by-day, we witness the presence of the moon and sun in a constant wave movement as daylight comes, goes, and returns, and as the full moon appears and recedes month by month—bold beacons of light rising and descending from our horizon daily, in a dramatic and continuing example of the waveform. With this ebb and flow of day and night, we witness our own shadows rising and falling, reaching heights and retracting, reminding us that we are inherently connected to the pulse of light by which the physical universe as we know it is sustained. In turn, rainbows—each wavelength of light forming a huge and spectacular waveform arcing through the sky—appear periodically as vivid witnesses, symbols for our minds and hearts. And always, our efforts to extend ourselves above the earth—whether it is simply by hopping, or throwing a hat into the air, or launching fireworks, or sending planes into the far reaches of the sky—are met with the resounding reminder of gravity, by which all motions away from the surface reach an apex sooner or later and come down again, in an enduring demonstration of the limits on our movements, and of the fact that there is a point where the wave will always break.

Throughout the earth, examples of the waveform are both scattered and abundant, as colours and patterns—all bound by waves—become the most intrinsic features by which we characterize our world. Birds, fish, animals and insects fill the air, land, and seas in constant motion, their migrations, which seem from our vantage point to be linear, actually forming perfect arcs, reaching an apex far from home and returning to the point of origin some day, some season. Moisture rises to its peak and returns as rain, in a constant pulse by which the earth is refreshed and nourished. And the land beneath our feet pulses, too, the earth experiencing continuous oscillations—volcanoes rising to their climax and receding, and pressures within the crust of the earth building to the point of breakage, then subsiding, forming hills and mountains, each articulating the perfect waveform by their shape, standing firmly as bold reminders of the pattern inherent in our world. Currents of heat rise through air, land and water, transferring and receding, sometimes causing temporary surges—heat waves, cold waves, floods, horrific storms and tsunamis—which, too, reach an apex and retreat. Meanwhile, the wind whips across the earth, shaping drifts of soil, sand, salt, and snow, creating waves on every stretch. And in a massive demonstration of power, ice ages overcome the earth in cycles, emerging, consuming, and withdrawing, in an overwhelming pulse of moisture across the globe.

In truth, every living thing depends on these waves of energy, light, heat, and water—every bacteria, tree, or beast upon the earth is driven by these pulses, great or small, which arise then dissipate, fuelling everything from the movement of salamanders to ion transfers. And organic growth itself mirrors the wave, as forms as varied as sunflowers and giraffes grow from seemingly nothing to their crest, then decay until they are returned to the earth—seeds grow to maturity, then become dust once again; fruit ripens slowly to perfection, then rots; and our own bodies reach their peak, then decline. In fact, not just individuals but entire communities and ecosystems reflect the waveform, cycling through stages of succession as they emerge or recover from massive catastrophes like fires and pollution. It is the same for other patterns of growth and physiological processes which are, by definition, described and predicted by waves— the beating heart, neural pulses, viral infections, bacterial epidemics, nausea, plagues, hypothermia, drug addiction, and drug withdrawal. And when creatures reproduce, the mechanism itself is facilitated by a rush of physical excitation which, too, is explained by a wave. Even inside each cell, it is the waveform which accounts for emergence, sustenance, and death, the process repeating itself in an infinite, cyclical arc as even the tiniest components of complex systems arise and die, allowing tissues, organs and bodies, in turn, to grow and die. And in a further, constant reminder, animal life is sustained at every instant by the steady flow of blood reaching corners of the body and returning, of nourishment entering and exiting, and of air rising and receding. In this way, every living thing experiences waves whereby energy extends out to its maximum and then is forced to retract, the pulse of each living thing, from its core to its surface, founded on an insistent arc.

In our everyday actions, we echo this wave, for we rise to eventually reach the peak of our endeavours, then wind down, returning to rest—sleep itself defined by a waveform. Workers exit their homes predictably, reaching their destinations, then return when their power has been spent. Our fishermen throw their nets and pull them home, as our farmers put out their herds and flocks and bring them in again. Even the machines we make are only capable of this kind of wave, operating for a greater or lesser time, until they assume dysfunctions or lose power. And even our best attempts to create perpetual devices are doomed to fail for they rely on the sun which—in fuelling everything from machines, to photosynthesis, to bioluminescence—inevitably creates waves of potential which day-by-day, cloud-by-cloud, extend and retract in an endless cycle. In our collective actions, we seem bound to the wave as well—the rise and fall of political power, dissent, poverty, resistance, racism, discrimination, crime, protests, conflicts, wars, independence, cultures, support, trends, innovations, and ideologies—in the patterns of settlement and migration, in market expansions and reductions, in the growth of local and world economies, and in the nature of change itself. And in the structures we erect, the arch remains the most pleasing, enduring, and inspiring form, adorning buildings of such beauty that they touch the heart beyond the eye, creating waves of marble, wood, and stone so distinctive and compelling that they are counted among the wonders of mankind.

Even careers follow the same rhythm, growing from nothing, building to success, and subsiding in time—and this is reflected in the cycles of popularity and talent of myriads of sports, music and movie stars, along with the fashions and values they advance, as icons of our generation continually ride the so-called "wave of popularity." In turn, our abilities to learn, think, understand grow slowly in time and reach a peak, only to recede again eventually. And the very nature of how we communicate—speaking and listening—are both defined in terms of waveforms, as is the manner in which we organize and store our memories, which come forth in waves triggered by the events in our lives, then recede again to the farthest corners of our minds. We experience the difficulties in our lives in such arcs, too—pain, doubt, anxiety, concern, fear, panic, shock, chaos, grief, resentment, remorse, loneliness, devastation, despair, and hatred—all begin slowly and build to a climax, only to subside mercifully in time. And it is the same for what we regard as positive: love, bliss, hope, relief, relaxation, compassion, charity, sympathy, praise, pleasure, peace and passion all follow the predictable curvature, rising and falling, again and again—just as our tears and our laughter, upon good or bad, begin, build, and then diminish along this same curve. Thus, in every aspect of our existence, we are held in the arc ourselves, riding a multitude of waveforms and defining harmony as a synergy between waves by which we experience deep feelings of peace, security, and comfort. Inevitably, then, the pulse of our lives echoes the pulse which enervates the physical universe, and we are bound together most fundamentally with the world which has been created for us.

Why is it that our world is defined so uniformly by the wave action of particles, processes, and phenomena rising and receding? Why is our world so harmonious that a plain shape which even a child can draw can explain a heartbeat, the path of a bee, thoughts, the colours of the rainbow, the life of the sun, the decay of radioactive isotopes, the beauty of music, the diffusion of radio and television broadcasts, the cycle of weather, the mineral composition of a rock, plant growth, fire, blood pressure, lightning, infections, and virtually all of existence, whether organic or inorganic, past or present? How else but by design could this world echo a single form at the essence of everything, whether it seems to stand in one place or vibrates at dazzling speed—and whether we can see it, or not? And where would the energy for the generation of so many waves, one interacting with the other, ever come from in a closed system where, among unifying principles, all agree that energy can be neither created nor destroyed? Surely, a wave requires an origin.

And as there is an origin, so must there be a point of return. If we learn only one thing from our reflections on this life, it must be this. For every single thing, whether living or non-living, embodies the waveform in its essence, and we are a part of this universe. Why should we expect something different for ourselves? On the material plane, we move from dust to dust, from tiny bits of cells, to our maximum ability, and back to specks of bone in the ground. But beyond this plane, our souls move from their source, creation, through the opportunities and tests offered to us in this life, then back towards our origin, to our meeting with our Creator. For it has been explained in all of the scriptures handed down to man that we have been deliberately set upon this world and we will all be brought back as in a harvest at the end of time, as and when God wills. We are here, after all, only for an appointed time, the outer limit of the wave defining our farthest reaches—the apex of our faith, and of our worship. And in the very shape of each wave rests our individual destinies, the actions controlled by our wills culminating in our sure return to God along a path which was defined for us at the moment of creation, as the loop curves slowly inward, imperceptible to our senses. For in this arc is written the very name of God, the only One Who existed before the multitude of arcs by which we exist. And always, our souls are moving, wave upon wave, with the pulse of creation.

THE MOSQUITO

As a Canadian, I have gotten used to the summer mosquitoes, and I can overlook a great many of them. But as a relatively new Muslim, I find them harder to ignore. My youngest child asked me, "Why did God put mosquitoes on this earth, if they just annoy us?" I began to look for an answer.

Perhaps one lesson to be learned from these creatures is the importance of *humility*. All power is from God alone, and we are so vulnerable. It takes us years to build strong ships to discover new lands, yet mosquitoes simply hop on trade winds and travel faster than we ever could; using only their muscles, they can cover 120 km in search of food. We imagine we are capable of so much, yet a tiny insect weighing only 2.5 mg is stronger than any of us, responsible for more human death than all other forms of animal life—including us. A bite injects saliva into the skin as an anti-coagulant, transferring parasites from one person to another and spreading malaria, heartworm, dengue fever, encephalitis, and yellow fever. Malaria alone infects half a billion people every year and kills someone every 30 seconds, up to 1.5 – 2.7 million people per year—or about 200 million in the last century. In contrast, armed conflicts only killed about 175 million people in the last century.[12] In fact, more than any single factor, the mosquito has limited settlement and immigration throughout history, and it continues to impede the economic stability of many developing countries. In some remote areas, where bite rates can reach 9000 per minute, unprotected people could lose half of their blood in two hours. And many famous men who thought themselves invincible have died from a single mosquito bite: Nimrod who fought the Prophet Abraham; the Roman emperor Titus; Alexander the Great; Dante Alighieri[13]; Oliver Cromwell, the "Lord Protector of England"; and Jefferson Davis, President of the Confederacy. Different species carry different diseases and will attack at different times of the day—and not all mosquitoes are deadly (only about 60 species carry malaria, for instance).

Different species also have specific habitats, particular ranges of attraction, preferred body parts for feeding (head, torso, face, etc.), and an attraction to slightly different scent combinations or "kairomones." In turn, people differ in their ability to attract mosquitoes, and each person's attractiveness changes over time. Individuals can develop partial immunity to different degrees, but the immunity is species-specific and strain-specific; as well, it tends to be temporary, fading when people move from one area to another. The human sickle-cell gene confers some immunity from malaria, but only if it occurs on one and not both chromosomes. A bite takes only .25 millionth of a litre, but the resulting illness may wipe out a person's memories, intellect, mobility, or life. Overall, the likelihood of luring a deadly bite from these so-called "flying syringes" certainly seems quite arbitrary. Columbus himself confessed in his journal that every mosquito troubled him, despite the perceived grandeur of his mission to claim the New World for Christian Spain, and they almost caused him to lose his religion. Yet the mosquito is strong argument for faith, rather than against it for it teaches us that there is awesome power in every form of life on earth, no matter how small. It also reminds us that our time on earth is limited, and we have no control over the moment of our death.

A second lesson we can learn is about the importance of *vigilance*. Beginning with Adam and Eve, the world has been a mixture of good and evil, as every aspect of the mosquito's life reminds us. The female mosquito's proboscis carries the blood protein which gives life to its infants and the saliva which brings death to its host. The clean water which is so essential to a man's life also births the mosquito which matures to kill his neighbour. The folic acid in a mother's womb feeds her baby as well as the malaria parasite that will eventually kill them both. The carbon dioxide by which plants grow and sustain our lives also draws the deadly mosquitoes which take life. The malaria which can kill us is also capable of killing the deadly syphilis bacteria and saving lives. Thus, the mosquito provides examples for a better understanding of a complex world where good and evil are often in the same place, at the same moment.

A third lesson is about the importance of *gratitude*. The mosquito, despite causing so much suffering, also brings benefits. Both genders eat nectar, so the mosquito is an active pollinator for tiny plants, and its larvae function as highly developed filter feeders, cleaning polluted water. Mosquitoes are an important food source for many beneficial animals: as larvae and pupae, mosquitoes supply aquatic ecosystems; and as adults, they feed frogs, birds, bats, dragonflies, and spiders. Incredibly, the mosquito is even able to eliminate AIDS in its own body as it digests HIV to prevent reinfection in the next host. The message is clearly that there is goodness in everything. For example, only the female bites, while the male is perfectly harmless. And though the mosquito may not seem attractive on your arm, its scaly wing under a microscope is exquisite in its detail, and its body is the ultimate in refinement, with six long legs, flight muscles, compound eyes, and a compound heart.

And for every difficulty God has placed before us, God has provided a remedy: naturally occurring vitamin B in human blood is a better deterrent than commercial repellants; and a one-kilometre-an-hour increase in the wind speed, a one-degree drop in temperature, or a slight acceleration in water currents, can eliminate more mosquitoes than any costly eradication project. Quinine, from the bark of the South American Cinchona tree, has been used for centuries to cure malaria. And the most important remedy is the 2000-year-old Qinghaosu, a relative of the wormwood tree which grows wild in the fields of China. The currently popular DEET products work only on contact, after the mosquito lands; however, a range products found in nature will actually keep them at bay: catnip oil, tea tree oil, eucalyptus oil, pennyroyal, basil, geranium, citronella oil, peppermint, and marigolds. Even more basic, washing hands and feet frequently is helpful as mosquitoes are highly attracted to methanethiol and isovaleric acid, the chemicals given off by the Brevibacterium Epidermis on dirty, smelly feet, and sweaty hands emit appealing trace substances. In truth, the best defenses against mosquito populations are inside the creature itself: it only lives about two weeks in the wild, and there are more than 200 parasites which destroy its larvae, preventing them from overwhelming the world. And so, the mosquito is a clear witness to the truth of the Holy Qur'an—the world has been created as an integrated unit, with many parts in balance, and there are naturally occurring solutions for every natural threat.

A fourth lesson is about the importance of *reflection*. There are 3400 species of mosquitoes; 100 trillion are alive at any one time; they (and their parasites) have been around for at least 30 million years; and they occur on every continent but Antarctica. In the US alone, the population is about 41,000 for every citizen! Their ubiquitous presence among us is a constant reminder to find meaning in ordinary things. Studying mosquitoes for even a short time, the idea that evolution and creation are mutually exclusive becomes absolutely untenable. The importance of natural selection is clear, but it is highly illogical—in light of the complexity and diversity of life—that all species would have evolved somewhat accidentally from common ancestors. For example, mosquitoes grow through four highly specialized stages, from egg, to larva, to pupa, to adult, and each stage has a unique apparatus for breathing; male and female mosquitoes are of distinctly different sizes, with major differences in antenna structure and mouthparts, so that each gender is adapted to its task; the female uses a receptor in her abdomen to sense humidity and temperature for egg-laying; and the eggs respond to water temperature, taking 7 – 60 days to mature, accordingly. In adulthood, their delicate sensors navigate by responding to minute differences in convection currents; and different insects have specific positions when they bite, with varying angles of the proboscis, according to their target prey. They respond to semiochemicals received by their antennae, seeking a ratio of key substances which is specific according to their species and habitat, and they remain completely disinterested if proportions are even slightly off. In particular, they sense carbon dioxide (which we exhale); dimethyl disulfide (issuing when thousands of species of human skin microflora break down proteins through oxidation); lactic acid and acetone (from sweat); estrogen and testosterone (which vary according to our gender); and various fatty acid esters (which adult fingers give off more than children's). At astounding distances of up to 30 – 50 metres, the mosquito can detect minute traces of these substances with more efficiency than million-dollar research programs and complex bioassays.

Even the mosquito's parasites are complex: at the Walter and Eliza Hall Medical Institute, they have been trying to unravel the malaria parasite's genetic structure since 1996. And interestingly, while the science of malariology advances through animal research, the model cannot be transferred to humans. Dr. Richard Levins, of Harvard states, "This may be a system where animal models don't teach us what's important for human disease.[14]" Thus, again, the mosquitoes provide us with knowledge so essential to life: humans are unique in this world, and the incredible diversity and specificity found in our world cannot plausibly be only the result of chance—there must be a divine origin.

Ultimately, mosquitoes are living evidence of three critical concepts for our existence. First, *time is relative.* We really have no definite idea about how long the universe has or will exist, or how long each of us will live. There are worlds within worlds, and in the time it takes me to earn one-week's salary, cook a meal, or blow my nose, an organism will have been born, lived its full life, and died. This is a parable for life on earth, which may feel like a long time, but on Judgement Day, will seem to have been merely a fleeting moment (23:112-114). Second, *space is relative.* We may selectively spray areas with pesticides and check air travellers for diseases, but the winds bind us all together, carrying parasites across the world. We have no thorough understanding of the size of the universe, and we need to see our earth, at least, as one single community, one creation—not a set of separate, self-sustaining "countries." For Europe, the first cure for the Old World's malaria came from the New World's quinine. Now, malaria may seem primarily like Africa's problem, where three-quarters of species and deaths occur, and shamefully, the World Health Organization's budget for the disease is only about 2 cents per infected person. But it is here, in the developed world, where we have the research tools—and the obligation—to provide a remedy to alleviate this staggering suffering. Third, *life is a test of faith.* It is surely no accident that the parable of the mosquito is mentioned at the very beginning of the Qur'an (2:26), as mosquitoes demonstrate an essential truth of Islam—that a short time of reflection can be worth more than a multitude of prayers. Truly, God has created this world for us—not so that we can abuse the environment according to our whims, but so we can make use of every detail to perfect our spiritual understanding and deepen our belief in God.

CHAPTER VII

Evolution

"O humankind! In due reverence for your Lord, keep
from disobedience to Him Who created you from a single human self, and from it created its mate, and from
the pair of them scattered abroad a multitude of men
and women. In due reverence for God, keep from disobedience to Him in Whose name you make demands
of one another, and (duly observe) the rights of the
wombs (i.e. of kinship, thus observing piety in your
relations with God and with human beings). God is
ever watchful over you." (4:1)

* * *

"Whoever uses sophistical arguments knowingly continues to be the object of God's wrath until he desists."
(From the hadith collection of Abu Dawud)

ORIGINS – PART ONE: IT BECOMES A BIRD

"*D*avid slew Goliath… And did not God check one set of people by means of another, the earth would indeed be full of mischief.*" (2:251) *"By the mystery of the creation of male and female…"* (92:3) *"He created you all from a single person."*(39:6) *"And in the creation of yourselves and the fact that animals are scattered through the earth, are signs for those of assured faith."* (45:4) *"It is He Who begins the process of creation, and repeats it."* (10:4) *"Or do they assign to God partners who have created anything as He has created, so that the creation seemed to them similar?"* (13:16) *"Now show Me what is there that others besides Him have created: nay, but the transgressors are in manifest error."* (31:11) *"Our Lord is He Who gave to each created thing its form and nature…"* (20:50) *"The variations in your languages and your colours: verily in that are Signs for those who know."* (30:22) *"He adds to Creation as He pleases: for God has power over all things."* (35:01) *"Just ask their opinion: are they the more difficult to create, or the other beings We have created?...Truly does thou marvel, while they ridicule…and when they see a sign, [they] turn it to mockery and say, 'This is nothing but evident sorcery!'"* (37:11-15) *"O Jesus the son of Mary! …Thou make out of clay, as it were, the figure of a bird, by My leave, and thou breathes into it and it becomes a bird."* (5:110)

The odds are that somewhere in the world, in any given week, a magician is showing his audience how he can make a beautiful dove appear seemingly out of nowhere. People have a fascination for magic shows, don't they? If you've worked backstage, you'll know there's a small cage being taken from town to town, and hundreds of hours of practice. But in a moment of receptive innocence—for children, and for the child within—it truly seems extraordinary how a person can make the loveliest of creatures from nothing—a pure, white, perfect bird—and then set it aloft above the audience, to perform one of the most breathtaking actions any living thing is capable of doing—flying. It's easy to be dazzled, and we can't help wondering how it's done. We're looking for that "Ah-hah" moment, right? These days, a lot of people are feeling similarly bewildered at the rapid course of scientific progress. In my lifetime, scientists have cloned a sheep, for example. The sheep has now died, so I guess it wasn't some kind of a super-sheep, and it might not even have been particularly content. But it was still a good-looking sheep. It cost millions and millions of dollars to make—"Dolly" she was called—and countless hours of energy and direction from some of the world's most brilliant minds, but they did manage it. The news went out quickly around the globe, and a kind of collective "Ah-hah" rang out among the public. It seemed to be the ultimate anti-God statement, for sure. If we can do what God supposedly did, then life is a lot less mysterious than what the scriptures say. If we can make these things, then maybe creation doesn't require God at all. Maybe, it's just a sort of logical scientific process. So now, evidently anxious to prove mankind is all-powerful, scientists keep cloning all kinds of things, both publicly and privately, as a lot of scientific energy and funds are being pumped into proving, either deliberately or incidentally, that God is either not responsible for creation or nonexistent. And while they haven't yet been able to make a man out of a monkey, or a bird out of a reptile, I'm sure that's on the to-do list in some lab somewhere.

In fact, the whole spectacle of creating animals from clones is starting to look quite a bit like, well, a spectacle. Scientists turn up like showmen on the nightly news, and faced with the increasing complexity of knowledge in the digital era, we all start to feel like an innocent audience ourselves. On the whole, it's becoming more than somewhat reminiscent of the period of human history when alchemy was held as a legitimate branch of science, and everyone from Aristotle on down tried to make gold out of virtually every kind of rock, while the willing public waited with baited breath to watch man demonstrate his power over matter. Even Isaac Newton found himself attempting to create gold from mercury, silver, lead and sulphur. So it seems the temptation to control by one's own hand is pretty strong. While Newton never succeeded, a certain Judith Temperley apparently did, in the 1960s. The reason we don't see a lot of mock gold on store shelves, though, is that she had to use an extremely expensive electron accelerator under considerable safety constraints to bombard mercury repeatedly with high-energy neutrons so that she could eventually displace just one proton in order to reduce one single atom of mercury (atomic weight of 80) to a single atom of gold (atomic weight of 79). Using this process, it would apparently take about 10 (add 23 zeros) years to create one penny's worth of gold[1] — not a very practical process, really. And since it turns out that changing things to gold requires atomic conversion rather than a lot of heating, stirring and incantations, there really isn't any other way. Therefore, it isn't that we can't make gold at all, but the way in which we make it isn't mathematically realistic. And so it is with genetics. It isn't that we can't create organisms, but when we do, it takes a really, really colossal amount of time and effort. Yet according to evolutionary theory, these things must have, and did, happen spontaneously, without direction or organization from outside, in a sort of primitive environment of loose molecules and turbulent weather. Really, just thinking about this stuff should make us feel at least a bit humbled by the awesome diversity around us. But instead, it just fuels further debate about whether God had anything at all to do with us all being right here, right now.

Yet speaking out against current evolutionary theory these days is dangerous. The line between creationists and materialists is drawn right at Darwin's feet, and the court system is being liberally applied to silence anti-evolutionary sentiments as a kind of modern heresy. The funny thing is, though, that no one is denying the idea of natural selection— the phenomenon that Darwin originally witnessed while watching finches on the Galapagos Islands. Without a doubt, Darwin was rightly inspired in concluding that some traits within the expressive range of a creature's genetic make-up help it survive better than others in a particular environment. And a creature which survives has a chance to find a mate, through which the offspring have the opportunity to inherit this characteristic. This is a demonstrable fact. Everyone also agrees that mutations can and do happen. What's not quite so much of a fact, however, is whether or not successions of small (and not necessarily or immediately adaptive) changes caused by random mutations can actually result in the evolution of a whole new species eventually, and then another, and so on. Right now, the fact that we can look at the human genome and figure out some of the genes responsible for common diseases is seen to support evolutionary theory because it shows us the connection between genetic material and the material world. And, in essence, as we understand more about genetic coding, the implication is that we just need a bit more time and the right computers to be able to model how the very first unicellular organism mutated, and its offspring mutated, and eventually all this serial mutation resulted in life forms as diverse as a praying mantis, a jellyfish, a crocodile, a hummingbird, a rhinoceros, a man, and all of the other various species on earth. And for over a hundred years, anyone resisting the theory has been labelled as unscientific, undereducated, religiously fanatical, or worse.

A most interesting point about all of this, however, is that in a personal letter, Darwin actually admitted the possible weakness of his theory: "The sight of a feather in a peacock's tail, whenever I gaze at it, makes me sick."[2] Was Darwin intuitively concerned that he might never properly account for the refinement of some intricate features such as the feather? Proponents simply explain that he initially found it hard to justify why "expensive" (energy-demanding) structures on some animals—like the peacock's tail—would be selected through evolution. So to try to explain the preservation of apparently impractical traits, he conceived the idea of sexual selection—that the peacock's elaborate tail gave him an advantage in attracting a mate. While this idea couldn't account for vestigial (useless) organs such as the human appendix—of no apparent value in mating—it did establish the importance of effective breeding as a cornerstone of evolutionary theory. Ironically, however, the truth would turn out to be quite different. For it is precisely because of sexual reproduction that Darwin's theory begins to falter rather than fly. The reason is that species complexity is not so much *impossible* as the result of small, random, sequential processes. Rather, it is a statistical *improbability* of the highest magnitude, especially when we consider how traits are passed on hereditarily. To understand why this is so, we need to refer to one of Darwin's contemporaries, an Augustinian monk considered to be the father of genetics and the first-ever bio-mathematician, Gregor Mendel.

Thanks to the discovery of DNA in the 1950s, it's now common knowledge that each living cell carries genetic data. During reproduction, genetic material from each parent is split in half, so the offspring gets a combination from both, and inheritance refers to this transfer of information from one generation to another. Mendel didn't have an electron microscope, but he nonetheless brilliantly inferred the existence of genes (he called "factors") in his critical work with hybrid pea plants in 1865. His ground-breaking discovery was that heredity produces mathematically predictable patterns—in other words, we can anticipate the characteristics of the offspring statistically based on parent characteristics. Further, since each gene works in tandem with the corresponding gene at the same location on its pair chromosome, we can also observe that some forms of a gene are dominant, while others are recessive. For example, if a pea plant with two identical forms of the gene for determining yellow pea côlour (YY) is cross-pollinated (sexual reproduction in plants) with another pea plant with two identical forms of the gene for green pea colour (GG), all the offspring of the first generation (F1) will be YG, obtaining one chromosome from each parent. Critically, however, since yellow is the dominant pea colour, the first generation (F1) will all be yellow, and the green "recessive" trait will be completely masked. If the F1 generation is then self-pollinated (inbreeding YG with YG), then four combinations will occur every time in a highly reliable 1:2:1 ratio: 1 YY (yellow): 2 YG (yellow): 1 GG (green). It is of vital importance to notice that the recessive green pea colour trait finally becomes evident only in this second generation (F2), only with inbreeding, and even then, only in ¼ of the offspring. And if the F2 generation were the result of cross-pollination instead (combining YG plants with random YY, YG and GG plants from the "gene pool"), then the green trait would be even less visible. This is because YY plants pollinated with YY, YG, or GG plants yield only YY or YG offspring, all of which will be yellow; and YG plants pollinated with GG yield ¾ yellow plants. In fact, only GG plants combined with other GG plants ever consistently demonstrate the green-coloured pea. In all other cases, the dominant gene masks the recessive gene, especially if breeding is not restricted to related individuals. Put another way, a recessive trait will be completely invisible to the naked eye unless it is expressed. And if the mother and father are unrelated, it will remain recessive for generations. Yet a trait which is not expressed cannot be selected. Further, the yellow pea colour will be represented by more than one "genotype"—both YY and YG. This means that a specific genotype, by definition, could never be reliably selected over another, though evolutionary theory requires exactly that. What Mendel proved critically, then, is that the physical expression of some genetic variations is not mathematically favoured by inheritance. So sexual reproduction actually makes evolutionary theory much harder to prove, not easier.

This brings us to the consideration of mutations. A change in genetic material is normally one of four kinds: single base mutation (a base along a single chromosome is substituted by another base); insertion/deletion ("indel"— bases are added or removed, singly or many at a time); duplication (segments of a chromosome are repeated); or translocation (a piece of chromosome is moved to the matching chromosome in the pair, sometimes entailing a reciprocal change). Under normal life conditions, mutations can and will occur, yet most are hardly noticeable for two main reasons. First, a lot of DNA apparently has either very little regulatory or identifiable function—perhaps 95 -98% of human DNA, for example.[3] Secondly, and most importantly in terms of evolutionary theory, chromosomes work in pairs; so if there is a change only on one of the chromosomes, the intact chromosome will often compensate for the function and mask the problem. This phenomenon is frequently observed by animal breeders, for example, when mutations occur on the sex-linked chromosome pair. In these cases, the gender with two variants of the gene (the XX human female; or the ZZ bird male; etc.) demonstrates the variation much less often statistically than the individual with only one of the genes (the XY human male; the ZW bird female; etc.). Compensation means that an offspring which inherits a mutated chromosome from one parent and a standard one from the other parent will be more likely to have the new trait repressed rather than expressed. And a trait which is not manifested cannot give an individual a selective edge—where there is no competitive advantage, in other words, evolution should not be observed. This poses particularly significant challenges for the supposed evolution of complex structures, like a bird's wing. The prerequisite genetic changes presumably would have happened in stages— no lone reptile woke up one morning suddenly capable of flight. Yet at each phase, any genetic change which was not physically evident or applicable (e.g. a slight shift in the shape of the sternum, the minor elongation of an abdominal muscle, a minute increase in lung volume, etc.) could not give the individual a survival advantage, and could not deliberately be preferred by a mate. Add to this the fact that most body functions are controlled not just by one gene but by many; dog breeders, for example, have identified nine genes just for coat colour. And consider, too, all of the necessary changes at the cellular level—the increase in glucose and oxygen intake for a rising metabolism, for example—which wouldn't be evident nor confer any kind of immediate advantage. Clearly, the odds of all the required genetic changes—most of them invisible, actually—being selected at the same time is extremely minute because mathematically speaking, each of these intermediate stages in development clearly would not be favoured by inheritance. Yet evolutionary theory requires just that: the preferential selection of countless subtle, silent, and even simultaneous genetic variations.

We must also consider whether or not a mutation will compromise an individual's health. The consensus among researchers, across thousands of experiments and investigations, is that mutations are usually harmful. In all except very rare cases, mutations lead to an impairment of function rather than an enhancement, as even common logic dictates that changes which are accidentally introduced into any complex mechanism will interfere with normal processes. Hermann Muller won the Nobel Prize in 1946 for his experiments on millions of fruit flies under intense radiation, yet he never found even one useful mutation. The reality is that most mutations are silent and when they are expressed, the change is usually too small to be detected. But when the change is detectable, it normally confers a disadvantage (Ho-Stuart, 2003)—rather than the advantage which Darwin's theory presumes. Evolution requires millions of beneficial mutations all working together to enhance and create delicate living systems, somehow accumulating elegantly to steer species differentiation. Yet modern mathematics exposes a quite opposite reality, for mutations are statistically seldom favourable, and therefore fail to reliably confer the survival benefits which evolutionary theory demands.

For the sake of argument, however, let's assume a situation where a beneficial mutation is actually manifested because the mutant gene functionally dominates the normal gene (eg. Mn—M =dominant mutation; n = recessive normal). As mutations typically don't have a blanket effect on a population, the variant individual will likely only have access to mates which are unmodified (nn), resulting in offspring which are 2 (Mn) and 2 (nn)—only half exhibiting the mutated trait. Through normal breeding for the second generation within the gene pool (other nn),

the F2 generation would be even more diluted—2(Mn) and 6(nn)—
only ¼ exhibiting the mutation. In other words, random selection of
mates yields mathematical results which reduce the prevalence of the
mutation in a population rather than increase it. The F2 generation would
only favour the mutation if the population were isolated and mating
were artificially restricted to those exhibiting the variation (like in Mendel's
experiments). In such closed populations, where inbreeding is prevalent
for several generations, so-called "founder's effect" does actually result
in the over-representation of the variant genes. This explains how Darwin
found evidence of unusual traits in the local finch populations of the far-
flung Galapagos Islands. But rather than confer an advantage on the population, the loss of genetic variety which results from such a limited gene
pool—as noted in the world's cheetah populations—is widely acknowledged to lead to poor health and lower reproductive rates. In any event,
without scientists to manage segregation scenarios, or massive geophys-
ical changes isolating each and every population on earth at every stage
of a mutation, the reality is that mathematical models of inheritance
make evolution-by-cumulative-mutations a statistical implausibility.

Perhaps more tenuous still, this model assumes that a visible variation will be attractive to both the caregiver and to prospective mates. But
can we assume that any mother would happily raise an offspring with an
unusual trait? Or, as it often witnessed in the animal kingdom, would
she simply neglect the care of the child perceived to be the lesser of her
brood? Would she, in fact, abandon it to the closest predator or to starvation, assuming the difference to be a liability? Yet for evolution to
occur, variations must minimally be accepted by rearing adults. And
what of the search for mates? Would a pea hen really be attracted to the
first male who had a huge feather sticking up his back side, over the others who looked normal? Or would her mating instincts drive her to continue her species within her own instinctual understanding of species
parameters? The natural world is surely full of evidence that mate choice
is based primarily on compatibility, and that a lone variant individual is
more likely to be discriminated against rather than favoured. And if an
animal fails to breed—no matter what mutation has occurred—evolution will not happen. This problem is especially acute where intermediate structures are concerned. A huge set of abdominal muscles or an

alternate hand formation are just disabilities without the accompanying wing function—and that's just how animal mothers and mates would be most likely to see it. In other words, the idea that emerging variations are a positive thing is a cornerstone of evolutionary theory, yet there is little substantiation that sudden oddities would be anything other than a cause for concern among the community. Variant individuals, then, would become statistically reduced rather than reinforced, and this would be especially true during the transition stages in the proposed evolution of sophisticated structures.

It's no small wonder, then, that the peacock's tail made Darwin feel ill. For rather than creating new species, it seems that natural selection actually preserves existing ones. For as Mendel uncovered, the mathematics of genetics demonstrate that even if a beneficial mutation were to occur, it might not be visible in the offspring. If it were not visible or immediately useful, it could not confer a selective advantage in life or mating, and could not reliably be selected. Even if it were visible, a mother might not accept it. Even if a mother supported it, a mate might not still prefer it. Even if a mate preferred it, it would be underrepresented in the next generation. And even if it were represented in the next generation, it would be even less well-represented subsequently, except with inbreeding. And if there were inbreeding, within a few generations (if not immediately), the loss of genetic diversity would reduce population health and fertility—hardly an ideal start for a new species. Yet unless mutations—most of them invisible and ineffective for generations—can somehow be selected, there is no way for them to proliferate. And without effective breeding, there is no Darwinian evolution.

Far from changing species, therefore, natural selection actually seems to stabilize them. In a way, it's almost as though natural selection and evolution are completely incompatible. After all, natural selection states that variations which confer advantages will be preferentially selected over forms which either are not competitively beneficial, or less so. Yet exactly contrary, evolution requires that variations which are not apparently advantageous and do not confer any immediate benefits will somehow be preferentially selected. Ultimately, the mathematics of inheritance really stretches the credibility of the theory of evolution to its breaking point, for at every turn—from Mendel's Laws to mutations, mothers, mating, and midway structures—the odds are simply astronomical against different species arising simply from successions of randomly generated changes. In fact, and most ironic of all, evolution actually seems to require a kind of visionary planning so that invisible, nonsensical, and impractical modifications be supported in the population because the end product—a whole new organ or function which none of the intermediate carriers will ever enjoy—is worth the wait. And while in every field of experience and knowledge, we use mathematics as the ultimate frame of reference for establishing objectivity and accuracy, somehow, where evolution is concerned, we seem to want to hold on to the illusion. It's not the first time we've opted for this path, of course. For throughout recorded history, we've often considered "scientific" what turned out to be not much more than wishful thinking and quick slights of the human hand and eye. As a species ourselves, we often seem to prefer it when someone moves the paper cups fast enough so we'll lose track of that one green bean and think there are lots and lots of them—instead of yellow ones—under each of those cups. Because if we think evolution can happen easily enough, given sufficient time, then we don't have to admit that the diversity we witness each day in the world all around us is really a spectacle for our senses, minds, and hearts, perfectly orchestrated by visionary planning of the highest order. Wouldn't the wiser person pull aside the curtain right about now and seek the hand of the Creator?

ORIGINS – PART TWO: THE WING OF HUMILITY

"O*mankind! Reverence your Guardian-Lord, who created you from a single person... and reverence the wombs that bore you."* (4:1) *"Thy Lord has decreed... that you be kind to your parents...and out of kindness, lower to them the wing of humility."* (17:23-24) *"Do they not observe the birds above them, spreading their wings and folding them in? None can uphold them except God, Most Gracious."* (67:19; 16:79) *"Each one knows its own mode of prayer and praise."* (24:41) *"And God did create you from dust; then from a sperm-drop; then He made you in pairs."* (35:11) *"Glory to God, Who created in pairs all things that the earth produces, as well as their own human kind, and other things of which they have no knowledge."* (36:36) *"He has established relationships of lineage and marriage, for thy Lord has power over all things."* (25:54) *"O Adam, dwell with your wife in the Garden and enjoy as you wish but approach not this tree or you run into harm and transgression."* (7:19) *"Travel through the earth and see how God did originate creation; so will God produce a later creation."* (29:20) *"Do they not travel through the earth and see what was the end of those before them?"* (40:21; 40:82, 35:44) *"And remember David and Solomon."* (21:78) *"[Solomon] took a muster of the birds, and he said, 'Why is it I see not the Hoopoe? Or is he among the absentees?'"* (27:20) *"We gave in the past knowledge to David and Solomon...And Solomon was David's heir."* (27:15-16) *"Thus, whomever God wills to guide, He expands his breast to the Surrender; and whomever He wills to lead astray, He causes his breast to become tight and constricted, as if he were climbing up the skies."* (6:125).

The truth is, evolutionary science has had more than its fair share of intrigue, and Dolly the cloned sheep was hardly its first poster child. For at least a hundred years, anthropology and palaeontology have witnessed a series of characters presented almost like movie-stars, and in the end, just as fictitious and problematic. Nebraska Man, Piltdown Man, Neanderthal Man, Turkana Boy, Java Man, Peking Man, Handy Man, Taung Child, and perhaps the most popular evolutionary pin-up girl of all time, Lucy. Each was offered as the solution to man's evolution—a sort of missing link to apes. Yet each ended up creating more problems than it solved, as dates were skewed, bones were misassembled, and most turned out to be hoaxes. That in itself is not surprising, for all of the grandiose conclusions drawn about man's evolutionary tree are really based on a stack of fossils small enough to "be displayed on a dinner table."[4] Predictably, then, the Leakey family, the very researchers who established the field in the 50s and 60s, became seemingly more doubtful themselves as time passed: "I would have to state that there is more evidence to suggest an abrupt arrival of man rather than a gradual process of evolving"[5]; "All these trees of life with their branches of our ancestors, that's a lot of nonsense."[6]

Yet apparently undeterred, evolutionists continue to advance new icons for their theory. Among the most recent is "Mitochondrial Eve." It turns out that while nuclear DNA comes from both parents, the rest of what makes up the fertilized egg is inherited only from our mothers. Curiously, among these inherited cellular components, the mitochondria actually have their own genome, with a fairly steady mutation rate. This means that researchers can construct ancestral "trees," using the number of mutations to estimate the genetic distance (time) between the descendents of various females. Using samples of mitochondrial DNA from around the globe, scientists established that all of mankind descended from either a very small founding population, or from one single woman.[7] Not surprisingly, she's been nicknamed Eve, and she's a bit of an awkward discovery for evolutionists—not what they expected to find. First of all, she refutes the idea that humans could have evolved from apes in a variety of settings worldwide because now everyone can be traced to Eve's community somewhere in Africa. Somewhat tongue-in-cheek, evolutionists have dubbed the idea the "Noah's Ark Hypothesis" –and certainly, it's hard to hide the fact that this all sounds a lot like the scriptural version of events. Meanwhile, creationists are probably starting to ponder how the evolutionary tree is oddly similar to the tree Eve was warned about in the first place—the one which would bring about man's utter downfall. Because inevitably, the more anyone tries to demonstrate how an undirected, self-perpetuating mechanism called evolution supposedly accounts for everything from unicellular plants to man, the more it becomes obvious that both fossil and genetic evidence just don't offer up the required proof. Or, as Darwin, himself, anticipated: "Often a cold shudder has run through me, and I have asked myself whether I may have not devoted myself to a fantasy."[8]

A great example of the problem with evolutionary theory comes from the study of feathers and flight. If Darwin felt sick just looking at a peacock feather, it's a good thing the electron microscope hadn't yet been invented, for we now know that they are truly ultimate masterpieces of engineering—not just pretty ornaments to draw a mate. The number of feathers is pretty constant within a species, but varies greatly between species: the Canada goose, for example, has about 33,000 feathers, while the Ruby-throated hummingbird has only about 940. Each feather has a precise and complex structure based on a central shaft (vane), to which is attached over 300 million tiny barbs. In turn, each barb has thousands of smaller strands called barbules along its sides, with each barbule ending in a specialized barbicel, consisting of tiny microscopic hooks called hamuli. The hamuli collectively act like a zipper, allowing each barbule to hook into another. Considering how complex a feather is, it's not surprising to learn that there is no single gene for its production. In chickens alone, three genes have already been identified in barb production: a gene named "noggin" affects the number of barbs on a shaft; "bone morphogenetic protein" (BMP4) affects the separation between barbs as well as their number; and "sonic hedgehog" (SHH) creates a perfectly measured webby membrane between barbs. It's a bit revealing of the mood in the field of genetics when such important—some would say miraculous—structures are given humourous names. But the reality of these findings is actually a serious matter. If three or more genes are responsible simply for the alignment of barbs, how many more genes regulate feather production in its entirety?

Of course, if all feathers were identical to each other, the odds of creating one from chance mutations would already be incredibly small. But there's actually more to it than that. It turns out that the barbs are specialized in terms of length and rigidity according to function and species, creating a number of different types of feathers: body feathers, flight feathers (which can be contoured, stiff, asymmetrical, or notched), ear coverts, semi-plumes (between the contour and down), and downy (with no interlocking barbicels), bristles (with stiff shafts and barbs only on the proximal portion), and filoplumes (with very fine shafts and only a few short barbs at the end). The feather provides the bird not only with the capacity for flight but also with much-needed sensory information. For example, the filoplumes serve as pressure and vibration receptors, sensing the position of other feathers and readjusting them as required. And down, which protects from cold and gives chicks their best chance for survival, is in itself a highly organized and complex organ: natal down has the same shape all over the young chick, but differs between species; definitive down is specialized to come in when the natal down molts; uropygial down is specific to the base of the tail; and powder down is waterproof. How could these all these different feathers arise by evolution alone? How could definitive down be selected, for example, in animals too young to survive on their own or mate? And how could such a continuum of specific structures evolve so synchronously simply by chance?

Again, if there were no more complexity to feathers than this, it would be sufficient to raise doubts about evolution. But there's more. Consider the fact that feathers are self-replacing. If they're lost through injury, they're replaced easily in a matter of weeks. And molting, which happens about 2 – 3 times in the first year of a bird's life, and once or twice annually after that, results in dramatic colour changes between winter and summer plumage, and even a higher feather count in the winter—all specially suited for insulation, heat absorption, mimicking, disruption, advertising, etc. The question of how such precision and diversity could have arisen accidentally defies evolutionary explanation. In fact, molting is a very expensive process by which a bird replaces 25 - 40 percent of its dry mass, drawing on protein and energy reserves to synthesize feathers and counter reductions in insulation and flight ability. The onset of molting is triggered hormonally by day length and depends on breeding cycle, habitat, and whether the species is migratory or sedentary. Common white terns actually have fairly fragile unpigmented feathers which are easily worn, yet these birds are able to fly 40,000 km annually from pole to pole due to the fact that they molt almost continuously. It boggles the mind to think of an intermediate step, for birds who failed to molt continuously would simply have drowned in the Pacific, and birds who molted continuously without migrating would simply have been huge energy wasters. And what of the common Canadian Ptarmigan—pure white in winter, and brown in summer? Is it really plausible that these birds slowly changed colouration over the generations—during which time they would all have been very visible in both summer and winter? And how did they ever begin to time their molts to the amount of sunlight? A mistake of even a few days could have easily proven deadly. Molting is dangerous in other ways, too. In loons, waterfowl, and gulls, all flight feathers are lost simultaneously, as these birds become temporarily flightless. What possible evolutionary benefit could there be from being temporarily a quintessential "sitting duck," as it were? Without doubt, any intermediate stage would have meant certain detection, vulnerability, and death.

Over the years, the idea that intermediate forms for birds must exist has actually consumed a lot of research time. Another icon of evolutionists, Shenzouraptor Sinensis (S.S.), recently found in China, was originally proposed as a transitional form, but now seems to be simply an early bird. It was a feathered dove-sized creature dated 140 million years ago (mya), with a relatively large cerebellum and visual cortex, pneumatized vertebrae and pelvis (bones full of air pockets, essentially), as well as cervical and abdominal air sacs, with feather and foot structures compatible with modern flying birds. Besides, if S.S. were really a transitional form, then how could we explain the older Archaeopteryx, first thought to be a transition, too, but now also considered a primitive bird, dated 150 mya (older than S.S.)? It also had feathers and a flawless flight mechanism. And what about Yixian Dromaeosaur? Alive about 130 mya, this small dinosaur was apparently flightless, yet feathered, though the individual found was a juvenile. If feathers were primarily for courtship—Darwin's sexual selection—why would they be prominent on an individual too young to mate? As feathers are such expensive structures to make and maintain metabolically, how could it ever be adaptive to have a bunch of feathers with no visible purpose? Meanwhile, fossils of 100 mya primitive flying cranes have been found, as have 60 mya flying herons and storks, as well as Cenozoic flying birds from about 65 mya—though some of their descendents, such as the kiwi and ostrich, are flightless. Ultimately, then, the fossil evidence is saying that flight was developed, then lost, then developed again, then lost again. But how can something be both positively and negatively selected? And is flight really so simple a mechanism that animals can easily morph from flight-ready to flightlessness repeatedly across millions of years?

To account for the ever-growing confusion, evolutionary ornithologists are now seemingly trying to minimize the very idea of flight being important as they suggest that feathers evolved primarily for insulation, with flight being only a secondary adaptation. Yet surely there are simpler structures than feathers which would have had fewer intermediate forms and better function if the only goal were body heat—like increased fat, for instance. How could the feather, a structure whose very complexity is designed to allow flight, lead to flight only accidentally? Most recently, Protoavis, dated 225 mya, was uncovered in Texas. It is a remarkably fossil find which features more than 20 bird-like attributes, including a large brain and visual cortex, binocular vision, and critically, a portal from the rear of the skull to the eye socket like a modern bird—a feature never seen in dinosaurs. Not only does this push back the so-called evolution of birds from reptiles further than anyone had ever speculated. But it also begs the question, at what stage would a hole in the skull have been an adaptive mutation which could be selected for, to allow transitional birds to flourish? More and more, then, a number of prominent evolutionists are declaring that the origin of birds is not as clear-cut as once was thought. The overwhelming conclusion is that there is an absence of intermediate forms between reptiles and birds, and as Dr. Alan Feduccia one of the most quoted researchers in the field, has stated, the therapod origin of birds is likely to turn out to be one of the great embarrassments of the 20th century.[9]

Further, there are a lot of physiological differences between birds and reptiles where it's virtually impossible to imagine how a successful intermediate would have looked or stayed alive. Feathers actually consist of about 91% fibrous protein with relatively short amino acid sequences, of a completely different shape and with different protein-coding sequences and control regions than scales, genetically speaking. If scales are similar to anything on a bird, they are more like claws. Second, birds have hollow, aerated bones while reptiles do not. In fact, their skeletons are lighter than all other land-dwelling animals. The frigate's skeleton, for example, weighs only about 118 gms, less than its feathers. What possible advantage would a reptile experience with fragile bones incapable of flight? Birds also have some of the fastest metabolic rates of any living creature, while reptiles have among the slowest rates. As a result, birds must make highly effective use of food. A stork baby, for instance, increases 1 kg of weight per 3kg of food, while land animals put on only about 1 kg of weight per 22 kg of food. What advantage would a reptile have expending much more energy than his neighbours trying to sustain a higher metabolism, constantly eating and fighting to stay warm—yet unable to benefit from flight?

Not only that, but birds are unique in being able to concentrate fat between tissues so that it doesn't impact on the flight muscles. What good would layers of fat be to an organism which had no ability to fly, except to make him a much slower—and likelier—prey? And how would modified fat metabolism ever begin? The changes required at the cellular level are too many to count, yet these would somehow have had to occur in complete synchrony and been mathematically selected, even though they could not, in fact, be seen, and therefore chosen by mates. And what about the thin skin of birds, with its complex receptors for temperature, pressure, and vibration? It's completely the opposite of reptiles, which are consistently distinguished by their fairly sturdy outer layer. What possible evolutionary advantage would there be to a mutated thin-skinned reptile which was more vulnerable to dehydration and attack? The bladder of birds is unique, too—it's gone. Birds just excrete uric acid directly—and look out below. The idea that an intermediate form, armed simply with a dysfunctional bladder, could be adaptive is a real stretch of credibility. And consider, too, that bird lungs are unique, with air going in and out via two different passages so that the lungs are never empty. In reptiles and virtually all other creatures which breathe, like humans, the air goes out the same way it came in. But how could any animal have survived the transition of its lungs? It doesn't take much thinking to know that lung malfunctions of any kind are one of the surest ways to die. Any transitional forms, in other words, would have been useless liabilities or acute dysfunctions. And without intermediate forms, there is no evolution.

Yet what birds are actually capable of doing is nothing short of fantastic, and man is always trying to figure it out. We've put birds into wind tunnels to see how they manage, we've used medical scanners to analyse their bones, we've taken high-speed X-rays of their wings at work, we've used MRIs to record movements in their soft tissues, we've tracked their flight patterns with radar, and we've even built all kinds of wings—from DaVinci's flying machines, to robotic wings. Yet not only can we not replicate bird flight ourselves—we can't even understand how they do it themselves. Birds are, in fact, more complex than the most exotic aircraft. A hummingbird can produce 90 flaps per second, flying even backwards or upside down. Large birds like seagulls have perfected gliding and soaring to save up to 70% of the energy required for flight—by far the most expensive process which any animals is capable of—using their wings as natural airfoils. Birds have a perfected metabolism which allows them to use the sparse oxygen at high altitudes, though even limited heights cause our own breasts to constrict. And the actual range of wingspans among birds is itself a wonder—from the 10 cm span of the tiny hummingbird, weighing just under 2 grams, to the gigantic Kori Bustard, weighing in around 20 kg, with wings spanning about 3.5 meters. More amazing still, there are only four possible mathematical patterns in the relationship between the wing area (squared) and wing breadth, called the "aspect ratio," and different ratios lead to different types of flight: an aspect ratio of 6.8 allows slow flight, poor gliding, but an explosive start, such as the flight of a pheasant; an aspect ratio of 9.3 allows the use of updrafts to avoid flapping, such as the flight of an eagle; a ratio of 12.5 allows for a slower takeoff, a faster top speed, good gliding and migration, such as the flight of a wader; and a ratio of 13.8 allows the optimal use of wind direction to vary speed and gliding close to land, such as in the flight of a gull. It is really an adventure in conjecture to speculate that such precise relationships between form and function could have arisen out of genetic accidents.

The supposed evolution of flight muscles also raises its own difficulties. For example, if man were to fly, he would need wings about 50 metres across and a chest 2 metres thick just to hold the flight muscles. As delicate as they seem, then, birds actually have the largest muscle tissue to body mass ratio on earth. When the ability to fly is lost—such as in the case of the now-absent Dodo and St.Helena hoopoe, and the more recent ostriches, enus, elephant birds, and kiwis—animals do not compete well since they're burdened with unnecessary muscles and structures. Typically, they tend to thrive only in limited environments, such as islands, where they are most at risk of extinction when conditions change or new species arrive. Consider Alvarezsaurid, dated 80 mya. It was a scrawny creature, feathered yet flightless, retaining most if not all of its flight muscles. Researchers struggle to explain how such a creature could have remained viable evolutionarily speaking as it ran around frantically in search of food, trying to maintain its high bird-like metabolism, while carrying a good deal of useless anatomical cargo. Their best conclusion is that maybe no one really understands the advantages of flightlessness after all. Yet if flightlessness is so adaptive, why evolve flight at all? The ability to fly is surely subject to enormous negative selection pressures when circumstances permit survival without it—after all, it requires extensive physical changes and drains body energy. And if a flight-abled creature can escape or change its environment in the first place—migrate, in other words—then how could it ever be forced evolutionarily to abandon its flight due to environmental pressures? Wouldn't it be simpler—and faster—just to pick up and leave? More recently, researchers have suggested, in fact, that rather than being an adaptive change, flightlessness may be the result of an adverse mutation widely known as neoteny, whereby full-grown adults actually look like overgrown infants. Far from being beneficial, the condition is highly limiting and can hardly be considered an intermediate stage in the evolution of flight or of stronger or more successful species.

In the final "swan song" to evolutionary theory, it turns out that bird cells actually have less DNA than reptilian cells. One has to wonder how all of the new functions could have evolved from a smaller genetic substrate—two-way lungs; modified bladders, arms, hands, and muscles; pneumatized bones; keeled sternums; and a myriad of feathers. Even Francis Crick, co-discoverer of DNA, a confirmed atheist who set out trying to disprove God, ended up changing his tone a bit in time: "An honest man, armed with all the knowledge available to us now, could only state that in some sense, the origin of life appears at the moment to be almost a miracle, so many are the conditions which would have had to have been satisfied to get it going."[10] And even when we see creatures which seem to have a mix of external characteristics—like Lucy or the

Yixian Dromaeosaur—can we automatically assume these are intermediate forms? If every single walking stick insect was wiped off the earth and we were left only with grasshoppers and twigs, would we be right to assume that one had evolved from the other, the first time we stumbled on a walking stick insect fossil? And without some sort of central direction, creation should have resulted in countless errors and partial attempts which we should easily find littering the fossil layers—evidence which is conspicuous by its absence, in fact. Darwin himself was puzzled: "Why, if species have descended from other species by fine gradations, do we not everywhere see innumerable transitional forms?"[11] Why, indeed.

Ultimately, as useful as the electron microscope really is, we might sometimes be better off without it. Because with all of our studies of tiny processes, components, and changes, we have become somewhat like the critic who is staring intently at one tiny spot of coloured paint on a magnificent impressionistic canvas. We can't really see the artistry anymore at all. We've got things broken down to such micro-levels that we're convinced the portrait is relatively easy to create, simply because we can understand something about how to motion one stroke of the brush. Looking at things up close like this, we're really missing the big picture, literally. For while it may be possible to recreate a dot of blue or green, or a genetic change here or there, it is beyond the limits of both logic and imagination to conceive the incidental orchestration of all the necessary elements, subtly blended and interacting to perfection, to create an image as big as our universe and beyond, constantly animated in multiple dimensions, moving not only across space but through time, from the very origins of life to this very moment. That is surely an accomplishment much greater than a single brushstroke, much more complex than a solitary line from a feathered pen. Yet it's only when we try to step back from the finite edges of our knowledge, and get a real bird's-eye view of our world, that we can appreciate the splendour and grandeur of creation in its entirety—neither simple nor accidental.

ORIGINS – PART THREE-THOSE WHO
COMPASS IT ROUND

"*Sanctify My House for those who compass it round…and proclaim the pilgrimage among men…that they may witness the benefits provided for them.*" (22:22-34) "*God finds you wandering and gives you guidance.*" (93:7) "*To God belong both east and west. He guides whom He wills to a way that is straight.*" (2:142) "*There is not an animal that lives on the earth, nor a being that flies on its wings, but forms part of communities like you.*" (6:38) "*He created the sun, the moon, and the stars, all governed by laws under His command.*" (7:54) "*It is He Who makes the stars as beacons for you, that you may guide yourselves… through the dark spaces of land and sea.*" (6:97) "*He who forsakes his home in the cause of God, finds in the earth many a refuge, wide and spacious.*" (4:100) "*And in the mountains are tracts white and red, of various shades of colour, and black intense in hue.*" (35:27) "*We sent down iron.*" (57:25) "*And We made the iron soft for [David].*" (34:10-11) "*And the birds gathered in assemblies; all with [David] did turn to God.*" (38:18-19) "*It was Our power that made the violent, unruly wind flow tame for Solomon, to his order, to the land which We had blessed.*" (21:81) "*But the Hoopoe tarried not far; he came up and said [to Solomon]: 'I have compassed territory which thou has not compassed.'*" (27:20-22) "*And Solomon …said: 'O you people! We have been taught the speech of birds, and on us has been bestowed a little of all things: this is indeed grace manifest from God.'*" (27:16) "*Then, when We decreed Solomon's death, nothing showed them his death except a little worm of the earth, which kept slowly gnawing away at his staff.*" (34:14)

It's easy to look back on the life of Charles Darwin, no doubt the most representative figure in the evolutionary field, and speculate about what he would have thought, given access to modern-day technology. Evolutionists expect, no doubt, that he would have found what they have found: the inner workings of complex systems reduced to interactions between simple proteins––life defined as a series of exchanges of materials whose substance seems clarified by tools which allow us to look intimately into what we presume to be the heart of things. But no one really has the right to make any assumptions about what Darwin might really believe, were he alive today. He was, seemingly, a cautious and humble man—The Origin of Species, his life's monumental achievement, was over 20 years in the making and did not actually go to print without a lot of prompting. And he seems, almost better than anyone, to have anticipated the shortcomings of his own proposals: "I am quite conscious that my speculations run beyond the bounds of true science....It is a mere rag of an hypothesis with as many flaw[s] and holes as sound parts."[12] Yet this reluctant icon single-handedly raised biology from what it was then—the hobby of horticulturists and horse breeders—to a science no one could ever marginalize again. And his self-doubts were refreshing in contrast to the arrogance of our times. More than an electron microscope, though, what Darwin could have really used was an airplane. Had he managed to fly through the clouds above the Galapagos, to follow the path his feathered subjects took migrating to that remote place, it would have given him another perspective. There's something about looking at one's home from a place where rivers look like dark threads and mountains seem smaller than one's thumb that can change a soul forever. It's really simply amazing how much reflection there is to be had from looking at life with a wider, rather than a narrower, lens. While we cannot anticipate what Darwin might have felt or learned, aloft amid a flock of finches rather than eye-to-beak, one hundred plus years of experience and research have taught us what he might have witnessed.

First of all, he would have seen the sky as a gigantic set of flyways—four altogether—which allow birds of all kinds to compass the globe in a way no other creature on earth is able to. Following their Pacific, Central, Mississippi, or Atlantic pathways, migratory birds travel 1000 to 3000 km each way to their destination, though distances of 6000 km, one-way, are not uncommon, and the American Sandpiper, among others, travels over 16,000 km to his seasonal home. Covering such distances demands a huge daily output—flight extending over 600 km per day for Lesser Yellowlegs, for instance—and consuming a huge amount of body energy. The Golden Plover, for example, loses 82g of its 200g body on its 4000 km journey—about 40% of its mass. To reduce the amount of energy required, birds rally together into formations—serial,

V-shaped, or group, taking turns being at the apex of the V to achieve a 23% energy savings. Succeeding with such expensive undertakings obviously takes a considerable amount of planning, metabolically speaking. A case in point is the Sedge Warbler, which doubles its size prior to migration—an increase in 100% of its body weight. The timing of the journey also becomes critical—responding to a balance of ultimate clues, such as the need for food and habitat, hibernation, breeding, climate, and the migration of prey, as well as proximal clues, such as the length of day. And as they travel, birds become the inadvertent chroniclers of our planet, for researchers have found that as they eat, they incorporate geographic "tags" into their feathers, which can then be studied like the rings on a tree, in the new science of ptilochronology—the study of feather time—as an index of global environmental pollution.

With so many factors to calibrate, synchronicity is nonetheless miraculously achieved. While most humans sleep, seldom witnessing the scope of the miracle, the volume of bird life moving across the globe is staggering—in one night alone, up to 12 million songbirds may be recorded on their journey south, and ducks and geese numbering up to 60 – 80,000 have overwhelmed airport radar systems. Shearwaters pass at a rate of over 60,000 birds per hour over some spots, somehow arriving from all over the world to their common destination during the same 11-day period each year, like noble pilgrims. And from one species to another, from one generation to another, birds demonstrate a remarkable fidelity towards stopover points, wintering sites, and breeding sites. Terns from Tortugas Island were shipped in different directions and freed 800 to 1370 km away over an unfamiliar sea, and yet most returned in a few days. The results were the same even if the birds were anaesthetized and/or the cages were rotated continuously during the journey. Manx Shearwaters were flown on commercial aircraft from the Atlantic to the coast of England, and returned in just under two weeks.

Researchers have conducted all kinds of experiments on bird navigation, but the phenomenon remains largely a mystery. When chicks are separated from adults, for instance, they still fly the same journey. Adult Bristle-thighed Curlews migrate when their chicks are only five weeks old, from Alaska to the tropics—yet their young follow their path weeks later. The Short-tailed Shearwater parent also leaves its young, who also later follow along. Do they not need to be taught? Yet European Starlings were once taken by the thousands from The Hague to Switzerland; the adult birds somehow understood they had been displaced and returned to normal wintering grounds, while the infants flew 90 degrees off their usual course.[13] Similar experiments moved birds from the eastern Baltic to Germany; the Hooded crows recognized the displacement and adjusted for it, but the Buntings did not adjust.[14] Do they need to be taught?

The evolutionary explanations for all of this, unlike the ever-present bird songs which fill our skies, are surprisingly silent. Trial-and-error in journeys over such distances, costing so much metabolic energy, would have meant far too many losses. Intermediate forms would have simply dropped into the oceans, never to breed. The interweaving of environmental clues to timed migrations would have left transitional forms as easy targets for predators and bad weather. And without beneficial genetic modifications of entire generations simultaneously—not just individuals—effective flocking would simply not have occurred, stranding all to a probable death. It's also genuinely hard to imagine what environmental pressures would have convinced entire species to just pick up and head west for 10,000 km, for instance, hoping for suitable land. What kind of inter-animal communication could have initiated the first migration? And if only a few survived those transitional years, wouldn't inbreeding and the reduced genetic variety which results make it so much harder for the next generation to adapt back at the first location? In fact, what migration requires is the temporary alteration of a bird to something much bigger and stronger than its usual self—along with an incredible sense of navigation and communal goals. When the animal arrives at its second location (or third or more, in the case of multiple stopovers), it must continue to be in a position of advantage, if only temporarily, sometimes even requiring a molt and a shift in colouration. It must then undergo another cycle of storing body fat and expending incredible amounts of energy to reach the next (or original) location, where it must, according to the season, now also find itself with strategic benefits.

At the very least, then, migration demonstrates the range of variability which is inherent in a species—the capacity to grow and change, to adapt to new homes, climate, and conditions—while still retaining one's identity as a species. A lot of variation is possible, in other words, without speciation. Second, birds are proof of clear instances where evolution has not occurred—for these creatures have hereditarily altered their surroundings rather than themselves. And if evolution were, in fact, primarily a response to localized pressures, how would it ever work on migratory birds anyway—creatures who must be able to meet the requirements of not just one but at least two very different settings? How could natural selection operate to optimize a body type in location A—for example, the shape of a beak, or feather colouration—which would turn out to be a huge liability in location B, where food, habitat, prey, and predators might all be very different? Critically, evolutionary theory cannot satisfactorily demonstrate how natural selection would operate under competing environmental pressures. Of course, there are other examples in the animal world where creatures have very different body types according to habitat and age—from the metamorphosis of insects to the seasonal colouration of wild hares. These alone are hard enough to explain based on the action of single genes and breeding advantages. But to try to account for why animals which can just pick up and resettle wherever they want right across the globe would ever evolve the complexity to change their appearance and strategies—to the point where even the colour of their eggs is ideally suited to temporary locations—is clearly beyond evolutionary theory. Further, to insist that all of this, plus the high level of communication and co-dependence required for the success of migration, could have occurred as the result of a series of fortuitous genetic accidents is clearly beyond reason.

Even more fundamentally, migration demonstrates that species are not well represented as discrete nodules on the so-called evolutionary tree, moving ever-distant from their ancestors. Rather, their origins are inherently connected to the very origins of the earth, rooted in the same fabric and purpose, in a way which suggests a continuum of design more than a continuum of adaptations. Nowhere is this more clearly exemplified than in the consideration of iron. It is common knowledge that iron makes up the core of the earth, around which the rest of the planet has formed, and it is the most abundant element by mass in the universe. The banded iron formations (BIFs) which can be seen like strips of colours through the mountains are a history of how oxygen first was released into our atmosphere, somewhat like a geological script of our planet, and much of the colouration in soil is caused by iron compounds and their interaction with oxygen, heat, and organic matter—red in warm, tropical climates; yellow and orange during periods of cooling; and grey, blue, or green in low-oxygen (aquatic) phases. In addition, from its first appearance in the historical record in the Middle East, in about 4000-3000 BCE, and from the Iron Age to the Space Age, iron has been the basis of human civilization. Iron has the highest binding energy per nucleon of any element known to man, and Iron 56 is the most stable nucleus in existence, the only element which cannot be subjected to either fusion or fission to liberate energy. It also forms the bulk of all the meteorites which fall to earth—as well as the essence of supernovas. And most relevant to the discussion of migration, the iron at the core of the earth is the source of our planet's magnetic field.

Of course, it's long been an established fact in ornithology that birds fly with reference to the stars and sun as well as topography. An experiment placed Warblers in a planetarium and artificially moved the sky about 300 km per night. After two weeks, the birds stopped their pre-migratory restlessness, apparently pleased with a night sky showing them to be in Middle Africa, where they expected to be after migration.[15] Another experiment at Cornell rotated the planetarium sky artificially around Betelgeuse instead of the North Star; the chicks then released demonstrated a false understanding that Betelgeuse was the North Star.[16] Homing pigeons were held under artificial light cycles to skew their biological clock from local time; released, they flew predictably off-course in relation to the clock-shifting.[17] And many experiments on Bobolinks by numerous researchers have shown them to respond differently to varied wavelengths of light. The physiological basis for such navigation systems has still to be explained.

More recently, however, the picture has become even more complicated. Numerous experiments have demonstrated that avian navigation, in addition to the suite of cues already counted, hinges critically on a kind of internal compass system which can detect even a .5% variation in the earth's magnetic field. Pigeons wearing magnetic bands lose their way, but only on overcast days[18] or in places where the earth's field is unusually strong. Pigeons wearing Helmholtz Coils around their necks (devices generating a magnetic field) also experience predictable disorientation: if the artificial field rotates clockwise (corresponding to the earth's normal field), the homing pigeons fly home successfully whether the weather is sunny or cloudy. But if the field is counter-clockwise, they fly home correctly only on sunny days—flying 180 degrees off-course on cloudy days.[19] In cement cages, birds will orient themselves properly for flight, but in metal cages, they will not.[20] And Bobolinks treated with short-term magnetic fields change their orientation: prior to the pulse, they hop southeast, but after, they hop northward.[21] Curious about the phenomenon, some researchers have begun to uncover an astounding fact: birds respond to magnetism thanks to trace amounts of magnetite— iron—in their own bodies.

The September, 1979, issue of Science reported the finding of magnetic tissues in the brains of pigeons—up to 10 million tiny crystals of iron oxide, called magnetite—the same material which makes up compass needles. The magnetite apparently provides the animals with both a compass sense, for orientation, as well as a map sense, for establishing position relative to a destination. There are new speculations that there may also be magnetite in the olfactory epithelium (sense of smell) of some birds and other animals prone to long-distance travel. In Yellowfish Tuna, for example, magnetite has been found in the sinus cavities near critical nerve centres. Another locus may also be in the visual system, since cutting optic nerves has been demonstrated to reduce the response to magnetism, and cells in the nucleus of the basal optic root respond to magnetic fields. To date, magnetic iron oxide has also been found in some bacteria, bees, sea turtles, trout, sharks, and salmon, among others. The magnetic crystals are about one millionth of a centimetre across, positioned essentially like tiny bar magnets which twist into alignment with the earth's magnetic field and somehow interact with neighbouring cells to communicate information to the nervous system. The field generated by these tiny crystals is remarkably strong, permeating many biological tissues, and few biomaterials seems to affect it. Most importantly, the growth of the crystals is physiologically controlled somehow and incredibly precise: if they grew even slightly bigger than they are, the magnetic domain would inevitably divide, with opposing poles at either end, cancelling the effect.

There is simply no evolutionary explanation for how such a refined structure, so deeply connected to the fabric of life, could emerge accidentally. Consider a few facts about iron metabolism, too. In all creatures, iron volume is highly regulated, and any imbalance leads to dysfunction: haemosiderosis, haemochromatosis, aceruloplasminemia, and so on. Birds, like other creatures, are extremely sensitive to iron overload. Captive birds, for instance, commonly die from hepatic iron storage disease, iron accumulation which damages various tissues and organs. So how would an intermediate form have survived the increased iron stores required for magnetite crystal metabolism? And how would the iron have gotten to the right place, into the right formation, in the first place? Iron tends to be re-circulated rather than absorbed, so iron transfer is critical to all life and very complex, involving many carrier molecules. So far, 30 genes have already been linked to iron metabolism in humans.[22] And given their superior navigational abilities, birds should metabolize iron with even greater complexity. With so many genes committed to iron balance in the body, is it reasonable to speculate that magnetic orientation, requiring not only genetic compliance but also the co-operation of systems such as vision and balance, could have arisen simply from chance?

It becomes even more mind-boggling to calculate the odds of all of these changes happening not just in one bird, but in a number of birds at the same time—because avian migration isn't a solitary activity. And if a change happened only in one individual, there wouldn't be any way to guarantee it was passed along to the next generation in sufficient numbers to ensure migration back from the breeding grounds to the original location. Even if the change happened in a few individuals, it wouldn't necessarily be selected because the capacity would be invisible on the surface unless an individual could communicate that navigational expertise—rather than just fluffing a tail to attract a mate. Presumably, one could assume some sort of a leader bird, a lone mutant with newfound skills, but why would everyone agree to follow? On what basis would whole generations risk their lives in this way, unless they were gifted with the ability to reason and make decisions? Ironically, then, it becomes necessary to presume the evolution of highly complex communication and social behaviours just to rationalize the possible evolution of migrational abilities. Yet these sophisticated skills are, by definition, even less likely to have evolved as simple genetic accidents.

Evolutionary theory, in fact, does not even begin to deal with complex interactions between organisms of the same species, or of differing species with each other. The field has seemingly satisfied itself with trying to explain sex and sheer survival, really. It has not even started to account for the phenomena of speech; co-operation; social behaviours; host-parasite systems; symbiosis (itself a complex of nutritional, shelter, transport, pollination, or/and defensive support systems); mimicry; predator-prey relationships; or the inherently co-dependent life of social insects. All of these arrangements require some sort of concept of co-evolution, after all, for which there is absolutely no plausible explanation. The very notion of evolution, in essence, is founded on selfishness and self-interest, whereas successful co-existence requires at least some ability to be altruistic. In scientific circles, they're talking about the difficulty of reconciling "global optimization with subsystem optimization," and they speculate about whether individuals might keep score of favours, or simply incline to behaviours which coincidentally favoured both themselves and the community at the same time. It's hard to imagine, though, how a flower would keep track of its favours in its co-evolution with a myriad of bee species, or how the parasite in the stomach of a horse would keep track of its favours in returning to the horse the ability to digest the cellulose in hay. And we can't even begin to discuss the life of the flower, the bee, the horse, the hay, the parasite, or the bird unless we can also fathom how the very first chlorophyll cell acquired the necessary energy to live without photosynthesis, so that it could live long enough to evolve photosynthesis. More and more, evolution becomes the quintessential example of the riddle of which came first, the chicken of the egg.

Ultimately, the truth about the supposed slow and gradual evolution of diverse species, ecosystems, communities, and interdependence, as the fossil record shows, is that it was never slow or gradual at all. About 530 million years ago, during what is termed the "Cambrian Explosion," the earth witnessed the rapid emergence of countless complex species, virtually all at once. In fact, all but two living phyla with fossilizable skeletons are represented at this time, and genetic divergence studies confirm the extremely abrupt appearance of innumerable life forms. Prior to the Cambrian Explosion, the planet was home to very few animals other than bilateral worms which burrowed through the earth, recycling plant and animal remains, contributing to a liveable earth. Yet Darwin himself said, "If numerous species belonging to the same genera of families have really started into life all at once, the fact would be fatal to the theory of descent with slow modification through natural selection.[23] Researchers today are somewhat more guarded, stating only that the Cambrian Explosion remains a difficult strategic problem for the theory of evolution.

It's worth returning to Darwin's island one last time. The evening is late, and birds are sitting quietly in their nests, guarding their young, as water laps slowly against the rocky shore. Stars beckon those who wait for the right moment to leave this beautiful place and fly to another, equally lovely but boldly different. For millennia now, parents and children have left each other to travel far, trusting they would find each other again, and find their place again, believing they would be provided for. They are drawn by an ancient instinct, an immeasurable gift, which allows them to open their arms and ride the wind from one corner of the world to the other. And even as night covers everything in darkness, each feathered face still knows which way is east, sensing the pulse of the earth with every fibre of its being. There is calm about their humble motions, as they preen a feather here and there and prepare to sleep. For all their life experiences have given them the wisdom to know that safety comes not when you are watchful over everything, but when the Creator is watching over you.

THE BLIND SPOT

Ask anyone which sense they would most hate to lose—it's their eyesight. I grew up around vision issues—my mother has been completely blind in one eye since infancy, and as my father was dying, a brain tumour took away his sight, one day at a time. Though I lived thousands of miles away, I found myself thinking, "What could I show him?" Each thing seemed more beautiful than the other—orchids, a drop of rain, a baby's hand—but there was so little time. With only a few hours of sight left in this life, what would you want to see? Our eyes, after all, are the key way in which most of us experience the world: *"God gave man the gifts of hearing and sight."* (76:2)—*"The hearing ear and the seeing eye, the Lord made them both."* (Proverbs, 20:12)

The mechanism of sight is actually one of the strongest arguments against an "evolution-only" view of the world. It's just too complex to result from random mutations and anatomical serendipity. Even Darwin confessed the eye made him feel "cold all over." As the evolution-creation debate rages on, evolutionists advance two main points. First, they argue the human eye is deeply defective—a "badly constructed apparatus[24]" because the retina is "inverted" away from the light, behind neural matter and blood vessels. These nerves and vessels then have to pass through the back of the eye to the brain, like a sort of cable, creating a "hole" in the photoreceptor layer on the retina. This results in a "blind spot" of 3 – 5 degrees in each eye (about the size of a small orange held at arm's length). Second, they argue that colour vision systems are not terribly complex.[25] Ironically, then, evolutionists are actually admitting that anything God made *should* be complex and perfect. Also, they are saying that evolution of the human eye led to a simplistic, maladaptive structure, even though their own evolutionary theory states that systems develop towards greater complexity which is *necessarily* adaptive. So is vision rudimentary and flawed, as they insist? And if that's true, why don't we notice the blind spot each moment of our lives?

Quite simply, it's because even in animals, sight is spectacular. Cat eyes have mirror-like plates (tapeta) which double light, increasing night vision. Bees have 15,000 facets for multidirectional flight. Fish have a refractive index of 1.6 to see size accurately under water. "Flashlight fish" house bioluminescent bacteria in pouches under the eyes, and black loose jawfish produce red light to see while invisible. Jumping spiders have eight eyes to attack at 20 times their length, and giant clams have thousands of eyes around their shells to detect motion. Buzzard eyes have 1 million photoreceptors per square mm to see a mouse 5000 metres below, and falcons can see a mole 1.5 km away. It's a statistical impossibility for millions of specific and sophisticated vision systems to arise from handy genetic "accidents." Besides, research clearly demonstrates that living things emerged with complex structures already intact: honey possums and dunnarts—so called primitive marsupials—have full colour vision from red to ultraviolet[26], and primitive brittlestar skeletons form crystals, each with hundreds of lenses, like the compound eyes of trilobites, 350 million years ago.[27]

How complicated is colour vision? First, consider "colour." Colour happens because of how materials react to light—how much they absorb, reflect, or transmit. Plants contain huge amounts of a "pigment" called chlorophyll, which reflects green and absorbs the other colours of light, so plants "look" green. Pigments are special substances which almost everything contains, and they give objects their particular colour(s) by reflecting one or more wavelengths of light, depending on the molecular structure of the pigment. Pigmentation varies a lot even within species, and it is under genetic control.[28] Further, each pure material on earth has a unique spectrum of its own, even without pigments—like a light signature—because of the particular wavelengths of light it transmits, absorbs, and reflects. And while humans only see part of the spectra (the "visible light" band), other organisms are sensitive to different wavelengths, like infrared (snakes) and ultraviolet (penguins), which they can use to detect food and threats. Spectra are really very specific. For example, leaves from the same plant have different spectra if they are light green, dark green, orange, dry, damaged, or dead.[29] The Qur'an gives clear notice of these facts: *"He has multiplied everything in varying colours and qualities"* (16:13), and *"for all things, God has appointed due proportion"* (65:3).

And how does the eye receive this colour? It contains pigments, too, in each of the two kinds of photoreceptor cells ("rods" and "cones"). Here, genetic changes in pigment proteins regulate which wavelengths the pigments will be sensitive to. Even primitive mantis shrimp have eight kinds of pigments, each with specific spectral sensitivity. And over 195 visual pigments have already been identified in fish.[30] Certain vertebrates (like birds) also have tiny pigmented oil droplets in their eyes, forming filters. In these animals, colour sensitivity is particularly hard to analyse because it depends on the transmittance of the oil, the absorbance of the pigment in the oil, and the pigments in the eye itself. Adding to the mystery, one pigment may be associated with different types of oil droplets, there are variations in oil droplets between species, and proportions of pigments vary with diet and habitat.[31] In short, "colour" is complicated, and no one can explain it exactly. The evolutionists themselves admit, "it is not clear how the expression of photopigments is regulated in individual cells.[32]"

So after centuries of research, there is still no complete theory of human colour vision.[33] The terms used to describe it confuse most people: supersaturation, hue cancellations, tristimulus space, retinal illuminance, luminance channels, neural conversion zones, photon noise, and channel overloading. In summary, 40 basic eye parts situated in 11 strata work together, including the retina's 6 – 7 million cones and 130 million rods. The rods and cones change light into chemical impulses through "phototransduction": light is absorbed by a protein which is coupled to an isomer of retinaldehyde, which activates a rhodopsin protein molecule to change shape so it can bind with transducin, which then activates phosphodiesterase to break down cyclic neucleotides in order to change the ion concentration in the cell, which produces electrical energy (neural impulses) which travel through 800,000 fibres in the optic nerve to the brain at the rate of 1 billion per second.[34] How can anyone call this mechanism simple?

Then when the impulse reaches the brain, the real process of vision begins—and it is even less well understood and more complicated! Consider that you can see clearly even when you are running and that you can recognize your children even if they are standing on their heads. Consider that you can recognize people you haven't seen for awhile, even if they change their hair, and you don't scream, "What happened to your other arm?" if you see a friend from the side. Consider that you recognize your house (3-D) even in a photograph (2-D), and when you hold a bottle with your hand spread out, you don't feel holes between your fingers. As a volunteer at the Montreal Neurological Hospital years ago, I met brain-injured patients with perfect eyesight who worried about someone's hand if it was buried in a purse and who could not recognize family members when photographs were inverted. The scientific journals are stuffed with theories to account for these types of phenomena. For example, it seems that through a process called "amodal completion," we can fill in objects which are incomplete or imperfect in our visual field—only scientists cannot agree about how or where in the brain this "filling in" happens. And most scientists agree that we can freely rotate visual objects "in our heads"—but they can't even begin to explain what these mathematical transformations might look like at the neurological level.

Finally, consider that you never notice the blind spot in each eye. Unconscious saccadic (rapid) eye movements apparently cause images to "slip" as much as 4 degrees per second. This helps to compensate for the blind spot. Also, "completion neurons" on opposite sides of the brain can process information about the blind spot for each eye.[35] It also turns out that the structure which creates the blind spot is a critical adaptation for supplying the extremely active photoreceptor cells of higher vertebrates with oxygen. Per gram of tissue, the mammalian retina has one of the highest metabolic rates—three times greater than the cerebral cortex, and six times more than the heart muscle. The specific positioning of the photoreceptor layer in higher vertebrates, in front of the retina, allows a unique network of capillaries to bathe the photoreceptors in blood, in order to maintain the necessary oxygen tension in the retina. So the blind spot is clear evidence of design, not defect.[36]

It's clear that Darwin thought that vision is relatively simple, but modern science proves otherwise. And since colour vision will not work without every component—and the components have no value on their own—how could it "evolve" in steps? The eye forces evolutionists to reconsider a few other points, too. In some insects, the larval and adult stages have different eye structures—did both types "evolve" at once, then? And what about lobsters, prawns, and shrimp? Their eyes work on reflection rather than refraction, with little squares positioned to focus light on a single point. Yet other members of the Class Crustacea have refracting eyes with hexagonal or round cells refracting light onto the retina. Coming from the same ancestors, why didn't all crustaceans "evolve" similar eyes?[37] Finally, the so-called "evolution" of the human eye violates the Second Law of Thermodynamics (the "Law of Decay"). This law states that change always happens from a condition of higher to lower energy. Evolutionists suggest the ancestors of man were tetrachromatic (seeing four colours) at first, then became dichromatic (seeing two colours) when some colours were meaningless. Apparently, these ancestors to man then later became trichromatic (seeing three colours), as we can see now, to better assess ripe fruit.[38] Perhaps the Qur'an anticipates this absurd logic when it invites a different reflection on ripe fruit: *"Feast your eyes on fruit and ripeness, for in these things are signs for all people who believe."* (6:99) For it is thermodynamically impossible for a system to "evolve" from more complexity, to less, then back to more again. Simply put, the fact that humans are trichromatic is part of our design and evidence of planning from the start: *"God has made for man a pair of eyes."* (90:8).

Newton, the "father" of thermodynamics, put it best when he said, "There is no other way, without revelation, to know God but by the manifestations in nature." Perhaps the real blind spot, then, is the one preventing some people from seeing the truth—*"it is not their eyes that are blind but their hearts"* (22:46). The human eye is hardly dysfunctional or simplistic. Rather, the human colour vision system is clear evidence of "irreducible complexity" which can only be the product of creation. For science strengthens believers, bringing *"proofs from the Lord, to open your eyes, if any will see."* (6:104) And even without the invention of retinography, microspectrophotometry, biochemistry, and neuropsychology, we could still know the same truth just by using our eyes to look all around us. The incomparable beauty of an orchid, a drop of rain, and a baby's hand, are proof enough, for *"everything has been sent from the Lord as an eye-opening message."* (17:102). All we really need to do is look.

CHAPTER VIII

Ethics and Values

"(Remember) when Luqman said to his son by way of advice and instruction: ...'O my dear son! Establish the Prayer in conformity with its conditions, enjoin and promote what is right and good and forbid and try to prevent the evil, and bear patiently whatever may befall you. Surely (all of) that is among greatly meritorious things, among matters of great resolution.'" (31:13, 17)

* * *

"You see the believers as regards their being merciful among themselves and showing love among themselves and being kind, resembling one body, so that, if any part of the body is not well then the whole body shares the insomnia and fever with it." (Sahih Bukhari, Al-Adab 'Good Manners and Form,' Hadith 40)

THE JOURNEY

L istening to Muslim teens, both as a teacher and public speaker, I
have noticed they have a recurring complaint: the boundaries set
on their behaviour seem much narrower than those on the kids
around them. Meanwhile, parents worry that teens are already following
trends too closely, getting drawn into lifestyles which will make them
suffer now and later. Religious parents are especially worried about teens
selling out eternity easily, as a life of self-restraint seems less appealing
than music videos and multimedia advertisements. New immigrants talk
about returning home, where the influences on teens may be better. But
are they really? One glance at satellite television reveals a basic truth: in
every culture, restraints on behaviour are dissolving. And, ultimately,
teen rebellion is something that can only be guided, not suppressed, for
it is part of an age-old human phenomenon: the journey.

The literature available on the "journey" is staggering. Teen rebellion,
research says, reflects a simple need to experience risk in travelling from
childhood to adulthood—or, as Stephenson (2002) puts it, to "put a boy/girl
in a situation that requires a man/woman to complete." The key objectives
of the journey are to generate community acceptance and establish one's
independence. Typical rites of passage for teens in this culture—which are
supported by adults in their lives—include commencing high school;
obtaining a driver's license; a first job; a first date/love; admission to col-
lege/university; and marriage. The Muslim teen's journey will necessarily be
different: the first date/love will not be encouraged, and the first job, especially for female teens, may not be either. So while those around them celebrate these events with their families, our teens may feel "short-changed,"
and parents of friends may echo this emotion, teasing covered girls, for
example, that they would look prettier for the boys without the *hijab*, or
judging Muslim parents because a teen cannot attend a mixed event.

However, one has only to channel-surf for a few minutes, or visit the
nearest public high school, to notice another staggering truth: there are
additional, darker, rites of passage which exist in western culture: the first

cigarette; first drink; first drug use; first fake ID; first alcohol purchase; first drunk driving and/or first ride with a drunk driver; first entrance to a club or X-rated film; losing one's virginity; first weapon; first act of vandalism; first gang; first fight (mostly boys); first diet (mostly girls); and first body manipulation (dyes, piercings and tattoos). In fact, in some subcultures, pregnancy is a rite of passage[1]; as is the first Employment Insurance cheque; the first suicide attempt; and the first incarceration.[2] These are hardly actions which develop positive attributes in any person or community, yet youth are lining up and encouraging each other to perform many, if not most, of these acts. Why? It seems that they are actually trying to journey from childhood to adulthood, but what they seek is not the mainstream community. Through a tragic combination of circumstances, the youth have defined for themselves a sort of alternate adult community to which they are journeying, one terrifying step at a time.

The first problem is that the mainstream community has become particularly unappealing for youth—more so, perhaps, than for any previous generation. The routines of work and family life cannot compete with the variety and speed of the digital world to which teens have become accustomed. In turn, computer technology has compromised, mechanized, or accelerated almost every form of employment, and advertisers continually generate new idols and desires, so adults themselves are complaining more than ever about their spouses, children, jobs, and salaries. Why should a teen seek to have the life of his or her parent, when that parent is complaining every night? This situation is further complicated for Muslim families, many of whom are recent immigrants, particularly dissatisfied about unfulfilling employment, as neighbourhood families, with greater disposable time and income, seem to be having more "fun" than Muslim households.

Second, television has stepped in to redefine a sort of "fantasy" adulthood, a desperately attractive and exciting place where responsibility is rarely, if ever, demonstrated. Television relationships are changeable, exciting, and full of sex, intrigue, and the continuous search for pleasure. Seven media conglomerates, responsible for 80% of all media output, have created a world of open personal boundaries and limited consequences. In an average year, television exposes a teenager to 1000 murders, rapes or assaults; 10,000 other acts of violence (73% unpunished); 2000 beer or wine ads; and 15,000 sexual references. In turn, teens will witness 20,000 advertisements, on which companies spend $153 billion yearly on the teen market.[3] Of these, 70% of those directed at girls revolve around appearance-related products, and 32% of the girls portrayed are overly thin.[4] Between advertisers and networks, a new reality has been clearly articulated in which the main objective is to be beautiful, through which one will have fun, rather than worrying about tomorrow. Thus, teens have become victims of a sort of "anticipatory culture"[5] in which expectations are that the journey will consistently bring novelty, physical gratification, and inconsequential risks—in clear opposition to the values required for a life of faith and devotion.

As part of this media-defined "journey", the new rites of passage yield devastating results. A study of 37,500 young British women aged 12 – 15 reports that 58% believe "appearance" to be their biggest concern[6]; and the Harvard Eating Disorders Center (2001) states 80% of American women wake up depressed about their appearance, while advertisers feast on the results, spawning a $33 billion per year weight-loss industry! In turn, the Journal of the American Academy for Child and Adolescent Psychiatry (2000) reports that 52% of girls aged 11 – 17 consider "sex and boys" their major worry, and Cornell University (2001) reports that romantically involved teens have higher levels of depression, as 42% of the emotions caused by young love are negative: anger, worry, hurt, anxiety, jealousy, and frustration. The study of over 8200 teens in grades 7 - 12 found that teenagers who "fall in love" are at a much higher risk for depression, alcohol-related problems, and delinquency. The Heritage Foundation (1996) reports a similar finding with over 6500 American teens, aged 14 – 17: those who have sex are consistently more depressed and suicidal. According to the Allan Guttmacher Institute (1999), more than 50% of 17-year-olds have had sex every year, 3 million American teens get sexually transmitted diseases and 1 million young women aged 15-19 get pregnant—a rate higher than in any other developed country. In fact, teens are responsible for 13% of all American births—with almost 80% of these occurring outside of marriage—and more than 275,000 abortions yearly.[7] Teen marriages end in divorce 50% of the time, contributing to an embarrassing $28 billion per year divorce industry, and 40% of American children being raised without a father.[8] A frightening 49% of children in Grade 6 have been pushed to try alcohol[9], and 78% of kids begin drinking before the age of 16. Drinking driving, in turn, results in over 100,000 teen deaths per year, while 49% of traffic fatalities in the first week of prom are alcohol-related. Escalating the problem, teens who drink are 50 times more likely to use cocaine, and 8 times more likely to use harder drugs.[10]

Clearly, with peer pressure fuelled by media pressure, teens are caught in an increasingly dangerous journey from childhood to adulthood. Suddenly, the rituals of traditional peoples like the Masai, where young men are sent alone to the forest to hunt or be killed, don't seem quite so dangerous after all, compared to what our children face in so-called "modern" society. And while it seems everyone agrees that teens need better rites of passage than the ones they now have[11], no one seems sure how to generate solutions. Certainly, you can shop online for a "Journey Camp" for your youth, as providers offer everything from drum therapy, to art therapy, and even ecotherapy, where teens are thrust into survival situations. Unfortunately, as Stephenson (2002) states, there is little or no value to a paid journey experience which takes the youth to an artificial environment—being able to cook a rabbit over an open fire, in other words, is hardly going to be a recognized value for an inner-city community. And without this relevance to the adult community, the journey becomes pointless.

So how can we generate real meaning for our youth as they transition to adulthood? First and foremost, we need to demonstrate that we are happy with ourselves as adults. We must try to minimize visible dissatisfaction with the current situation in our lives—despite the continuing stream of negativity around Muslims since 9/11—and we must work for positive emotions and attitudes in our homes and families so that our youth feel optimistic about their futures as adults.

Secondly, we need to constantly draw our youth's attention to the flagrant hypocrisy of media images of adulthood. The obvious, short-term solution is to reduce television viewing and encourage critical viewing (Is that realistic? Do you know anyone who looks like this for real?). A longer-term solution is to get our youth to understand hypocrisy, for which there is no better source than the Qur'an: *"You may like something which is bad for you"* (2:216), but *"don't incline towards those who do wrong or the fire will touch you"* (11:123). Remember, *"Don't get excited by those who have no certainty of faith,"* (30:60), for *"on Judgement Day, it is the hypocrites who will say, 'Let us borrow from your light' "* (57:13).

Third, we should work collectively to try to offer alternatives to youth—games, sports, academic and interest-based enrichment, volunteerism, and outdoor activities. We could even set up media criticism classes and encourage discriminating shopping. The viability of an Islamic lifestyle has never been clearer, but success will only happen when we care for all teens, not just our own children, as we try to raise both opportunities and expectations. Perhaps we could even redefine rites of passage—much as the Scout, Guide and Cadet movements have done so successfully, with "badges" to show stages of learning and growth—elaborating our own steps in positive religious growth as youth work towards light, not darkness.

Fourth, we need to explain to youth that peer pressure doesn't stop just because you give in. The youth who are being conservative are pressured to try a beer. The youth who drink are pressured into drugs. The youth who take drugs are pressured into vandalism, etc. Whatever boundary a person establishes, there will always be pressure to exceed it. So giving in does not generate any relief whatsoever. Holding on to a personal boundary means you only have to defend one boundary. Give in, and you are forever defending each new boundary you try to set up along the way, as you go further into compromising situations. As the Qur'an warns us, *"If you were to follow the common run of those on earth, they would lead you away from God."* (6:116)

Ultimately, we can also remind our youth—and ourselves—that peer pressure is nothing new. Prophet Noah faced ridicule as he built his boat over those many years, and Prophet Abraham defied his own father and his community to do what he believed was right. Prophet Joseph, in turn, withstood the temptations of youth to keep his dignity intact. In fact, in one way or another, every prophet's story is about peer pressure—resisting overwhelming forces in the community to walk a clear path to God. And the path—the journey—is also a key element of prophethood in every case, as it becomes necessary to leave one world behind in order to complete the mission. Clearly, God has provided us with a huge mercy in the way of a defining understanding: the pressure to assimilate is a dangerous force along the necessary journey to the fulfilment of our fate on this earth. As such, the journey of each one of our teenagers is the journey of all mankind, at all times. Taken in this context, it may be easier to guide our teens rather than to judge them, to see the door to adulthood as opening rather than closing—and to pray for, rather than condemn, the culture which they call their own.

MY HUSBAND—MY BROTHER

When I left Christianity for Islam in 2001, I became fascinated by how my new friends spoke so little about their husbands, other than for a few kind, inoffensive comments. Gone were the girl-talks about sex or insufficient help around the house, which defined the "bonding" within my previous circle of women—and my first marriage. In the relative simplicity of time spent with my new sisters, I came to realize that the kinship of marriage is both a test and a means of devotion. There is a famous saying of the Prophet Muhammad (PBUH): "Marriage completes half of one's religion." Far from meaning that we should invest half our time or resources in planning a wedding, the point is that marriage is the setting which God provides for us as adults, by which we can best grow and demonstrate our faith—and by which a wife becomes a man's sister, and my husband becomes my brother.

It's obvious that marriage, if kept honourable, prevents people from committing major sins like fornication, indecency, and adultery. These are grievous errors for all People of the Book, as the Bible warns, *"do not commit adultery"* (Ex 20:14) and *"do not covet your neighbour's wife"* (Ex 20:17). Marriage is considered to have been instituted in paradise (Gen 2:18), and there is a stern warning to *"honour marriage and keep the marriage bed pure"* (Heb 13:4). However, statistics reveal that the majority ignore this advice: 50% of marriages end in divorce[12], while 72% of men admit to extramarital affairs within the first two years of marriage, and 70% of women within the first five years. In turn, 15% of women and 25% of men have more than four affairs while married.[13] According to an Angus-Reid Poll (2001), 17% of Canadians have either cheated on their spouses or been cheated on, and 61% have family members in this situation. Given these figures, it is no surprise that youth are cynical about marriage—as 5.5 million couples yearly choose to cohabitate rather than marry.[14]

There are also more violent consequences of unsuccessful marriages: 380,000 men stalk their ex-wife each year, while 52,000 women stalk their ex-husband.[15] Four million women are assaulted yearly by their sexual partners, and each day, in the United States, four women are murdered by their boyfriends or husbands. One quarter of all crime in America is wife assault, while 67% of all marriages experience domestic abuse at least once.[16] Ironically, many non-Muslims see Muslim marriages as being male-dominated at the expense of women while, in fact, western women continue to be punished in dysfunctional marriages, perhaps ever since the Bible blamed Eve for giving the fruit to her husband (Gen 3:6), and thus promised ongoing enmity between wife and husband (Gen 3:15).

Contemporary thinkers seem torn on how to deal with the problem—there are countless Internet sites about the sad realities of broken homes and fatherless households. Amid all this, conservative voices are calling for reforms to divorce legislation, requiring longer wait times and counselling, and restricting divorce on demand. A few clicks away, however, are scavengers—legal professionals vouching to help you get everything you deserve out of your divorce settlement—including vengeance. Click again, and companies are competing with each other for the ever-expanding "speed-dating" service—selling packages of multiple dates of a few minutes each, boasting reduced "search and rejection costs" in finding your life's mate. Click a bit more and you will find bounty-hunters— psychological professionals promising to help you build a meaningful life with your spouse by teaching you to fulfil each other's "needs." Through all these approaches, the true value of marriage is lost, for what is really important is not how well marriage secures contentment in this life, but how well it ensures success in the next life. The dismal divorce statistics speak to a basic truth about marriage, so eloquently stated in the Holy Qur'an: if piety is not the foundation, we will always have suspicion and shakiness in our hearts until our hearts are cut to pieces (9:110).

First, our spouses are mates created for us (39:6), and the relationship of marriage has been established by God (25:54) so we can live in tranquility (30:21). In fact, our spouse has been created from a single soul, from which we, too, came (6:98), and it is God who put love and mercy between our hearts (30:21). Our spouses are such that they complete rather than duplicate us—as the great Prophet Moses found happiness married to a simple farmer's daughter. And as our spouses are a blessing, we should treasure them by being righteous ourselves (21:94), being true in word and actions (3:17), and by being careful to avoid acts of indecency (3:135) or following our lusts (4:27). As a first step, both men and women should lower their gaze (24:30-31), to try to keep themselves as modest and pure as possible, for it is our responsibility to prevent suspicion (49:12). Trust in a marriage can only come when we avoid deception among ourselves (16:94) and we do not strain our eyes longing for the things which God has given to some people (20:131). Thus, at all times, we need to be honourable in our contract (2:235), and though men and women are inherently creatures of impulse (21:37), as a couple, we need to engage in the mutual enjoining of truth, patience, and constancy (103:3). The example of Prophet Adam's (PBUH) marriage is all-revealing, for when spouses enjoin each other towards evil, both will suffer.

Even if we are not fully satisfied with our spouse's character or appearance, we should remember that our shapes are from God (40:64), as are the variations between peoples (49:13). So we should gently cover over each other's faults (2:263) because it is our duty to preserve a healthy marriage and not to pull apart what God has ordered to be joined (2:27). It is also true that we may sometimes dislike something in our spouses which is actually good for us (2:216), as God checks each one of us by means of the other (2:251). Equally, we should accept graciously when our spouse admonishes us for a legitimate fault (26:214), for it is each our duty to strengthen other believers (3:200) and to protect belief in God in one another (9:71). Even if our spouses bring challenges into our lives, we need to remember that God has made them, too, as a trial for us, and we need to have patience (25:20). If a spouse refuses to improve his/her own conduct, then we must accept that we have done what we can, for none can bear the burdens of another (53:38). After all, the Prophet Lot's (PBUH) wife was left behind among the unbelievers, and perished, despite having a prophet full of apt advice as a husband. And if ever we feel our marriage experiencing severe difficulties, we should simply ask God for help, for if a family in breach wishes for peace, God will cause a reconciliation (4:35). Always, we should pray that our spouses will be the comfort of our eyes (25:74), and we should never give up hope of God's soothing mercy (12:87), for God sends nourishment to all things in due proportion (41:10).

If our spouses engage in vain talk or futile pursuits (52:12), we are advised to walk away quietly (28:55) and avoid disputing with each other over trifles (18:56). We should also refrain from annoying each other (33:58), and if we have an argument despite our best efforts, we should not retaliate to any greater extent than the injury received (22:60), and restrain our anger (3:134). For one who forgives even when angry will be entitled to a life with God (42:37), and patience and forgiveness are courageous acts of will (42:43). We should always speak to each other with kind words (2:263) because it is a virtue to be compassionate (90:17), and we should neither laugh at each other nor be sarcastic (49:11), nor should we call each other by offensive nicknames (49:11). As well, the spouse who has greater assets or a greater salary should avoid boasting about having more wealth than the other (18:34). We should always conduct our marital affairs through mutual consultation (42:38), and deal with our mates in a moderate way, lowering our voices (31:19). Even if we are troubled by an earlier tension, we must welcome each other honourably when coming home (24:61) and return a greeting at least as courteous as the one given to us (4:86). When we are trying to negotiate with each other, we should speak fairly (2:83); and if one spouse inclines towards a peaceful resolution following a dispute, it is the other's duty to also incline towards peace (8:61). Then, once we have come to an agreement, we should keep our promises (2:100).

Yet if a spouse is harsh or cruel, we don't need to acquiesce (68:13), nor do we need to listen to violence or swearing (68:10), because it isn't right for either spouse to oppress the other (42:42). Instead, we should try to understand that the agitated spouse may not be fully aware of what he or she has done, for the deeds of transgressors always seem fair in their own eyes (10:12) and it is human nature to be contentious (18:54). So, we should simply try to forgive them and ask God to forgive them (3:159) and whatever faults in us may be contributing to the problem (47:19). The Pharaoh's wife, for example, prayed for mercy, though she was unable to detract her husband from his evil ways. At the same time, we must be wary not to hold ourselves as purified (53:32) simply because we appear to be the "victim" in a dispute—for only God can judge between

252 *Bridge to Light*

us (4:141) and it is always best to be humble (25:63). Likewise, when we are generous towards each other, with gifts of any kind—even words—we should never follow our generosity with reminders or injury (2:262), which would only cancel the charity (2:264). What is most important is to try to be at our best with our spouses, even if efforts sometimes fail, for what really counts is the intention in our hearts (33:5).

When we are among others, we should never speak ill of our spouse (49:12) nor ridicule him or her (9:79), and we should say only those things which are best (17:53), for God knows all the hypocrites (29:11), and they will be in the lowest depths of the fire (4:145). Actually, it is best not to speak too much of our spouses at all, to prevent scandals from circulating (24:19), and to avoid gossiping about possible indiscretions (24:16). Always, it is best to overlook any faults in our spouses with gracious forgiveness (15:85), and be thankful to God for all our benefits (2:152). We should not be jealous of our own or another's spouse's success either, for some people have simply been bestowed gifts more freely than others (4:32). And we should never regret our marriage, even in hard times, for we need to trust God through blessings and calamities (2:177), as there will always be days of varying fortunes (3:140). We can always remember Prophet Job, whose wife stood by him despite devastating difficulties.

Most critically, we should always regard our spouses with the highest dignity, not as individuals who are somehow "inside our personal boundary" and therefore exempt from the respect we show others, but as the ultimate recipients of our best virtues. For we spend more time with them than anyone else, and we experience a broader range of emotions with them than we do otherwise. If we consider them to be our closest sister or brother in faith, then we turn our homes into sanctuaries, and our families into witnesses to our goodness. Surely this is part of the lesson of the Prophet Muhammad—whose large household became both a school for believers, and a test of his own and his family's attributes, rendering every moment of married life into an act of worship. Ultimately, our spouses are our garments and we are theirs (2:187)—for they are our best protection in this world. And by simply recognizing marriage as an environment rather than just an agreement, we can ensure that our bond is the most ideal opportunity to earn rewards, in this life and the next.

THE ELDERS

On Christmas Day, years ago, I sat on a beach in British Columbia with my three children and watched an aged couple walk past. They looked like a magazine cover, loving and healthy, with time and money to spare. It was a clear contrast to the dozens of women, shrunken with time, who counted their coins to buy half a cabbage and sausages two at a time, eating Christmas dinner alone. The week before, my children's school had gone to the local nursing home where my neighbour "changed big diapers for a living," as she put it, to sing holiday carols. As their voices echoed across a room of vacant eyes, many crying or sleeping, they breathed in body fluids and decay. The staff offered the children treats, but most declined, preferring to leave. For they had witnessed the tragic promise of old age in western culture—and it looked nothing like a magazine cover at all.

The elderly have the highest suicide rate in the west—every 90 minutes, someone over 65 commits suicide in the US, not including those who just stop eating or discretely overdose.[17] "Gray crimes" include 46,000 purse snatchings, 166,000 robberies or assaults, 1000 murders, and 2.5 million property crimes per year on average.[18] And in the US, 15-20 million cases of elder abuse are reported yearly (19/20 cases are unreported), 85% involving family members[19] who underfeed, forcibly confine, or beat almost two million elderly every year.[20] In addition, almost 30% of psychotropic medications prescribed to the elderly are unnecessary[21], and many are forcibly given "shock treatments" (ECT) to make them more compliant towards routines which simply heighten their feelings of helplessness. In Ontario, in 2000-2001, for example, almost 5000 shock treatments were administered to elderly people—the "chief targets of ECT"—and ironically, many elderly commit suicide just to avoid these "treatments."[22]

The problem thrives in cultures that foster independence over interdependence, where people cite housing, income, work and school as impediments to caring for their aged. Over 80% of the world's elderly are actually in developed countries[23], where seniors are usually expected to take care of themselves. A typical reflection is the current reference to a "sandwich generation"—as though caring for both children and elders were a new and unique burden. Yet worldwide, up to now, every generation has been "sandwiched"—caring for its young and old at the same time, usually in the same house—and current voices simply seem to be looking for ways to get out of the sandwich. In Britain, for example, the majority feel burdened by the health demands of their seniors[24], 22,000 elderly are on powerful sedatives for no reason[25] and one-fifth of pensioners are starving[26]; in China, despite marriage laws forcing couples to support their elderly, increasing numbers of seniors require care by non-family members[27]; in Singapore, authorities are desperately trying to encourage families to keep their elders at home[28]; and in Japan, so-called "assertive daughters-in-law" are being blamed for vanishing family care.[29]

We should nurture our elderly, yet we rationalize until it seems to be in everyone's best interests if we "allow them their independence." In addition, cultural values which prioritize youth, ego, and desire convince our elders themselves that only unthinking adults become "burdens" on their families. This perspective is completely different from that in the Muslim world. The Qur'an upholds the care of the aged as a sacred duty: *"Treat in kindness your parents"* (2:83), and *"Be reverent of the wombs that bore you."* (4:1) And in Islam, serving one's parents is second only to serving God: *"Show gratitude to God and to your parents."* (31:14) The instruction is all-encompassing, in that it is not sufficient simply to provide a home and food, but also necessary to support them and to suppress irritation, even when they may become difficult to handle: *"Say not to them a word of contempt, nor repel them, but address them in terms of honour, and lower to them the wing of humility out of kindness."* (17:23-24) Thus, Muslims are compelled by their faith to care for their elderly, no matter how impractical the demands.[30] The result is a noticeably low rate of senility among aged Muslims, who live comfortably, gain status with age, and do not suffer the loss of self-esteem associated with growing older in western culture.[31]

Yet as a result of prevalent ideologies in the west, half of all Americans and Canadians will end their lives in a nursing home. And what does group care look like? The average nurse's aid in the US cares for 30 people a day, earning minimum wage, and the yearly staff turnover rate is 93%.[32] The Harvard School of Public Health found that typical contact time is appalling— about one hour per resident per day in a not-for-profit institution, and 30 minutes a day in a profit-based institution[33] — insufficient for basic personal care and feeding. Despite high daily costs of $100 – $300, only 38% of fees go to patient care (including staffing), and five of the 10 biggest nursing home chains in the US filed for bankruptcy in 2000. In 2002, 30% of nursing homes in the US were cited for harming or jeopardizing residents, and 25% of nurse's aides prosecuted had prior records. Malnutrition affects up to half the patients, and in 1999 alone, 500,000 deaths occurred in nursing homes, with starvation, dehydration or bedsores cited on thousands of death certificates. In Canada, 33% of nursing homes have a history of neglect and abuse, with an average of 30 complaints filed per week—and more complaints unreported for fear of reprisals on family members.[34] Ironically, Ontario government funding is $117 per resident-day for nursing homes—but $140 per resident-day for jails. And in Ontario, regulations entitling the elderly to one bath per week were recently discarded—but prisoners are legally entitled to a shower a day. Most tragic of all, many residents never receive a visit from anyone at all.

The status of elderly women, in particular, is a concern around the world, as officially expressed in 1989 by the UN General Assembly. Generally, women live longer than men and are paid less during their working lives, so that even in the west, the poverty rate among elderly women is twice that of elderly men.[35] Of additional concern is the rape or assault of bedridden or demented elderly women, often by caregivers and co-residents[36], and the fact that elderly women become alcoholic or addicted to anti-depressant medication much more frequently than elderly men.[37] Elderly women are also especially vulnerable to abuses of ECT, receiving shocks two or three times as frequently as men.[38] Further, almost 80% of elderly living alone are women[39], and in problem-plagued nursing homes, 70% of residents are women.[40] In contrast, Islam ordains the dutiful care of every single elderly woman. This is actually the basis of the so-called "four wives issue" (by which opponents frequently try to discredit Islam), which originates as an act of welfare to reduce the number and plight of women living alone, especially in later years, when they outnumber men dramatically.

Interestingly, a few very exclusive "Eden Alternative" nursing homes, conceived by Dr. Bill Thomas in 1991, are springing up in the west. These include a children's daycare, gardens, pets, open hours for dining, home-cooked meals, the residents' own furniture, and a stream of visitors and varied activities. Not surprisingly, these centres do better than standard facilities on key indicators: fewer drug prescriptions and anti-depressant medications, lower infection and pressure sore rates, lower mortality rates, less staff turnover, and reduced staff absenteeism.[41] Once again, research dollars uncover the obvious, for it turns out the best place for elders looks and feels like a real home.

In fact, however, the care currently given to the aged in Canada and the US stains not just their hearts but ours, for it is a legacy of shame—and part of a concerted effort by the majority to ignore death. The elderly are segregated from homes and communities to make it easier for us to forget we are aging. The few who stay in circulation are rich and well enough to look great despite their age, so we avoid facing the reality of our finite wealth and health. And hair loss, greying, skin changes, and reduced energy—all natural conditions of aging—are considered medical problems requiring treatment, exemplifying the motto of materialism: "With enough money, we can fix anything." The myth is carried to the grave, as financial "security" buys better caskets and full-service embalming, where carcinogenic formaldehyde props up every vein and theatrical makeup creates the perfect face for a luxurious open casket—bringing peace and comfort to everyone who looks on. What people say to each other in funeral parlours echoes the sentiment—comments on how good the person looks and how death was for the best manage to successfully trivialize what happens when we die.

Compare this with an Islamic burial. Rather than invasive manipulations by strangers, the family gently closes the eyes, quietly washes the body in scented water, then wraps it completely in clean white cotton. Rather than exposing the body to comments, no one may look upon the deceased's face after the ritual washing, and witnesses are compelled to be calm or simply whisper blessings. Rather than spending $5000 - $10000 on caskets, tombstones, and funeral rites, Muslims are buried directly and quickly in the ground, without ornamentation, while family members pay off the debts of the deceased and contributions to charity are made in the person's name. Then, rather than assuming that death is for the best, Muslims pray for mercy on each passing soul with humility, for only God knows how each person will be judged.

Years ago, I watched my grandmother's decline from her house, to a nursing home, to her grave. Everyone told themselves they had done the best they could, selecting a good facility from stacks of glossy brochures. But, ironically, the dining room overlooked the Catholic cemetery where she would soon lie. I had said, "I'll see you again at Christmas," but she had answered clearly, "No, you won't." And we would never have the chance to speak again. I never forgave myself for leaving her that day, and for not taking her to walk on a beach on Christmas Day, holding hands with me. As a lapsed Christian, I had more excuses than faith at the time, and I had forgotten the Bible: *"Cast me not off in the time of old age; forsake me not when my strength fails"* (Psalms 71:9). It's absolutely true that caring for our elderly is a difficult burden, yet *"good deeds are best in sight of the Lord as rewards, and best as the foundation for hopes"* (18:46). As a Muslim now, I am inspired by the seniors I regularly meet in family homes and community functions, looked after with patience and dignity, and respected to the highest degree. As a Muslim now, I also find renewed hope in the meaning of life and death, and were my grandmother here today, I would remind her that *"the hereafter is the home that will last"* (40:39). As it was, I completely failed this tiny, tired woman whose womb engendered mine, as our western culture fails so many old souls by forgetting, or ignoring, our most basic obligations. May God teach us mercy—that we may give it and earn it.

CHAPTER IX

Diversity and Understanding

"O humankind! Surely We have created you from a single (pair of) male and female, and made you into nations and families so that you may know one another (and build mutuality and co-operative relationships, not that you may take pride in your differences of race or social rank, and breed enmities). Surely the noblest, most honorable of you in God's sight is the one best in piety, righteousness, and reverence for God. Surely God is All-Knowing, All-Aware." (49:13)

* * *

"Shake hands and rancour will disappear. Give presents to each other and love each other and enmity will disappear." (Malik, Muwatta, Book 47, Hadith 476)

IN GARMENTS OF SILK

When I was a very little girl growing up in Quebec, I believed that if I dug really, really deep into my sandbox, I would pop up in the kitchen of some Chinese family on the other side of the earth. China was, for most of my life, the opposite of my world. Yet as a Muslim, I am finding that China is actually an integral part of my life. In my work, I regularly meet newcomers to Canada. About 90% of the time when I am among the Chinese, I "feel" as though I am with Muslims. The men are deferential, responsible, and respectful, and the women are quiet, warm and conservative. There is an acceptance of fate and a submission to God that is remarkably familiar and comforting. Their eyes never focus on my head scarf, nor try to avoid it either. So why are they so comfortable for me, and me for them? A famous saying tells us to seek knowledge as far as China. If we do, what can we find?

To begin, we notice a very obvious, but little-publicized fact: China has one of the largest Muslim populations in the world, and maybe the largest, if an accurate count could ever be made. The 1990 official Chinese census put the Muslim population at an impossible 18 million. Yet in 1950, the government's own estimates were of 50 million, and McGraw Hill reported 70 million in 1969. As a "minority" in this country of 1.4 billion, many Chinese Muslims are reluctant to report their religion[1], and according to the World News (1999), up to 30-50% of all Chinese children may be unreported as citizens try to avoid complying with population controls. Given these facts, and assuming the current rate of growth of the Chinese population (2.2 fertility rate, according to the UN), the figure might well be over 150 million Muslims or more by now. The Asian Wall Street Journal (2001), for example, estimates that there are 400 million Muslims in China! Regardless of the precise number, the Muslim population is staggering. In 1998, there were 33,000 acknowledged mosques in China, as many as 40,000 imams, at least 8 different translations of the Qur'an, and 9 Islamic universities, according to the Chinese Muslim Society. Clearly, China is a Muslim country.

China's Muslims are a diverse set of peoples, primarily made up of two main ethnic groups. The Uyghurs are Sunni Muslims with Turkic roots, and they primarily live in the Northwest corner of China. Their homeland, mainly the autonomous region of Xinjiang, is the largest single province in China (1/6 of the entire country), and Uyghurs comprise the majority there, also holding most of the government posts. Their land includes 1/3 of the coal and oil reserves of China, leading to obvious political tensions in the region. Since 1949, Beijing has been encouraging non-Muslims to relocate to Xinjiang to alter the demographics, and over the years, the Uyghurs have turned to rebellion on a number of occasions to resist suppression. In fact, in 1949, the entire Uyghur delegation died in a mysterious plane crash on their way to meet with Chairman Mao, who made no secret of his desire to dilute both minorities and religion. Today, the Uyghurs adhere to core Islamic beliefs. Classified as a minority in a rural border area, the Uyghurs have been allowed to have three or more children, though since September 11th, 2001, many Uyghurs feel selectively targeted by officials in efforts to reduce their family size.

The second main group of Muslims in China are the Hui—"Those who shall return." The Hui are primarily devout Sunni Muslims who are allowed to have two children per family. The men usually wear caps and the women, closed scarves, and so they are easily recognized even though they are scattered throughout China. The Hui have proven to be extremely successful businessmen throughout China and have become China's entrepreneurial class. They honour Muslim holidays and prayer schedules, and wherever they are in the majority in an area, no one is allowed to breed pigs. Their prosperity is especially visible in southeastern China in areas such as Fujian, for example, where their enterprises have benefited entire cities. In turn, the business revival they have engendered throughout China has been dedicated to Islam, with yearly increases in funds for mosques and Islamic schools. Largely, the Hui are descended from Muslim soldiers and traders.

How the Muslims came to China in the first place is well-documented. The Silk Road stretched for 8000 km and almost 2000 years between the Mediterranean and eastern Asia and brought countless traders to China, looking for silk, jade, lazurite, spices, ginger, tea, porcelain, paper, and gunpowder—so much that the route was worn four metres deep in some places. In fact, the blessed first wife of the Prophet Muhammad, Khadijah, was a caravan merchant who may herself have traded in Chinese goods. Since the Sui dynasty (581-618), Arab sea merchants had been coming to the great ports of China. Then, in 650, Saad Ibn Abi Waqqas, the prophet's maternal uncle, arrived to spread the faith. The Emperor of the Tang Dynasty (618-907), Yung-Wei, believed Islam to be very compatible with Confucius and gave him complete religious freedom. Thus, the very first mosque in China was built, at Ch'ang'an— now a national monument which still stands after 13 centuries. In 710-715, Kalifahs Al Walid and Hisyamn sent ambassadors to China, and by 727, large Muslim ships were a common site in the port city of Kwang Chou (now Canton). Within 50 years, Muslim soldiers, known for their strength and loyalty, would be recruited to support various emperors: the Abassid Caliph in Baghdad sent 20,000 soldiers to the Tang emperor in 758 CE; the Abassid Caliph Al-Mansur sent 4000 Turk soldiers to Emperor Su Tsung in 760 CE; Tibetans hired 20,000 Muslim soldiers in 801 CE to strengthen their fight against the Nanchao Kingdom; the Northern Sung emperor depended on 15,000 Muslim soldiers for his defense; and the Mongol emperor, Khubilai Khan, brought as many as 30,000 Muslims to China as a military reserve. Typically, these Muslim soldiers remained in China and married Chinese women, many of them taking on distinctly Chinese names over the generations—Hu Xuan for Hussain, Mu for Muhammad, Ha for Hasan, etc—and integrating completely into Chinese culture, while proliferating their religion.

In the 9th century, the Persian Gulf was sometimes referred to as the "Gulf of China" because Chinese-Muslim trade happened on such a large scale. By the beginning of the Sung Dynasty (960-1126), Muslims dominated the import-export business in China, and the director of shipping, regardless of the emperor in power, was consistently Muslim. By the Yuan Dynasty (1279-1368), during Khubilai Khan's rule, 8/12 governors were Muslims and Seyed Adjail Shaams Ad-Din Omar, the 31st generation grandson of the Prophet, became the Governor of Yunnan province. Also during this time, Yehdardin, a famous Muslim architect, laid the foundations for the great capital city of the Yuan—now Beijing. Khubilai Khan's own grandson, Ananda, who was raised by Muslim foster parents, eventually became the Prince of Anxi. He converted to Islam in 1295, along with his cousin, Ghazan Khan of West Turkestan, and most of the 150,000-strong army of Anxi. As the leader of the "red turbans," a Muslim farmer named Zhu Yuanshang eventually displaced the Mongols to install the Ming Dynasty (1348-1644), the so-called "Golden Age of Islam" in China. One Ming emperor, Chu Yuan Chang, was a Muslim convert with a devout Turkish Muslim wife who kept a *halal* court. Every port city had imams, and Muslim welfare homes for war orphans of other minorities sprang up throughout China, along with incredible advances in agriculture, irrigation, communication, and education. The great Muslim Chinese Admiral Cheng Ho (Zheng He) led seven fleets of 20,000-30,000 men in trading ventures around the globe, in huge boats which dwarfed those of Christopher Columbus. Certainly, by the end of the Ming Dynasty, Islam had gained a permanent foothold in China.

What is less well-known that, from the beginning, Islam fit perfectly into the Chinese world view and was compatible with their central values. Confucius is probably one of the most often quoted people who ever lived, and his words have spawned countless different "schools of thought" through which he has been reinterpreted and sometimes misinterpreted, beginning almost right after his death in the 5th century BC. But during his life, Confucius expressed beautiful, important ideas which eventually formed the basis of Chinese ethics. He was a simple and conservative man, orphaned at a young age, who had a gentle humour and disliked pretentious talk. Considering a few of his beliefs, it is easy to understand why the Emperor Yung Wei, who received the companion of the Prophet, recognized Islam as both familiar and fitting to the Chinese people:

– It is a cardinal virtue to respect your parents, and filial piety is everyone's greatest obligation on this earth. The family is the basis of all social organization, and its success is based on unequal relationships and mutual and complimentary obligations, such as between husband and wife.

– A good man helps the needy rather than just making himself richer.

- Every situation in life is a lesson. If I am walking with two men, each will serve as my teacher. I will observe the good in one and imitate it, and I will observe the bad in the other and correct it in myself. Virtue lies in attacking the evil in oneself rather than the evil in others.

- Patience and perseverance are the key to a successful learning, and being humane requires a good knowledge of reality.

- People should only compete for goodness, and they should always choose virtue over comfort. Virtue means working hard, spending only when necessary, being modest and moderate, avoiding conspicuous consumption, keeping one's promises, and guarding one's temper.

- Sincere faith and dignity are of paramount importance. People should maintain friendships with those who are upright, and they should avoid idle talk.

- Beware of hypocrites. The best people are those who watch over themselves when they are alone, and the manifestation of sincerity is as a light that moves others.

- We should all treat others as we would want to be treated.

- All people are similar in nature at the beginning, for human nature is what is given to us by heaven. Following our true nature is the correct path.

Confucius believed that his mission was the will of heaven, and he hoped simply that if he were not recognized in this world, at least he would be known in heaven. He believed in prayer, for he said, "Whoever turns away from heaven has no one to pray to," and he didn't fear the numerous attacks on his life because he said, "Heaven has produced the virtue that is in me. What then do I have to fear from such a person?"

Most interestingly, perhaps, Confucius insisted that he was not revealing anything new, but that he was simply reviving an earlier religion of the Zhou Dynasty. This mysterious Dynasty lasted almost 900 years—longer than any other—from 1134 to 249 BC. At its peak, it subsumed all of the land which is considered present-day China. The Zhou were incredibly civilized with a sophisticated and relatively peaceful feudal system, allowing minorities to practise their own religion in exchange for the payment of nominal land taxes. They are still considered some-what of a mysterious "lost civilization" which had unusually high levels of development in medicine, weaponry, agriculture, animal husbandry, handicrafts, silkworm cultivation, and politics. Many non-Zhou chose to move into Zhou territory to retire because of the high quality of life. The Zhou believed the devil to be the harmful influence inside every man, that moral intention is the key to a successful path, and that only God can punish and reward. Significantly, iron emerged in China dur-ing this dynasty, and the Great Wall of China was initiated, to block moun-tain paths from "barbarians" who might destroy the harmony of their culture. Certainly, the Great Wall of China, which many people travel the earth to see, may be another living reminder of the important signs throughout our world. As far back as 1000 years before the Prophet Muhammad, the Zhou Dynasty upheld a world view very compatible with Islam: "Tianming"—the importance of ruling benevolently over a family which is morally worthy of the responsibility.

Ultimately, Confucius is regarded as "China's greatest teacher," and his views have established the basis of modern Chinese thinking. According to Geert-Hofstede's survey of current Chinese values (1991), the Chinese still believe that moral discipline involves moderation and keeping oneself pure, and long-term happiness requires persistence, respect, thrift, and a sense of shame. Integration in society involves tol-erance, trustworthiness, conservative behaviour, and being contented with one's life, and society should value filial piety and chastity. A good man should be patient, kind, and courteous, and a good woman should be righteous and loyal. A good person has integrity of character and abides by the greatest good. Was Confucius one of the unnamed prophets of the Qur'an? Only God knows the finest mysteries of this life. Yet our duty, ever and always, is to read and reflect, and to recognize our brothers and sisters, wherever they may be.

RED, BLACK, AND WHITE

My father's family was from England and France, and my mother's, from France. My family traces its roots in Canada to 1608, to Samuel de Champlain. I studied North American history for years, and I was, by the grace of God, an exceptional student. In summary, I learned that three types of peoples established the population base on this continent prior to the migratory waves of the 19th century and later: so-called "red" people (Aboriginals), black people (Africans), and white people (Europeans). No Muslims ever factored into this history, and my clear recollection is they were never mentioned. Islam was not a part of my continent, or my life, until recently—or so I thought. Ironically, my mother had been calling me "marabout" ("grumpy," in French) for years, because my studiousness clashed with her "joie de vivre" daily. Little did I know the word actually means "holy person of the Moors." She had been calling me a Muslim all along. Maybe other truths about Islam lay just under the surface. I decided to revisit the history I thought I knew.

Native people were the first to settle the continent. They originated from Mongolia thousands of years ago, via a land bridge linking the northwest tip of the continent with Asia, migrating further south over countless generations. Natives, I learned, were inherently primitive pagans, with a survival-based lifestyle. They were essentially illiterate until they were "educated" by Christian Europeans in the 300 -400 years which followed Columbus's landing in 1492.

In truth, Native people had significant contacts with Islam, though this is not in textbooks, and many were educated—and perhaps Muslim. The languages of the Pima and Algonquian include many words derived from Arabic.[2] Many American place names have an Arabic origin: Alabama (Allah Bamya) and Tallahassee ("Allah will deliver you eventually"), as well as 484 towns, including several cities Native Americans in Washington State named "Medina," and "Makkah." According to Thatcher (1950), many tribe names are based on Arabic: Anasazi, Apache, Arawak, Akikana,

Cherokee, etc. In addition, the crescent moon features prominently in Navajo jewellery, and is known to have originated from outside the Americas. Five tribes in the southeastern US were considered "civilized": the Cherokee, Creek, Choctaw, Chickasaw, and Seminole. These people were literate and clothed; until 1832, the men wore a turban and a tunic past the knees, and women wore full-sleeved, long dresses. Other Indian men also wore turbans: the Potawatomi, Shaunee, Sioux, Winnebago, Yuchi, and more. The chief of the northeastern band of Cherokees in New York early in the 1800s was Mahir Abdal-Razzaaq El. And the Cherokee Chief in 1866 was Ramadhan Bin Wati, a Brigadier General in the confederate army. His son, Saladin Watie, was part of the South Cherokee delegation which signed the end of the US Civil War. In fact, the Cherokee syllabary, assembled by Chief Sequoyah between 1809-1821, parallels Arabic sound structure, and some symbols look like rotated or inverted Arabic. How could this be possible unless Muslims came to the continent in significant numbers prior to the 19th century?

The black people I studied about came from Africa, either before or after Columbus. Some came on their own, motivated to get away from destitute countries and "lucky" to find land somehow. Most came as slaves, and they were an impoverished, illiterate people who were essentially pagans. I learned slave songs in music class showing me how sad their lives were and how they found salvation in Jesus.

The reality of black history on this continent is shockingly different. First, their homeland was thriving. West Africa was the centre of trade under the Muslim leader Mansa Musa (died 1337), who sent trade expeditions of 400-2000 ships to the west and elsewhere. Two great universities marked the height of literacy in a land which produced the most gold in the world, yet made more profit from the sale of books. In East Africa, prominent Muslims such as Malik Ambar and Malik Andeel dominated the history of Ethiopia, creating a society which was cultured and charitable, leaving mosques and water reservoirs which were still in evidence in 1813, hundreds of years after their deaths. And in North Africa, the great city of Fez featured mosques, palaces, irrigation and sewer systems, free colleges and hospitals, a sophisticated legal system, and social assistance for the destitute. Certainly, if any Africans travelled to this continent on their own, it was not through "luck" or coincidence:

the Atlas of Cresques, which Columbus himself used, was based on the extensive expeditions of Africans to "the Americas."

Second, 15%-50% of the more than 15 million African slaves were Muslim, with the first landing in Virginia in 1619. They were highly educated, and they tried to maintain their faith despite hardships, as historical anecdotes record slaves fasting on farms, prostrating in fields, and hiding copies of the Qur'an. Diouf (1998) chronicles archaeological finds of secret masjids and Islamic "maroon villages" of runaway slaves. Contentiously, in Haiti, a famous slave named "Boukman" (book man), who incited Haiti's independence, was accused of "voodoo" for reading a strange book backwards (the Qur'an?) and speaking in tongues (Arabic?) during ceremonies at "Bois Cayman" (the woods of the *Imam* [prayer leader] or *iman* [faith]?) Abdul Rahman, a slave, supposedly wrote out "The Lord's Prayer" in Arabic in 1828. Decades later, the text was revealed to be Sura Al-Fatihah instead. Similarly, Omar Ibn Said (1770-1864), a Muslim scholar sold to a North Carolina protestant in 1819, was given an Arabic Bible by Francis Scott Key, who composed the American national anthem. The Bible is in the Davidson College Library, and in the margins, Omar praises Allah (SWT) in Arabic. Just before Omar's death, a North Carolina newspaper published his writing of "The Lord's Prayer," in Arabic. It turned out to be Sura Al-Nasr—remembered though he had been in slavery for over 40 years.

In 1539, the first-ever land crossing of the US was completed by Azenmouri, a Muslim Berber. In 1654, English explorers reported a colony of bearded people in North Carolina who called themselves "Moors" and dropped to their knees to pray while working silver smelting operations. In 1670, "Turks and Moors" were excluded from slavery by the Virginia National Assembly. On March 3, 1753, Abel Conder and Mahamut petitioned in Arabic for their freedom from slavery in South Carolina. On June 28th, 1786, a Declaration of Naval Peace between the Moors and America was signed by Thomas Jefferson, John Adams, and Taher Ben Abdelhack Fennish. In 1787, A Treaty of Peace and Friendship between the Cherokees and the US government was signed by Abdel-Khak and Muhammad Ibn Abdullah. And on January 20, 1790, the Free Moors Act allowed Moors to be tried as South Carolina citizens rather than under the Negro Act. Islam was clearly thriving on this continent for hundreds of years before anyone ever heard of Malcolm X or the movie "Roots."

As for the white people, I learned that prior to the 19th century, they came from Spain, Portugal, England, and France, which wanted to expand their thriving economies. Many explorers were mentioned, primarily Christopher Columbus, a brilliant sailor who discovered the Americas and allowed Europeans to "civilize" the continent. I skipped rope to a popular rhyme: "In fourteen-hundred-and-ninety two, Columbus sailed the ocean blue." In retrospect, I think the rhyme should have been, "In 1492, Columbus sailed the ocean, too."

Without question, Muslims found the Americas long before Columbus. In 793, Al Biruni, a Muslim scholar, established the circumference of the world within 70 miles. In 889, Khashkhash Ibn Saeed Ibn Aswad, a Moor from Cordoba, sailed to North America, providing information for the map by Al-Masudi, a famous Muslim trader, published in 900. Between 929 and 961, Abdul-Rahman III, an Umayed Caliph, left Spain for the Americas. In February, 999, Ibn Farrukh, a Moor, sailed from Granada towards Cuba. Sometime between 1099 and 1166, Al-Sharif Al-Idrisi, a Muslim cartographer, reached an island off Central America, and a native spoke to him in Arabic. In 1291, Sheik Zayn-eddine Ale Ben Fadhel Al Mazandarani sailed from Morocco to the Caribbean. Between 1300 and 1384, Chihab Ad-dine Abu-Al-Abbas Ahmad Ben Fadhl Al-Umari, a Muslim historian, wrote an extensive history of Mali's explorations beyond "the sea of darkness and fog." In 1311, Mali's Sultan Abu Bakari I led to expeditions to the West Atlantic. Even Columbus found Muslim evidence: during his second trip, the natives of Haiti presented him with spears tipped with Guanin of the exact composition as shops in Guinea; on his third trip, in 1498, he witnessed the natives of Trinidad wearing Moorish fabric designs and he called the Carib people "Mohemmedans"; and on July 31, 1502, he reported finding "Indians" whose women covered their faces. In 1500-1509, Balboa, found black people in Central America calling themselves "Kabbas" and "Almamies" (Al-Imam). English explorers also reported "swarthy Moorish-looking natives" in Central America, and Moorish shipwrecks have been found off the coast.

Secondly, Columbus was perhaps not such a "great" man, and without the help of Muslims, he might never have even found America. Columbus's favourite book was "Description of the World," by Pierre D'Ailley, based on the measurements of Al-Farghani, a Muslim scholar. He also used maps from Al-Masudi's "History of the World" and the Atlas of Cresques, 1375, based on the travels of the Moors. His ships were built in Oman, and two of his three captains were Muslim—Martin Alonso Pinzon, on the Pinta, and Vincente Yanez Pinzon, on the Nina— relatives of Abuzayan Muhammad III, a Moroccan sultan. Columbus was reportedly moody, autocratic, and distant, and the research is clear that he made a number of fundamental errors in counting leagues and calculating the length of a degree of latitude. He was actually lost several times and notified his crew that their position was different from what they knew it to be, causing resentment and creating conflicts with Vincente Pinzon, who argued the route repeatedly. In short, Columbus seems to have been really just a sea-going entrepreneur who found the Americas despite himself.

In fact, by his own admission, Columbus was also nothing less than another crusader. He was inspired by the Edict of the Council of Cardinals of 1457, which sought to "reduce to perpetual slavery the Saracens (Muslims) and pagans." In one journal entry, he dedicated his voyage to "combating the religion of Mahomet" and expanding "the Holy Christian faith," and committed all the wealth gained to the conquest of Jerusalem, presumably to compensate for the military failure of the crusades. France and Italy had actually been trying to eradicate Muslims, Jews, and even Unitarian Christians for hundreds of years. Inquisitions caused millions to be tortured, burned at stake, or exiled—their property confiscated, and their books burned. Those left alive were forcibly baptized, and many Muslim families placed their daughters in convents rather than have them sold at auction. In 1481, the inquisition extended to Spain, which had been ruled by the Moors since 711, and was a thriving country of 30 million people in 950, with beautiful cities like Cordova, endowed with public baths, libraries, sewer systems, hospitals, orphanages, subsidized schools, and universities. The marriage of Ferdinand of Aragon and Isabella of Castille in 1469 had strengthened two warring Christian kingdoms, and Granada—last stronghold of the Moors—fell on January 2,

1492. In the euphoria, Columbus was given approval for his trip, though his request had been rejected twice before. And so began the fateful journey—inspired by a feverish impulse that culminated years of death and destruction, and intended as an act of greed and manipulation. It's no wonder that many consider the anniversary of the voyage of 1492, the occasion of massive festivities throughout the continent, nothing more than a celebration of genocide and exploitation.

In the end, it all comes down to one word: Timbuktu. Many idioms of my childhood used this word: "That's a lot of luggage. Where are you going, Timbuktu?" Or, "I don't care if you try to hide in Timbuktu. I'll still find you." And so on. It meant somewhere far, far away, and quite unreal. In fact, Timbuktu, in West Africa, was the very heart of Islamic culture for hundreds of years. The fact that this place was rendered fictitious in common language is only one more sign of the concerted effort to erase, severely minimize, or even ridicule the contributions of Islam to the history of the world, and the Americas in particular. God willing, we can all help our children and their teachers bring the distinctive and honourable heritage of Islam on this continent into the light, and we can encourage each other to maintain vigilance against systematic global amnesia by simply doing what the Qur'an so fundamentally directs us to do: read.

REFERENCES

Shared Sources for All/Most Texts, Directly or Indirectly

➢ *The Meaning of the Qur'an*, Translated by Abdullah Yusuf Ali, with Arabic Text. Charminar, Hyderabad, India: Elisiasii Family Book Service, 2000.

➢ *The Koran*, Translated by N.L.Dawood. London: Penguin, 1999.

➢ *The Meaning of the Glorious Koran*, Translated by Mohammed Marmaduke Pickthall. New York: New American Library, 1930.

➢ *The Noble Qur'an* (Qur'an three-way translation: Ali, Pickthall, Shakir) <http://www.usc.edu/dept/MSA/quran/>

➢ MSA-USC Qur'an Database (Qur'an word and text search courtesy of the Muslim Students Association at the University of Southern California) <http://www.usc.edu/dept/MSA/reference/searchquran.html>

➢ Qur'an Browser (2003) (Qur'an side-by-side translations with Arabic) <http://www.quranbrowser.org/>

➢ Bible Gateway (Copyright 1995) (Bible word and text search) <http://www.biblegateway.com/>

➢ Ontario Consultants on Religious Tolerance (Interfaith information and statistics) <http://www.religioustolerance.org/>

➢ BeliefNet (2005) (Interfaith information and statistics) <http://www.beliefnet.com/>

➢ World Values Survey (Interfaith information and statistics) <http://www.worldvaluessurvey.org/>

➢ Adherents.com (Interfaith information and statistics) <http://www.adherents.com>

➢ Geert Hofstede Cultural Dimensions (1967-2003) (Intercultural information) <http://www.geert-hofstede.com/>

➢ Statistics Canada (Canadian demographics and statistics) <http://www.statcan.ca/start.html>

➢ US Department of Justice Bureau of Justice Statistics (American demographics and statistics) <http://www.ojp.usdoj.gov/bjs/>

➢ Nationmaster.com (International demographics and statistics) <http://www.nationmaster.com/>

➢ Wikipedia (Online encyclopedia) <http://en.wikipedia.org/wiki/Main_Page>

> How Stuff Works (Online encyclopedia) <http://www.howstuffworks.com/>
> World Values Survey (Values and beliefs around the world) <http://www.worldvaluessurvey.org/>
> World Health Organization (WHO) <http://www.who.int/en/>
> Wrested Scriptures (Scriptural comparisons and commentary) http://www.wrestedscriptures.com/
> ThinkExist.com (Quotations by notable people) <http://en.thinkexist.com/quotations>
> The Way to Truth (General Islamic knowledge) <http://www.thewaytotruth.org/>
> Sound Vision (General Islamic knowledge) <http://www.soundvision.com/info/>
> Fountain Magazine (General Islamic knowledge) <http://www.fountain-magazine.com/>

Background Reading

> Al-Sadiq, Imam Ja'far. *The Lantern of the Path*. Longmead, Shaftesbury, Dorset: Element Books Ltd., 1989.
> Gulen, M. Fethullah. *Criteria or Lights of the Way*. Konak-Izmir, Turkey: Kaynak (Izmir) A.S., 1998.
> Martin, Richard C. *Islamic Studies: A History of Religions Approach*, Second Edition. Upper Saddle River, New Jersey: Prentice-Hall Inc., 1996.
> Mawdudi, Abul A'la. *Towards Understanding Islam*. Toronto: The Message Publications, 1986.
> Qutb, Muhammad. *Islam: The Misunderstood Religion*. Lahore, Pakistan: Islamic Publications Ltd., 1986.

NOTES

CHAPTER I
THE JOURNEY TO THE NATURAL CALL FROM DEEP WITHIN

1   "The Wind," Cat Stevens, *Teaser and the Firecat*, October 1971
2   "Moonshadow," Cat Stevens, *Teaser and the Firecat*, October, 1971
3   "Time," Cat Stevens, *Mona Bone Jakon*, April 1970
4   "Changes IV," Cat Stevens, *Teaser and the Firecat*, October 1971
5   "Morning Has Broken," Cat Stevens, *Teaser and the Firecat*, October 1971
6   "O Caritas," Cat Stevens, *Catch Bull at Four*, September, 1972
7   "Can't Keep it In," Cat Stevens, *Catch Bull at Four*, September, 1972
8   "Music," Cat Stevens, *Buddha and the Chocolate Box*, March, 1974
9   "Sun C/79," Cat Stevens, *Buddha and the Chocolate Box*, March, 1974
10 "Tuesday's Dead," Cat Stevens, *Teaser and the Firecat*, October 1971
11 Ibid
12 "The Wind," Cat Stevens, *Teaser and the Firecat*, October 1971
13 "100 I Dream," Cat Stevens, *Foreigner*, July, 1973
14 "The Road To Find Out," Cat Stevens, *Tea for the Tillerman*, November 1970

CHAPTER II
HEALING THE DARK AGES INSIDE THE MODERN SOUL

1   NewsTarget, 2005
2   World Health Organization (WHO), January, 2001
3   Journal of the AMA, June, 2003
4   Australian Institute of Health and Welfare, 1998
5   Psychiatric Services, April 2004
6   Harvard Mental Health Newsletter, February 2002
7   WHO, October, 2004
8   Archives of Internal Medicine, 2004; British Medical Journal, 2004
9   Association for the Advancement of Behavior Therapy, December, 1999
10 New Scientist, May 2003
11 American Journal of Geriatric Psychiatry, 1997
12 Al-Hikmah, V. 10, p. 92-95
13 Agriculture Canada

14 Ibid.
15 Ibid.
16 WHO, 2002; Food and Agriculture Organization of the UN, 2004
17 Schoental, 1983
18 Mitterbauer et al, 2003; Casanova et al, 1999
19 Surprenant and Brewer, 2004
20 Bulletin of the WHO, 1999
21 DeVenter, 2003
22 Tong and Draughon, June, 1985
23 Health Canada
24 World Safety Organization, Nov 2003
25 Holland, 2004
26 Gdanzki, Mar 2001
27 Geisler, 2004
28 OMAFRA, Murphy, 2000
29 Thrasher, Aug, 2004
30 Miss. State Univ, Nov. 03
31 Carruthers, Jan. 1998; Calabrese and Baldwin, 1982
32 Hawkins, 1999
33 NRC, 1979
34 Agriculture Canada
35 Hegazi, 1996; Lopez-Solanilla et al, 1998; Coghlan, 1999
36 GM Watch, 24, 8/03
37 Bigwood, 2003
38 Institute for Food and Policy Development, Spring, 1998
39 Bulletin of the WHO, 1999
40 Schwartz, Feb 2002
41 Thrasher, Aug, 2004
42 San Francisco Chronicle, May 19, 2002
43 BBC, Nov 1, 2002
44 Boston Globe, April, 2000
45 Toronto Star, July 7, 2004
46 Child Welfare League of America, 2004
47 Wilson, 1994
48 Washington Times, Feb 1, 1996
49 US Dept. of Justice
50 Mother Jones, 1999
51 Ibid., 1999
52 AI, 2001
53 AI, 1998

54 Ibid., 1998
55 Ibid., 1998
56 Ottawa Conference, Gendreau, 2000
57 (Wilson, 1994)
58 Figures from UN Survey of Crime Trends and Operations of Criminal Justice.
59 AI, 1998, 2001
60 National Centre for Injury Prevention and Control
61 Commonwealth Fund Survey, 1998; Statistics Canada, 1993
62 Federal Bureau of Investigation, 1996
63 National Victim Centre, 1992
64 Bureau of Justice Statistics
65 UN Survey of Crime Trends and Operations of Criminal Justice
66 US Bureau of Justice Statistics
67 MUDPC, 2002
68 US Bureau of Justice Statistics
69 UN Survey of Crime Trends and Operations of Criminal Justice
70 US Dept. of Justice
71 National Victim Centre, 1992
72 US Bureau of Justice Statistics
73 MUDPC, 2002
74 Ibid., 2002
75 NY Daily News, Dec 26, 2003
76 "Islam Behind Bars," CBC, July 7, 2004

CHAPTER III
THE EGO TRAP

1 WHO, 2003
2 Nationmaster.com
3 Ibid.
4 Happiness.net
5 Sax, 2000
6 Centre for Disease Control

CHAPTER IV
REFLECTIONS ON THE BASIC TENETS OF FAITH

1 Biblegateway.com
2 Ibid.
3 Newsweek, 1993; Reader's Digest, 2003

4   //home.flash.net/~hoselton/deadsea/deadsea.htm or www.webcom.com/~gno-
    sis/library/scroll.htm
5   www.restorationfoundation.org
6   www.bbie.org/WrestedScriptures/A08Islam.html
7   www.bible.org; Biblical Studies Foundation.
8   Doubleday, 1970
9   circa 167 BC
10 New International Version; from manuscripts selected by the Council of
    Nicea, 325 CE
11 7th century CE; Yusuf Ali translation
12 New Catholic Encyclopaedia, Encyclopaedia Americana, Illustrated Bible
    Dictionary, Encyclopaedia Britannica, New Encyclopaedia Britannica, New
    International Dictionary of New Testament Theology, Encyclopaedia of
    Religion and Ethics, Dictionary of Religious Knowledge, Encyclopaedia of
    Religion, Zonderyan Pictorial Encyclopaedia of the Bible, Colliers
    Encyclopaedia, Compton's Interactive Encyclopaedia
13 October 14th, 1997
14 Baez, 2000
15 Statistics Canada
16 Canadian National Incidence Study of Abuse and Neglect
17 Canadian Centre for Substance Abuse
18 UN Office on Drugs and Crime
19 National Survey on Drug Use and Health
20 US Bureau of Justice
21 US DHHS Census Bureau
22 Canadian Council on Social Development

CHAPTER V

NOURISHING FAITH: PRACTICE

1   Sullivan
2   Newberg, University of Pennsylvania
3   Sullivan
4   Christian Medical Association
5   Duke University, The Faith Factor
6   The MANTRA Project
7   University of Miami
8   kidsforgod.org
9   from the sayings of Prophet Muhammad in the collections of Bukhari and
    Muslim

10 Journal of Paediatric and Perinatal Epidemiology (2000; 14: 248-256)
11 New England Journal of Medicine (April 27, 2000; 342: 1250-1253)
12 Mayo Clinic Pro. (Dec. 1997, 72: 1133-1136, 1197-98)
13 Lancet (Aug. 29, 1998: 352:666-67, 692-702.)
14 The Saturday Evening Post (Jan 2000)
15 CNN.com (Jan 2002)
16 The Independent (Aug. 17, 2000)
17 Biomanufacturing, Dec. 19, 1999
18 www.tray.com

CHAPTER VI
CLEAR SIGNS AROUND US

1 Journal Sentinel, 1999
2 Behe, 1991
3 WorldNetDaily, 2002
4 "Superstition in the Pigeon," Journal of Experimental Psychology, #38, 1947
5 Cassidy, 2000
6 New Scientist poll, Autumn, 2002
7 Crabtree, 2002-2003
8 Ibid., 2002-2003
9 The Council of Florence, 1431-1437, and the Council of Trent, 1545-1563
10 CNN July 9, 2002
11 Science Daily, October 2003
12 Brzezinski, 1993
13 Dante's "Inferno"
14 Atlantic Monthly, August, 1997

CHAPTER VII
EVOLUTION

1 Washington Post, March 22, 1999
2 Charles Darwin, in a letter to botanist Asa Gray, April 3, 1860
3 Human Genome Project
4 New Scientist 20, May 1982
5 Richard Leakey, PBS Documentary, 1990
6 Mary Leakey, Associated Press, 1996
7 Ingman, 2001
8 Charles Darwin, Life and Letters, 1887, Vol. 2, p. 229
9 New Scientist 153, 27-31

10 Francis Crick, Life Itself: Its Origin and Nature, 1981, p. 88
11 The Origin of Species, 1859, Chapter 6
12 Letter to Asa Gray, in Darwin, Desmond and Moore, 1991
13 Perdeck, 1967
14 Ruppell and Schuz, 1949
15 Sauer, 1961
16 Emlen, 1970
17 Kramer, 1953, 1959
18 Keeton, 1971
19 Ibid., 1971
20 Merkel and Wiltschko, 1964
21 Beason, 1986
22 Human Genome Project, 2004
23 The Origin of Species, 1st ed., p. 302
24 O'Regan, 1992; Vuletic, 2002
25 Rowe, 1997
26 Arrese, 2003
27 Sussman, 2001
28 Martin, 2001
29 Zhou, 2000
30 Partridge and Marshall, 1998
31 Varela et al, 1993
32 Rowe, 1997
33 Ede, 1997
34 Calvert, 2003
35 Pessoa, Thompson, Noe, 1996
36 Denton, 1999
37 Behe, 1996
38 Bowmaker, 2002

CHAPTER VIII
ETHICS AND VALUES

1 BC Parents Online
2 The Australian Institute of Criminology
3 National TV Violence Study, 1996
4 Children Now 1997 Conference
5 Islamzine, 1995
6 The Independent, 2002
7 Allan Guttmacher Institute, 1999
8 Nappa, 2000

9   National Resource Center
10 Greater Dallas Council on Alcohol and Drug Abuse
11 Wolfe Centre for Media Literacy, 2002
12 US Census, 2002
13 Family University
14 Divorce Magazine
15 Ibid.
16 Women's Rural Advocacy Program
17 AH Wilder Foundation, 2004
18 US Bureau of Justice Statistics
19 Machuca, 2001
20 Parenti, 1996
21 Geriatric Times, March, 2001
22 Weitz, 2004
23 World Watch Archives (WWA), April, 2002
24 Ibid., April, 2004
25 Ibid., November, 2003
26 Ibid., February, 2001
27 Ibid., March, 2004
28 Ibid., June, 2004
29 Ibid., April, 2001
30 Ritts, 2000
31 Ibid., 2000
32 Burger, Kayser-Jones and Bell, 2000
33 AHCA, 2003
34 Toronto Star, December, 2003
35 Ohio State University, 1998
36 Brandl and Cook-Daniels, 2002
37 Blow and Barry, 2003
38 Breggin, 1998
39 Seniors-Site, 2004
40 AHCA, 2003
41 National Center on Accessibility, 2004

CHAPTER IX
DIVERSITY AND UNDERSTANDING

1   Gladney, 1995
2   Zoubeir, 1998

INDEX

A

Abortion, 42, 122, 245
Adultery, 248
Alchemy, 206
Alcohol, vi, 4, 6, 29, 31, 40, 41, 60, 111,
148, 149, 150, 151, 152, 153, 154, 158,
244, 245, 281
Allergies, 25
Amish, 148
Angels, 5, 66, 68, 73, 82, 83, 84, 85, 86,
99, 102, 118, 154, 164, 180
Arabic, vii, viii, 70, 101, 103, 267, 268,
269, 270, 273
Astrology, 5, 13, 174, 177
Atheism, atheist, 51, 163, 164, 167, 223
Avicenna (Ibn Sina), 24

B

Bees, 29, 88, 231, 236
Bio-terrorism, 25, 30
Boomerangs, 191
Boukman, 269
Boundaries, 40, 41, 49, 51, 66, 67, 68, 69,
81, 82, 83, 84, 85, 86, 139, 140, 243, 244
Buddhism / Buddhists, 5, 49
Burial, 256

C

Cambrian Explosion, 233, 234
Camels, 100, 188
Cells, 82, 157, 165, 188, 192, 196, 223,
231, 237, 238, 239
Cheng Ho, 264
China, 157, 175, 199, 219, 254, 261, 262,
263, 264, 265, 266
Cloud seeding, 93
Colour, 29, 33, 88, 89, 149, 209, 211, 218,
225, 229, 235, 236, 237, 238, 239

Columbus, 198, 264, 267, 268, 269, 270,
271, 272
Comforter, 98
Confucius, 71, 263, 264, 265, 266
Convert, x, 10, 12, 88, 129, 142, 264
Corner Stone, v, 102
Cosmic Dust, 90

D

Dante, 61, 178, 197, 279
Dark Ages, v, 17, 19, 21, 23, 24, 25, 27,
29, 31, 33, 35, 37, 39, 41, 43, 275
Dark matter, 121
Darwin, 167, 207, 208, 211, 212, 213,
217, 219, 224, 225, 226, 234, 235,
238, 279, 280
Day of Atonement, 150
Dead Sea Scrolls, 81, 97, 101, 102, 106, 119
Death penalty, 32, 33
Depression, 5, 19, 20, 27, 134, 245
Dervish, 19, 24
Diet, 29, 30, 60, 111, 155, 237, 244
Discrimination, 42, 111, 194
DNA, 27, 95, 167, 208, 210, 216, 223
Doctrine of Atonement, 115
Dolly, 206, 215
Drugs, 5, 6, 19, 25, 30, 38, 40, 122, 246,
247, 278

E

Eating disorders, 245
Eden Alternative, 256
Erickson, 49
Eschatology, 120

F

Fasting, 138, 149, 150, 269
Fate, 14, 54, 56, 83, 129, 169, 173, 247, 261

Fear, v, 21, 33, 42, 75, 76, 77, 78, 79, 80, 83, 92, 99, 122, 146, 173, 174, 175, 176, 179, 186, 195, 255, 265
Fibonacci numbers, 165, 166, 167
Firmaments, 94, 95
Forgiveness, 23, 56, 60, 73, 81, 113, 115, 126, 127, 128, 136, 178, 251, 252
Fornication, 153, 248
Freud, 50, 51, 59, 167
Fungus, 27, 28, 29, 30

G

Gambling, 153, 179, 185
Ghandi, 136
Gospel of Barnabas, 97, 98
Gossip, 63, 143
Gourd, 88
Gratitude, vii, 8, 14, 65, 79, 144, 159, 169, 170, 171, 198, 254

H

Hadith, 17, 45, 73, 121, 131, 161, 203, 241, 259
Hagar, 104, 105
Haram (prohibited), 139, 155, 158, 159
Hell, vi, 31, 61, 67, 69, 79, 84, 102, 116, 174, 178, 179, 180, 181, 182, 183, 184, 185
Hijab (head scarf), 138, 147, 243
Honey, 88, 236
Hui, 262
Hypocrites, vi, 67, 141, 142, 246, 252, 265

I

Idols, 68, 244
Illness, 48, 51, 62, 146, 198
Inquisition, 271
Iron, 92, 110, 121, 192, 225, 229, 230, 231, 232, 266

J

Jerusalem, 31, 99, 117, 180, 271
Jesus Seminar, 112, 118
Jihad, 68, 69, 70, 75
Jinn (spirits), 62
Journeying, xi, 244

Judgement Day, 80, 97, 102, 113, 123, 126, 134, 201, 246
Justice, v, 30, 32, 33, 34, 36, 38, 39, 41, 43, 69, 71, 100, 101, 122, 150, 273, 276, 277, 278, 281

K

Ka'ba, 106

L

Leakey, 216, 279
Luck / lucky, 14, 15, 173, 174, 175, 176, 177, 268
Lucy, 215, 223

M

Magic, 29, 110, 205
Magnetite, 231, 232
Malaria, 145, 197, 198, 199, 200, 201
Marwa, 66, 67
Mary, Mother of Jesus, 83, 114, 170, 188, 205, 279
Mecca, 35, 66, 99, 106
Medina, 58, 267
Mendel, 208, 209, 212, 213
Mennonites, 148
Migration, 98, 194, 222, 227, 228, 229, 230, 232
Mitochondrial Eve, 216
Moon, 91, 94, 95, 192, 225, 268
Mosquitoes, 197, 198, 199, 200, 201
Mutations, 207, 210, 211, 212, 213, 216, 217, 235

N

Native, 5, 143, 267, 270
Newton, 163, 206, 239
Noah's Ark Hypothesis, 216

O

Oil, 12, 117, 121, 199, 237, 262

P

Palm, 19, 29, 31
Paran, 99, 104

Pharaoh, 52, 67, 251
Phi, 164, 165, 166, 167
Phyllotaxis, 166
Pilgrimage, 35, 66, 225
Plague, v, 25, 30
Poison, 60, 65, 100
Polygamy, 107, 149
Polytheism, 51, 54, 56, 81, 110
Prophets (partial selection only),
    – Abraham, 51, 54, 67, 83, 102, 104,
    197, 247
    – Adam, 56, 67, 68, 102, 198, 215, 250
    – Jesus, v, 5, 6, 31, 51, 67, 81, 83, 97,
    98, 99, 100, 101, 102, 103, 105, 106,
    107, 112, 113, 114, 115, 116, 117, 118,
    119, 120, 125, 141, 142, 143, 158, 170,
    178, 181, 184, 188, 205, 268
    – Job, 37, 61, 62, 63, 66, 84, 117, 118,
    128, 136, 168, 169, 170, 173, 188,
    243, 252
    – Jonah, 87, 88, 171, 188
    – Joseph, 10, 129, 171, 188, 247
    – Moses, 25, 51, 67, 80, 83, 84, 98,
    99, 102, 126, 128, 136, 149, 150, 171,
    184, 188, 250
    – Muhammad, ix, 26, 36, 51, 58, 61,
    67, 83, 94, 97, 98, 99, 100, 101, 103,
    106, 107, 109, 110, 111, 117, 121,
    128, 133, 145, 146, 170, 248, 252,
    261, 263, 266, 269, 271, 274, 278
    – Noah, 51, 67, 102, 127, 170, 184,
    188, 216, 247
Pulse, vi, 19, 22, 191, 192, 193, 194, 195,
    196, 231, 234
Pycnoclines, 89, 187

Q

Quakers, 146, 149

R

Ramadan, 138, 140
Religiosity, 135
Resurrection, v, x, 125, 127, 128, 187

Revert, 12
Rocks, 4, 92, 93, 97, 109, 110, 138

S

Safa, 66, 67
Saul (Paul) of Tarsus, 112, 141
Shari'a (Islamic Code of Law), 36
Skinner, 176, 177
Slaves / slavery, 55, 111, 142, 268, 269, 271
Solar wind, 95
Stoning, 32
Submit / submission, ix, 3, 11, 13, 55, 79,
    105, 109, 115, 127, 128, 136, 150,
    152, 170, 171, 177, 189, 261
Sun, 3, 7, 11, 91, 99, 120, 121, 174, 189,
    192, 194, 195, 225, 230, 275
Superstition, vi, 5, 22, 173, 174, 175, 176,
    177, 279
Swearing, 251

T

Teenagers, 183, 245, 247
Television, 14, 55, 83, 122, 139, 148, 149,
    181, 195, 243, 244, 246
Torah, 92, 99, 106, 155
Trinity, xi, 5, 113, 119, 183
    – Son of Mary, 114, 205
    – Son(s) of God and other figurative
    uses of "son", 116, 119

U

Uyghurs, 262

V

Vanity, 47, 65
Vicegerent, 68
Vigilance, v, 81, 138, 139, 140, 146, 198, 272
Vision (eyesight), 24, 168, 220, 232, 235,
    236, 237, 238, 239, 274

W

Waveforms, 192, 195